Democratic governments are able to elicit, legally and legitimately, both money and men from their populations. Certainly there is tax evasion, draft evasion, and even outright resistance; yet to a remarkable extent citizens acquiesce and even actively consent to the demands of governments, well beyond the point explicable by coercion. This is a puzzle for social scientists, particularly those who believe that individuals are self-interested, rational actors who calculate only the private egoistic costs and benefits of possible choices. The provisions of collective good should never justify a quasi-voluntary tax payment, and the benefits of a war could not possibly exceed the cost of dying.

Consent, Dissent, and Patriotism explains the institutionalization of policy in response to anticipated and actual citizen behavior and the conditions under which citizens give, refuse, and withdraw their consent. Professor Levi claims that citizens' consent is contingent upon the perceived fairness of both the government and other citizens. Most citizens of democracies, most of the time, are more likely to give their consent if they believe that government actors and other citizens are behaving fairly toward them. Demonstrated fairness is therefore a critical element in effective and democratic governance.

CONSENT, DISSENT, AND PATRIOTISM

POLITICAL ECONOMY OF INSTITUTIONS AND DECISIONS

Editors
James E. Alt, Harvard University
Douglass C. North, Washington University of St. Louis

Other books in the series

Alberto Alesina and Howard Rosenthal, *Partisan Politics, Divided Government, and the Economy*

Lee J. Alston, Thrainn Eggertsson, and Douglass C. North, eds., *Empirical Studies in Institutional Change*

James E. Alt and Kenneth Shepsle, eds., *Perspectives on Positive Political Economy*

Jeffery S. Banks and Eric A. Hanushek, eds., *Modern Political Economy: Old Topics, New Directions*

Yoram Barzel, *Economic Analysis of Property Rights* (2nd edition)

Robert Bates, *Beyond the Miracle of the Market: The Political Economy of Agrarian Development in Kenya*

Peter Cowhey and Mathew McCubbins, eds., *Structure and Policy in Japan and the United States*

Gary W. Cox, *The Efficient Secret: The Cabinet and the Development of Political Parties in Victorian England*

Gary W. Cox, *Making Votes Count: Strategic Coordination in the World's Electoral System*

Jean Ensminger, *Making a Market: The Institutional Transformation of an African Society*

Murray Horn, *The Political Economy of Public Administration: Institutional Choice in the Public Sector*

John D. Huber, *Rationalizing Parliament: Legislative Institutions and Party Politics in France*

Jack Knight, *Institutions and Social Conflict*

Michael Laver and Kenneth Shepsle, eds., *Making and Breaking Governments*

Michael Laver and Kenneth Shepsle, eds., *Cabinet Ministers and Parliamentary Government*

Brian Levy and Pablo T. Spiller, eds., *Regulations, Institutions, and Commitment*

Leif Lewin, *Ideology and Strategy: A Century of Swedish Politics* (English edition)

Gary Libecap, *Contracting for Property Rights*

Mathew D. McCubbins and Terry Sullivan, eds., *Congress: Structure and Policy*

Titles in the series are continued at back of book after the index.

CONSENT, DISSENT, AND PATRIOTISM

MARGARET LEVI
University of Washington

CAMBRIDGE
UNIVERSITY PRESS

PUBLISHED BY THE PRESS SYNDICATE OF THE UNIVERSITY OF CAMBRIDGE
The Pitt Building, Trumpington Street, Cambridge CB2 1RP, United Kingdom

CAMBRIDGE UNIVERSITY PRESS
The Edinburgh Building, Cambridge CB2 2RU, United Kingdom
40 West 20th Street, New York, NY 10011-4211, USA
10 Stamford Road, Oakleigh, Melbourne 3166, Australia

First published 1997

Printed in the United States of America

Typeset in Sabon

Library of Congress Cataloging-in-Publication Data
Levi, Margaret.
Consent, dissent, and patriotism / Margaret Levi.
p.   cm. – (Political economy of institutions and decisions)
Includes bibliographical references and index.
ISBN 0-521-59055-8 (hb). – ISBN 0-521-59961-X (pb)
1. Allegiance. 2. Patriotism. 3. Democracy. 4. Draft.
5. Conscientious objection.   I. Title.   II. Series.
JC328.L44   1997
323.6'5–dc21   97-11414
                                                     CIP

A catalog record for this book is available from the British Library.

ISBN 0–521–59055–8 hardback
ISBN 0–521–59961–X paperback

For my father, Joe Levi
and
for my husband, Bob Kaplan

Two men with strong senses of political obligation who
fought their very different wars in very different ways.

It is hard to know what to do with all the detail that rises out of a fire. It rises out of a fire as thick as smoke and threatens to blot out everything – some of it is true but doesn't make any difference, some is just plain wrong, and some doesn't even exist, except in your mind, as you slowly discover long afterwards. Some of it, though, is true – and makes all the difference.

Norman Maclean, *Young Men and Fire*

Contents

Contents

Series editors' preface

The Cambridge series on the Political Economy of Institutions and Decisions is built around attempts to answer two central questions: How do institutions evolve in response to individual incentives, strategies, and choices, and how do institutions affect the performance of political and economic systems? The scope of the series is comparative and historical rather than international or specifically American, and the focus is positive rather than normative.

What makes citizens comply with various costly exactions of government, particularly those like military service in which citizens risk losing their lives? In a provocative effort to provide a rational choice perspective on democratic legitimacy, Margaret Levi argues that citizens will prefer to comply provided the personal costs of compliance are not too burdensome. However, she argues, citizen compliance is contingent, requiring a positive assessment of both government trustworthiness and ethical reciprocity, the likelihood that other citizens will also do their share. Her evidence is rich and varied. She shows how mutual distrust between linguistically separate subgroups during two world wars made ethical reciprocity and "fair shares" arrangements unobtainable. Moreover, institutional arrangements making government commitments credible are essential to getting people to act on the belief that any fair shares arrangements will be enforced, and variations in credibility explain differences in the success of conscription. Finally, she shows how different personal costs of obtaining the status explain varying extents to which people became conscientious objectors.

This is pathbreaking analytic comparative history at its strongest, combining qualitative and quantitative evidence spanning two centuries of wartime history in Britain, Australia, New Zealand, Canada, France, and the United States to explain differences in citizens' decisions about taking personal risks in complying with government policies.

Acknowledgments

This book was a long time in the making. My husband, Bob Kaplan, tells me I have promised it by "December" for at least four years in a row. When we first married, in 1990, I told him he would soon learn what it was like to live with someone completing a book. I never dreamed I would only be approaching that moment after our fifth anniversary. My colleague Donald Matthews continually reassures me that most books take seven years from initial gestation to submission to the publisher. This one began in 1988 and was sent off for review in the last hours of 1995, more or less on Matthew's track (although I worry that he has created a self-fulfilling prophecy, at least for me).

The research took me to two continents other than my own and introduced me to a vast historical and novelistic literature on wars and the home front. There were some remarkable moments along the journey. A few examples will have to suffice: walking through the battlefields of the Somme and experiencing all that is left of the trenches; stopping at the memorials to soldiers in small Australian outback towns, where the houses are few and the lists on the monuments extremely long; listening to the stories of friends who had to decide whether to go to Vietnam: some did, some left the country, some went to jail, some won exemptions, and some, like my husband, spent a year or two in VISTA in the battlefields of South Chicago. Perhaps the funniest moment came when my French failed me (I can only assume that is what happened). I had telephoned the Ministry of Defense in Paris to set up an interview with a particular general and understood from the person at the other end that the general was dead and that I should speak to the colonel on Monday. When I called the colonel, he said I needed to speak to the general, who was not *mort* after all; he had only gone to the *mer* for the weekend.

There were also some remarkable people who helped me. My especial thanks goes to Professor Patrick Troy of the Research School of Social

xi

Acknowledgments

Sciences, who encouraged the project and helped me see its larger implications. The Program in Administration, Compliance, and Governability that he established and ran was an important source of feedback, support, and intellectual growth. Michael McKernan, previously Assistant Director of the Australian War Memorial, introduced me to the international world of military historians and watched that, as a social scientist, I was aware of the critical issues of historiography. Without Shane Fricks and Stephen DeTray, research assistants and collaborators on two of the chapters, I would never have completed this book. Catherine Fieschi offered invaluable research assistance with the Canadian material. Daniel Valadez, Miguel Puente, and Steve Miller helped me organize myself, my office, and the materials I needed to complete this project.

Two opportunities slowed down the manuscript by making me seriously rethink aspects of it and learn what I needed to learn to make it better. James Alt invited me to give a series of lectures in the political economy program at Harvard in January 1993. As a consequence, the book I thought I had just about finished the previous December I had to rewrite – thus, the second December of which my husband speaks. However, in the fall of 1993 I became a fellow at the Center for Advanced Study in the Behavioral Sciences. Long discussions with Laura Stoker forced me to confront the questions posed by political theory both more directly and more clearly. What really slowed me down, however, was membership in a special project on historical political economy with Robert Bates, Avner Greif, Jean-Laurent Rosenthal, and Barry Weingast. The standards for comparative analytic narratives that we developed during that year and as we continue to work toward the production of a jointly written set of essays for an edited volume (in process) raised new issues and problems for me that took me to the next December and the next. My gratitude to all of these who slowed my project is immense, nonetheless.

I am grateful for generous financial support provided by the German Marshall Fund of the United States; the Australian War Memorial; the Canadian Embassy Fellowship Program; the National Science Foundation through grants SES-87049 and SES-911050; and the Graduate School Research Fund of the University of Washington. As a visiting scholar, I received additional support, collegial as well as financial, from the London School of Economics; the Maison des Sciences de l'Homme; the Havens Center at the University of Wisconsin; Center for Ethics, Rationality and Society at the University of Chicago; the Program in Administration, Compliance, and Governability at the Australian National University; the Max-Planck-Institut für Gesellschaftsforschung in Köln; the Schumann Center of the European University Institute; and Exeter College of Oxford University. This material was partially pre-

Acknowledgments

pared while I was a Fellow at the Center for Advanced Study in the Behavioral Sciences. I am grateful for financial support provided to me through the Center by National Science Foundation grant SES-9022192.

Cambridge University Press provided superb support. Alex Holzman's editorial advice was invaluable. The copyediting of Genevieve Scandone and Edith Feinstein may have shamed me but made this a far more presentable book; I am immensely grateful to them.

I received extremely useful feedback from colloquia and conferences at the above institutions and at Claremont Graduate School, Columbia University, Cornell University, Duke University, Harvard University, Humboldt University, McGill University, M.I.T., New York University, Northwestern University, UC Davis, University of Minnesota, University of Rochester, Washington University, University of Gotheburg, and University of Lund. Yoram Barzel, Fred Block, Thomas Borcherding, John Braithwaite, Randall Calvert, Dennis Chong, Karen Cook, Thomas Christiano, Stanley Engerman, Martha Finnemore, David Fitzpatrick, Barbara Geddes, Miriam Golden, Geoffrey Grey, Mark Hansen, Kjell Hausken, Ronald Jepperson, Ann-Mari Jordens, David Laitin, Michael Lipsky, Carl-Hampus Lyttkens, Mary MacKinnon, George Madaus, Peter May, Jane Mansbridge, Lincoln Moses, Avner Offer, Elinor Ostrom, Roger Petersen, Philip Petit, Thomas Pluemper, Samuel Preston, Bo Rothstein, Fritz Scharpf, Allan Silver, Peter Simkins, William Talbott, Craig Wilcox, Erik Wright, and John Zaller all offered comments of extraordinary usefulness to me in this project, as did several anonymous reviewers. So, too, did the members of PEDDS (Political Economy Drinks and Discussion Society) and of the Macrosociology Group at the University of Washington. I thank them all.

I am particularly grateful to those who read the penultimate draft of the manuscript in its entirety and who demanded that I sort out its confusions. If I have failed to do so, it is not the fault of James Alt, Robert Bates, Avner Greif, Anthony Gill, Russell Hardin, Ira Katznelson, Edgar Kiser, Mark Lichbach, Jean-Laurent Rosenthal, or Janice Thomson. They tried their best to convince me of the work still to be done; I have tried my best to satisfy them.

My two greatest debts are to my father, Joseph Levi, and to my husband, Bob Kaplan. My father, who died before this book was completed, instilled in me both a love for history and a desire to develop a capacity for critical thinking. His especial fascination was the U.S. Civil War; few fathers have marched their young daughters through as many battlefields. His interest in the 1860s combined with his experiences of the 1940s to make him think deeply about the reasons for war. One of his many legacies to me is the conviction that most wars should not be fought at all but that fighting in some wars is the awful yet necessary

Acknowledgments

complement of morality and citizenship. My debt to my husband is of a different sort. As a ratcho (what the graduate students in my department call those who use rational choice theory), I am extremely aware of the costs and the benefits of any enterprise. I fear I have made Bob bear far too many costs for all the benefits I have received from his generosity and love.

Earlier versions of some of the material in the book previously appeared as follows:

"The Institution of Conscription." *Social Science History* (special issue on "Institutionalism and the Historical Turn," eds. Eileen McDonagh and Phil Ethington) 20, 1 (Spring 1996): 133–67.

"A Weapon Against War: Conscientious Objection in the United States, Australia, and France" (with Stephen DeTray). *Politics & Society* 21, 4 (1993): 425–64.

"Are There Limits to Rationality?" *Archives Européennes de Sociologie* 32 (1991): 130–41.

"A Logic of Institutional Change," in *The Limits of Rationality*, edited with Karen Cook (Chicago: University of Chicago Press, 1990).

1

History as politics

In general I might agree with you:
women should not contemplate war,
should not weigh tactics impartially,
or evade the word enemy, or view
both sides and denounce nothing.

Women should march for peace,
or hand out white feathers to
inspire bravery. . .

Instead of this, I tell
what I hope will pass as truth.
A blunt thing, not lovely.

Margaret Atwood, "The Loneliness
of the Military Historian" (1995: 49–50)

A "blunt thing, not lovely" is an appropriate description for truth, or what passes for truth, in the social sciences. Stilted language and cumbersome methods contribute to its coarse features. More importantly, the homeliness of social scientific truth results from disinterestedly asking questions that lack clear answers. The beauty of science is its logic and parsimony. The beauty of literature is its expressiveness and involvement. Social science is generally messy and aloof. Yet it, and we its practitioners, continue to investigate issues about which people care deeply and act passionately.

One such set of issues is war and military service in democracies. Why do citizens sometimes enthusiastically give their behavioral consent to their governments and sometimes refuse it? Why at some times and in some places is there widespread protest or draft evasion and at other times and places considerable patriotism and volunteering? Why are some groups likely to support a particular war and others not? And how can a people consider a government democratic when it makes such harsh compulsory extractions of its citizens in money and life?

Military service is just one of many ways democratic governments demonstrate their immense power to tax. Democratic governments are able to elicit, legally and legitimately, both money and men from their populations. Certainly, there is tax evasion, draft evasion, and various other forms of disobedience and even outright resistance; yet it is remarkable the extent to which citizens acquiesce and even actively consent to the demands of governments, well beyond the point explicable by coercion. This is a puzzle for social scientists, particularly those who believe that individuals are self-interested, rational actors who calculate only the private, egoistic costs and benefits of possible choices. In this view the provision of collective goods would never justify a quasi-voluntary[1] tax payment; and the benefits of a war could not possibly exceed the cost of dying.

Such behavior may befuddle social scientists, but mobilizing support for their policies is a daily task for political actors. Few governments can survive without a high degree of quasi-voluntary compliance by their subjects and citizens. Sustenance of military, tax, and other political obligations depends on the willing compliance of large numbers of individuals who, albeit obligated to obey the laws and compelled to do so if necessary, comply because they choose to.[2] Otherwise, both the political and economic costs of governance become too high. Whether, for democratic government to thrive, acquiescence and conformity must translate into active behavioral consent remains an important empirical question with significant normative implications.

This book has two principal explananda: the institutionalization of policy in response to anticipated and actual citizen behavior; and conditions under which citizens give, refuse, or withdraw their consent. The central claims flow from the argument that citizen consent is contingent upon the perceived fairness of both government and other citizens. Most citizens of democracies, most of the time, are more likely to give their consent if they believe that government actors and other citizens are behaving fairly toward them. Fairness is a critical element in effective and democratic governance. Yet the standards of fairness vary over time and place and among groups within the polity; so, too, do the democratic rules that will determine whose and which standards of fairness dominate. Consideration of how the standards of fairness emerge and change is an additional theme of the text.

Understanding the role of consent in governance advances democratic theory. Recognizing fairness as an important influence on behavior helps put to rest critiques of rational choice as a model that unrealistically

---

[1] It has become common practice for the U.S. Internal Revenue Service and its counterparts in other countries to emphasize the importance of voluntary compliance. However, such compliance, although willing, is also compelled by law: An individual who chooses not to comply will suffer sanctions if caught. Thus, I prefer the term quasi-voluntary compliance, developed in my *Of Rule and Revenue*.

[2] This was the argument of an earlier book, *Of Rule and Revenue* (1988), in which I explored the institutional choices of government actors.

2

assumes only narrowly self-interested actors. An equally important goal of the book, however, is the development of an empirical model that combines the microfoundations of methodological individualism with historically grounded case studies of macroevents. The result is a book that aims to transcend the usual boundaries between normative and empirical political theory, between ethics and rationality, between choice-theoretic models and more sociological or historical research.

WHY STUDY THE HISTORY OF MILITARY SERVICE?

History shapes agents and their ethics; it contributes to the definition of group membership, individual identities, and what constitutes fairness. Why some groups of people are more likely to comply with the laws than others rests on a dynamic analysis in which the past informs the present. Crucial to the investigation of consent are historical events that are the bases of expectations of what others will do and what the likely outcome will therefore be. The sources of present beliefs are past experiences and practices. Prior institutions, prior strategies, and prior actions delimit current options, and stories of yesteryears reveal what bargains have been broken and which kept. Although the past is not necessarily predictive of the future, it is a guide to the possible pitfalls that lie ahead. Consequently, political entrepreneurs and government actors struggle over the meaning of the past for the present.

History also shapes institutions and regimes, and history can reveal the underlying causes for institutional change or stability. Democracies, at least some democracies, survive significant strains. This book documents some of those strains, particularly ones caused by revolutions, civil wars, external wars big and small, and the domestic politics of conscription. For France, Britain, Australia, Canada, New Zealand, and the United States, such pressures led to the evolution rather than destruction of democratic institutions. Although the investigation of the history of military service can hardly offer a full empirical account of the causes or compass of democratic institutional endurance and transformation, it does suggest some reasons why democracies survive, on the one hand, and why they change, on the other.

Although governments often evoke political obligation as one basis for compliance, few issues permit observation of both the decisions that produce government policies and citizen choices in the face of government demands. Military service satisfies both criteria.[3] To join the army, to be a conscientious objector, to resist the draft are publicly recorded

---

[3] Thus, once again I find myself studying armed young men in uniforms. My dissertation and first book (1977) was on police unions. My husband notes that *Of Rule and Revenue* was a study of old men in uniform.

behaviors. The data may be messy, but the data on who pays or evades taxes is even more difficult to obtain and often even more suspect. Moreover, military service is an important obligation of democratic citizenship, at least male citizenship. Noncompliance with this obligation has implications for the efficacy of government. Although each act of noncompliance may have a singular motivation, an ensemble can constitute a political statement and, on occasion, an actual rebellion.

There are further justifications for the investigation of military service. In recent years, scholars attempting to develop a more adequate theory of the state have given considerable attention to the relationship between states and citizens in regard to social welfare and taxation. Variations in the form of the military obligation and the institutions that enforce this obligation have received some descriptive but little or no theoretical attention. Yet military service is demonstrably as important an aspect of the state–citizen relationship as any that exists. There has not, of course, been total neglect. Several important historical and political sociologists have taken up the question to some extent but generally within the context of the role of the military in society (e.g. Janowitz 1980; Giddens 1985, esp. chs. 8 and 9; Mann 1986 *passim* and 1993 *passim*; Birnbaum 1988; Tilly 1990). There has been no systematic investigation of how governments induce citizens to accept military service nor explanatory theory of variation among states and citizens, even in important works like that of Huntington (1957) or Enloe (1980). International relations specialists and international political economists have certainly considered the importance of national defense and military power, but, with few exceptions (Thomson 1995), the state theorists among them have been more concerned with questions of hegemony, international cooperation, and trade than with why a state chooses the military format it does and what effects that has on citizen behavior. Thus, this study of military service further contributes to the construction of a more satisfactory theory of the state than is currently available.[4]

The history of military service constitutes an important subject for investigating not only state building (see, e.g., Gillis ed. 1989; Hooks and McLauclan 1992; van Holde 1993) but also what it means to be a

---

[4] Theorizing on the state has tended to be either extremely abstract, to concern itself with general issues of the state, such as its transformation over history, or to be inductively built from particular cases (for further discussion, see Levi 1988: 185–204). Some of this work begins the move toward an actual theory of the state that can specify why the state varies over time in the institutions that constitute it and what effect those institutions have on citizen behavior. However, there is still considerable ground to be covered in developing a satisfactory theory that links the actions of individuals to the structures and institutions in which they must act (Kiser and Hechter 1991). Nonetheless, these cases contribute to the literature that analyzes the microfoundations of state behavior.

liberal and democratic state (see, e.g., Cohen 1985; Silver 1994). Debates over the introduction of obligatory military service in democracies rehearses themes of ennobling self-sacrifice, nationalism, and the superiority of the needs of the state to the rights of the individual, on the one hand, and of the nature of full citizenship, fears of standing armies, and the superiority of the rights of the individual to the needs of the state, on the other. Military service is one of the central dilemmas for the liberal social contract as initially formulated by Thomas Hobbes. It is to protect one's life that an individual agrees to submit to the regulations of states. Thus, the demand by government that a young man potentially give up his life for his country puts a tension at the heart of political life, a tension Hobbes recognizes but does not satisfactorily resolve.[5]

The issues of consent, fairness, and obligation are clearly and unquestionably present in the institutions of military service in liberal democracies. Conscription is possible only with some form of permission by the citizenry. At the least, conscription, like taxation, demands representation. To what extent democratic conscription actually rests on the more exacting standard of consent is one of the empirical – and theoretical – questions at the heart of this book.

The focus on military service means the study is limited by issues of gender and, to some extent, age. Those making decisions whether to volunteer for the army, evade the draft, submit to conscription, or conscientiously object are both young and male. Nonetheless, the arguments developed here appear to have relevance for a broader range of cases, reviewed in the last chapter. From the investigation of a set of extreme extractive obligations, it may be possible to generalize the explanation of behavioral consent in one sphere to others in liberal democratic societies.

THE METHODOLOGICAL APPROACH

The approach of this book to the important philosophical and practical questions embodied in the concept of consent is by means of concrete empirical investigations informed by formal theory, especially game the-

---

[5] Sara Monoson pointed this tension out to me. Cohen (1985, esp. ch. 6) also recognizes this issue. See Kateb's (1992) critique of Hobbes, Locke, Rousseau, and Rawls for their lapses on this point (184–7) and his critique of the reasoning behind the United States Supreme Court decisions that upheld conscription (187–9); and see Walzer (1970: 82–6) on the ways Hobbes (1985 [1651]) attempts to reconcile men taking a risk and even dying to "protect their protection" (Hobbes, pt. II, ch. 29) with the fact that they are giving up the self-protection guaranteed by the social contract. Walzer (1970, 1977), Singer (1974), Kateb (1992), and Klosko (1992) are among the contemporary political theorists who have wrestled with the problem of when, morally, there is an obligation to die for the state.

ory. This description captures one of the meanings of "analytic narrative," [6] the approach advocated here. Analytic narrative combines detailed research of specific cases with a more general model capable of producing hypotheses about a significant range of cases outside the sample of the particular project. Reliance on the techniques of analytic narrative encourages sensitivity to the complexities of the case while providing sufficient analytical rigor to support carefully reasoned explanations consistent with the evidence and superior to the alternatives.

The use of analytic narrative is not, of course, restricted to those combining game theory and history. Much of the research in economic history fits this description (e.g. McCloskey 1991) as does that of those comparativists concerned with combining detailed contemporary case studies with formal theory (e.g. Laitin 1992; Golden 1996). Moreover, the term has currency in sociology, among those who are mathematical (e.g. Abell 1987, 1993; Abbott 1990, 1993; Fararo 1993), those more concerned with ontology (e.g. Somers 1992, 1994; Aminzade 1993), and those who consider themselves rationalists (e.g. Goldthorpe 1996; Kiser 1996).

Despite the interest in what is now called analytic narrative, however, there are still relatively few attempts to use the tools of modern political economy to provide sustained analyses of comparative political behavior in actual concrete settings.[7] For both area studies specialists and historical macrosociologists, case studies have been the major form of research and communication. Although case study work may correct the lack of adequate detail common to broad comparisons, it usually fails to offer adequate causal mechanisms. This makes generalization problematic. Indeed, too many of the proponents of case studies tend to reject general theory and all that implies about testing propositions, generalization, and prediction (Kiser and Hechter 1991; Collier 1991). To use case studies theoretically requires retaining sensitivity to the particularities and richness of the stories while actually offering the microfoundations that permit illumination of general theory. It requires translating the insights of game theory, microeconomics, and the "new economic institutionalism" into hypotheses that can account for important political events and decisions.

---

[6] Robert Bates, Avner Greif, Jean-Laurent Rosenthal, Barry Weingast, and I are currently completing a book that elaborates and develops this approach (in process).

[7] Among the exceptions not already mentioned are Bates (1991, 1997); Frieden (1991); Laitin (1992); Kiser (1994); Geddes (1994); Verdier (1994); and Kalyvas (1996). Although economic historians often claim to be political economists, there are still too few examples of sufficiently detailed cases in which politics and political institutions play an important role. Among the exceptions are Rosenthal (1992); Greif et al. (1994b); Milgrom et al. (1990); and North and Weingast (1989).

Methodological approach

In the analytic narrative used here, the tools of historical narrative combine with formal analytic theory to guide both the collection and assessment of information. The formal analytics require a deductive model in which rational actors strategically interact until they reach an equilibrium outcome from which no one has an incentive to deviate. This does not mean that all individuals are rational or strategic. Nor does it mean that there is a single equilibrium; it is more likely that there will be multiple equilibria. There are also instances where no equilibrium seems possible; cycles and chaos are more likely. Nonetheless, the presumption of equilibria permits the analyst to consider what would disrupt or inhibit a particular equilibrium.

Equilibrium analysis fosters the construction of comparative statics, which in turn produces a set of hypotheses concerning what exogenous shocks or alterations in the independent variables will have what effects on the actions of the individuals under study. For example, in *Of Rule and Revenue* (Levi 1988), a ruler, maximizing revenue to the state, must determine what kind of revenue production system to construct. Changes in the form of taxes and tax collection should, therefore, reflect changes in the transaction costs of collecting and enforcing certain kinds of taxes, the relative bargaining power of those likely to be taxed, and the expenditure requirements of the ruler. Moreover, particular outcomes should be predictable, that is, there will be no income tax until the costs of assessing and collecting income are sufficiently low to make it pay for the ruler.

The model indicates the links between independent and dependent variables and leads to an account of the mechanisms that are essential to a causal explanation. The logic of game theory is useful in simplifying the complexity of history, generating some testable, or at least observable, hypotheses, and providing grounds for generalization. A concern with the game logic builds both equilibrium analysis and institutions into the model. The new economic institutionalism clarifies what constrains or facilitates actions and what role information and beliefs play in affecting behavior (see, e.g., Tsebelis 1990; Ostrom 1990; Golden 1990; Bates and Krueger 1993; Firmin-Sellers 1996). The current infatuation among comparative political scientists, economists, and sociologists with institutions certainly gives institutions pride of place, but it is the fine grain of the links between institutions and behavior that rational choice scholars are attempting to model and that game theory helps to make plain.

An additional advantage of the game theoretic approach is that it permits specification of the counterfactual, the behavior that failed to occur because it is off the equilibrium path. In an important essay on "Objective Possibility and Adequate Causation in Historical Explana-

7

tion," Max Weber argued for the explicit and systematic use of counterfactuals as aspects of the empirical world that are contrary to fact but
not to logical or "objective" possibility (1949 [1905]). Counterfactuals
are indispensable in most comparative and historical work, since the
number of possible causal factors are so numerous and interrelated
and since the number of similar cases are seldom sufficient in number.
However, Weber's efforts to formulate some general principles for evaluating the plausibility of "objective possibility" lack adequate theoretical
grounds for justifying and circumscribing his counterfactual assumptions
(Elster 1978: 180).

Until recently (Tetlock and Belkin eds. 1996), there has been little
effort to systematically evaluate the role counterfactuals do play and can
play in social scientific analyses. Nor, until recently, has there been much
success in giving counterfactual assumptions theoretical justification.
However, game theory does provide a means to do just that. It outlines
the range of sequential choices available to the actors. To understand
why one of the paths becomes the equilibrium path, it is necessary to
understand why the actors did not follow other possible paths.[8] Thus,
the model generates testable hypotheses about: (1) what the beliefs of
the actors had to be and what they could not have been; and (2) what
the critical junctures were in the decision-making process.

Path dependence is the term social scientists currently use to capture
how past actions constrain present choices. Developed to account for
the persistence of suboptimal technologies (David 1985; Arthur 1989),
its applications to social and political arrangements are generally less
successful. Nonetheless, recognition of the persistence of suboptimal
institutions (North 1981, 1990; Putnam 1993) has begun to produce
models in which consideration of what is off the equilibrium path plays
a critical role in explaining how current arrangements are the effect of
past choices (Greif 1994a, b).

Of course, path dependence can have other sources as well. Game
theory also illuminates these. For example, the notion of focal points
(Schelling 1978) has proved essential for understanding coordination
without direct communication. Institutional arrangements and past
agreements often serve such coordinating functions and, moreover, make
it difficult to coordinate around alternatives, especially when mass mobilization is involved (Hardin 1995; in press).

While it is certainly the case that good theory often elaborates contingencies or points on the path where a different action or event may have
changed the outcome, it is also the case that theory should delimit the

---

[8] See, especially, the papers by Weingast (1996) and by de Mosqueta (1996). For a
discussion of counterfactuals in historical analysis, particularly as applied to revolution, see Kiser and Levi (1996).

possibilities. There is a tension in the work of most structuralists who, on the one hand, tend to make their theory extremely deterministic and, on the other hand, insist on conjunctural analysis that opens up too wide a range of possibilities. Here is where analytic narrative offers an important alternative approach. While it provides a causal model, it also illuminates the critical junctures or choice points. At its most successful, it can offer an account of why one path and not another is followed and then maintained.

The final problem that analytic narrative helps resolve is generalization and robustness. A wide range of cases in different places at different times provides a basis for presuming that the model is both general and robust, but more important is the derivation of explicit hypotheses from an explicit model. Such an enterprise permits the reader to reach her own conclusions about the persuasiveness of the evidence and to extend the model to other cases in other times and places. Particularities of cases may make generalizations across cases difficult, but theory helps sort the particular from the general. At this point in the development of analytic techniques, the complexity of the social world probably allows only "sometimes true theories" (Coleman 1964: 516–19; Scharpf 1990: 484). However, progress more often than not rests on the slow and incremental accumulation of knowledge.

The behavioral assumptions of an analytic narrative of citizen behavior

In the analytic narrative of variations in citizen consent and government policy-making, individuals are the decision makers. They can be narrowly egoistic or ethical, but they are rational in that they act instrumentally and consistently within the limits of constraints to produce the most benefit at the least cost. The variation in choice reflects the variation in constraints, often in the form of resources or institutions that delimit or enable action, promote certain beliefs over others, and provide or hide information.

Model building begins by identifying the key actors, positing the ends they are maximizing or optimizing, and then explaining their behavior by reference to the constraints and strategic interactions that influence their choices. The analysis of variations in state revenue production policies across time and place (Levi 1988) relies on the assumption that rulers maximize revenue to the state subject to the constraints of their relative bargaining power, discount rates, and transaction costs. Revenue maximizing is an intermediate end, instrumental to the achievement of any number of further ends. A ruler's ultimate goal could range from increasing personal wealth to enhancing power to promoting an ideolog-

9

ical agenda. The goals vary among rulers as does the concrete amount of revenue it is feasible to collect.

Military service policies have a similar structure. The ultimate end is to win a war or provide adequate defense or, possibly, pay off cronies with military contracts or stage a coup and become emperor. Recruitment and payment of soldiers is the means to achieve those ends. Thus, most rulers most of the time wish to enlarge their armies subject to their constraints, and the most important constraint is often the probable consent – or at least compliance – of the governed.

Focusing on the citizen rather than the ruler requires somewhat different assumptions, however. For one thing, there is likely to be considerably more variation in the information and beliefs, as well as preferences of citizens than of rulers. Whatever rule or norm informs the choice to comply is often shared and constructed by a group of actors who possess a common identity. This may mean shared interests, but it as often means a shared culture – racial, religious, or ethnic based – that may cut across interests. How such a group is defined and what norms it uses as behavioral rules are critical to the decision about how to act.

Nor does citizen compliance lend itself easily to a single maximand. Not only are there multiple preferences within the universe of citizens, a single individual may hold several goals. As has been often demonstrated with voting and as has been more recently demonstrated for regulatory strategies and public opinion (Kiewiet and Kinder 1981; Kiewiet 1983; Ayres and Braithwaite 1992; Stoker 1992; Scholz 1994), there may be both an ethical and egoistic element in the decision to comply (or not) or volunteer (or not). Certainly there are segments of the citizenry who maximize on one dimension rather than optimize on several. A large proportion, however, appear to have dual utilities.[9] They wish to contribute to the social good, at least as long as they believe a social good is being produced, but they also want to ensure that their individualistic interests are being satisfied as far as possible. Moreover, these interests cannot be ordered in the way a ruler's can. Achievement of ethical goals may not ensure achievement of self-interest, and ethical concerns may conflict with or undermine more egoistic ends. Sometimes institutional arrangements can ensure that ethical and self-interested concerns reinforce each other. Sometimes they cannot.

From the individual to the aggregate

Sufficient individual-level data to actually distinguish among causes of compliance are difficult (and usually impossible) to acquire. Even when

---

[9] Margolis (1990a, b) uses this term. Also see Margolis (1982).

10

there is information on individual behavior, there is seldom accompanying material on the tangible costs and benefits, ethical views, justifications, and attitudes of those same individuals. The one possible exception is the case of conscientious objectors, who must justify their behavior in a more or less public juridical process. What is more likely to exist are aggregate data on percentages of compliers, correlated with such factors as religion, geographical region, or occupation.

Using a model derived from individual action for explaining empirical variation among aggregates potentially runs afoul of the ecological fallacy. This would certainly be a problem if one is inferring the reasons for the choices made by the individuals who compose the aggregate from the behavior of the group. Alternatively, one can use the deductive methodology of the economist. Assuming that individuals act "as if" they are maximizing utility, one can hypothesize about behavior under varying constraints. This is the approach used by those who attempt to account for variations in organizational membership using hypotheses drawn from Mancur Olson's (1965) concept of the free rider. It is also the approach used here.

Even so, there are problems, particularly when using the logic of game theory. After rehearsing the range of objections to treating composite actors as a single player and while recognizing that aggregate actors have even less strategic rationality than corporate actors, coalitions, and collective actors, Scharpf (1991: 289) nonetheless claims that if the aggregated individuals have similar interests and situational constraints, ". . . it will make sense for others to anticipate their aggregate responses to a given stimulus as if they were a single composite actor." There is, however, one additional admonition: The game must be a sequential game in which the aggregate actor makes the second move (Scharpf 1991: 289–90).

In the analysis that follows, the games are among the government as a corporate actor and either a median legislature or aggregates of citizens. The government always acts first, and the citizens respond. The citizens can be an electorate as a single aggregate, simplified as the median or pivotal voter, or two aggregates of citizens with very distinct preferences, simplified as groups based on class, status, or party. In either case, the individual citizen is generally monitoring the behavior of other citizens as well as government actors.

THE SELECTION OF NARRATIVES

Explanations of variation in behavioral consent and government policy require detailed information about institutions, norms, policy content, and what people actually do. Cases drawn from six countries over the

11

past two hundred years provide the illustrative material. The countries are the United States, United Kingdom, Australia, Canada, New Zealand, and France. Five are Anglo-Saxon democracies. They all share a political tradition that affirms local rights and sets constraints on state incursions on those rights. Given that tradition, it is not surprising that they share a government ideology that makes conscription for a national military the exception rather than the rule. Even so, there are interesting differences among the countries that may account for differences in both government demands and citizen responses. While all are democracies, they have quite distinct histories in the granting and exercise of suffrage. They still differ in terms of the organization of both government and parties and in the nature of the cleavages that are politically salient. Australia granted suffrage to women with its Confederation in 1901 but excluded aboriginals until the 1960s, about the same time southern blacks gained an effective vote in the United States. Canada and Australia are the most markedly federal in organization. Among the five, only the United States does not operate with a parliamentary system. Nor has the United States ever had a serious labor party. Australia's Labor Party has periodically held power since 1914 and Britain's and New Zealand's for some part of the twentieth century. The francophones in Quebec and the Irish in Britain have territorial as well as linguistic claims that set them apart from groups in the other four countries.

France makes an interesting contrast, permitting exploration of the effect of underlying legal and state traditions. The Napoleonic Code, *étatisme,* and the numerous French experiments with forms of governance distinguish France from the common-law, more decentralized, and relatively more stable regimes of Anglo-Saxon countries.

To study military service in democracies and not include France would be indefensible. Modern conscription[10] has been an aspect of French national life since the Revolution. France, like Britain, is an old country with centuries of experience with military service that was more impressment than civic obligation. To establish an army of citizens required first the destruction of the army of the king and the lord. France was the first of the democracies to transform the very meaning as well as institutions of conscription; by the twentieth century, military obligation was a rite of passage to citizenship for young French males. Its purpose was as much nation building as nation protecting. This makes Jacques Chirac's abolition of required military service all the more interesting.

Military service is an important area of citizenship in which it is

---

[10] As Edgar Kiser reminds me, there were forms of earlier conscription: Medieval France had the *arrière-ban* and most other medieval kingdoms something similar.

possible to observe relevant behavior. Even so, good statistical data were difficult to locate. No country has kept comparable or complete statistics over time on who joins and who does not, and cross-country comparisons have proved difficult at best. Moreover, whole years and sets of records are missing. A fire in the St. Louis depository that held all the U.S. draft records is one kind of reason. More arcane is the account of a small fire that destroyed relevant materials from World Wars I and II in the Australian War Memorial. The representatives of the British government operate under strict rules of secrecy concerning a very large amount of military-related material, and they uphold those rules rigorously. The Australian government operates with a greater openness. The problem arose because in the Australian War Memorial were records that the British deemed secret and the Australians did not. The problem was resolved by the British, or so my reliable source tells me, by planting a mole archivist in the War Memorial. This mole lit a small fire in the relevant stacks and then disappeared.

The second obstacle was the accessibility of data even when there is reason to believe it is not missing. Having spent weeks meeting people who could introduce me to people who could give me a proper introduction to the head archivist at the Service Historique de l'Armée de la Terre at Vincennes and then spending days clarifying with her precisely what I needed, we discovered that the relevant material had, but a few years before, been transferred from the central to *departement* archives. When I returned the next year with further and different inquiries, a new archivist was in place. He listened to my questions and then had a young soldier usher me into a private room, set several unmarked file folders on my desk, and permitted me to photocopy as much of the material as I wanted. I photocopied it all. Who knows what I will one day need and if I – or anyone else – could ever locate those files again? The British posed a very different sort of access problem. They, like most of the countries in my sample, operate with a rule that closes records on military personnel for up to 50 years after the relevant war. However, when I asked about personnel statistics from World War I, the military historian in charge of the records informed me that, one, they were not aggregated, and, two, the only way I could get access to the individual attestation papers was to get permission from each recruit or his closest living relative. I concluded that even the National Science Foundation might consider the cost too high for what might prove a very low return on the investment.

Data problems confirmed investigation of the model by means of case studies with statistical illustrations rather than some large cross-national, cross-historical time series analyses. However, it was the reliance on case studies that posed a third obstacle to the research, particularly in Canada, Australia, and New Zealand. These are countries with very small populations and very long histories of European colonization. Consequently, the secondary literature is spotty. On some issues it is very good, on other issues nonexistent. This is in marked contrast to France, Britain, or the United States, in which so much of the history has been mined in great detail.

THE ORGANIZATION OF THE BOOK

As with most instances of analytic narrative, the logic of exposition is distinct from the logic of inquiry, to loosely paraphrase Marx.[11] The process of inquiry begins with a deductive model, but the inductive investigation transforms and produces a fuller elaboration of the deductive model. However, in the written text the presentation of the model precedes the presentation of the cases. Thus, it is important to evaluate the model in terms not only of the cases presented but also in terms of out-of-sample cases or of cases developed by other analysts.

Elaborating the deductive model of contingent consent is the project of Chapter 2. The purpose of Chapters 3–7 is to explore the implications and plausibility of the model through examination of particular puzzles. The last chapter explores the implications of the model of contingent consent for theories of political consent, political obligation, and democracy, and it reconsiders and refines the model in light of the findings here and in the works of others.

Consent, Dissent, and Patriotism represents an exploration of the very real tensions experienced by the citizens of democracies confronting decisions to expend considerable personal resources on behalf of a collective good, by government actors aiming to be both effective and popular, by social scientists seeking both good theory and good explanation, and by rational choice scholars who recognize the reality of both self-interest and ethics. This book heightens rather than alleviates these tensions. It reveals the contradictions faced by the historical actor and the analyst of history and insists on their reality. Instead of evading the obligation to confront these problems, this book makes them the centerpiece of attention. *Consent, Dissent, and Patriotism* represents a grand ambition. It is an attempt to use rational choice models to explain

---

[11] In the actual words of Marx (1974 [1867]: 19), "Of course the method of presentation must differ in form from that of inquiry. The latter has to appropriate the material in detail, to analyze its different forms of development, to trace out their inner connection. Only after this work is done, can the actual movement be adequately described."

phenomena not usually considered susceptible to rational choice analysis; it insists on the combination of model building, attention to the complexities of history, and empirical tests; and it aims to contribute to both empirical and normative democratic theory.

2

The contingencies of consent

We are coming, Father Abraham, three hundred thousand more,
From Mississippi's winding stream and from New England's shore;
We leave our ploughs and workshops, our wives and children too.
With hearts too full for utterance, with but a silent tear;
We dare not look behind us, but steadfastly before;
We are coming, Father Abraham, three hundred thousand more!
    James S. Gibbons, "We Are Coming, Father Abraham," 1862

Hell, No!
We won't go!
    Chant of protest against the War in Vietnam, 1965

When are individuals actively consenting and when are they more pas-
sively engaged in conforming or acquiescing? How much difference does
it make to the everyday practice of democratic governance whether it is
consent or not? How is policy-making influencing and influenced by
behavioral consent? The model of contingent consent offers a means to
begin to answer these questions both logically and historically. When
citizens believe government actors promote immoral policies, have ignored their interests, or have actually betrayed them, citizens are unlikely
to feel obliged to comply with the laws. The discovery that some citizens
are failing to contribute reduces the willingness of otherwise willing
citizens to comply. Failure to achieve contingent consent constrains
policy-making, but government actors can affect the extent of contingent
consent by means of their policies, institutional arrangements, and administrative practices. These are the central arguments of the book.

    The first part of this chapter offers a model to account for empirical
variation in behavioral consent, the second some alternative models, and
the third some specific hypotheses concerning military service policy.
Throughout there is a concern with distinguishing behavioral consent –

or its refusal – from other acts. Not all compliance is consent, and compliance often has multiple motivations.

THE MODEL OF CONTINGENT
CONSENT: COMPLIANCE

"Silence gives consent" (Goldsmith 1921: Act II, 19) is a false aphorism, if by silence is meant the failure to choose. Consent implies a choice, a choice perceivable by the outside observer. Sometimes this choice leads to inaction, but consent and, correlatively, refusal to consent always demands a decision. As Burawoy argues in regard to the labor process (1979: 27):

... consent is expressed through, and is the result of, the organization of activities. It is to be distinguished from the specific consciousness or subjective attributes of the individual who engages in those activities. Within the labor process the basis of consent lies in the organization of activities as though they presented the worker with real choices, however narrowly confined those choices might be. It is participation in choosing that generates consent.

Burawoy is not alone is his effort to study consent as a behavioral choice. In his rich account of the reaction of peasants to landlord-initiated changes in their work relationships, Scott (1985) describes a repertoire of choices that highlight noncompliance as a form of dissent with the new status quo.

The emphasis on consent as a behavioral choice transcends the political theory debate over tacit or express consent.[1] The observer, whether an interested government or a disinterested scholar, infers consent by observing behaviors. The number of supporting votes is one indicator of the extent of behavioral consent to government, but, as both Presidents Johnson and Nixon learned, electoral mandates do not represent blanket permissions. In terms of specific policies, a better indicator is compliance. Compliance represents a behavioral response of citizens that is likely to have an effect on the substance of government policy. By significantly raising the costs of implementation, noncompliance is an attack on a policy, whether or not it is an explicit act of resistance.

Compliance and noncompliance are not the simple dichotomous variables they at first appear to be, however. All compliance is not consent; nor is all noncompliance the withdrawal of consent. Most compliance and noncompliance engender ambivalent readings: Tax payment may connote approval of the government or fear of being caught and pun-

---

[1] A discussion of the political theory and philosophical literature appears in the concluding chapter.

ished for nonpayment; draft evasion can be a form of conscientious objection or of free-riding; a milling, angry crowd may constitute a rebellion or a riot. Such acts have multiple interpretations and multiple interpreters. Witness the shirking and vandalism that James Scott (1985) so skillfully convinces the reader are "weapons of the weak" in a political struggle.[2] Noncompliance may simply be opportunism; it may also be resistance. In the hands of the powerful, it may reflect a capacity to ignore the rules that apply to others. In the hands of the relatively powerless, it may indeed be a "weapon of the weak." Compliance may simply be a response to incentives; on the other hand, it may reflect citizen authorization of government action. Perhaps what we have come to call consent, even when it takes the form of risking your life for your country, is simply submission and involves no consent at all. Perhaps what we have come to describe as compliance is actually a means of expressing consent.

The difficulty in interpreting compliance and noncompliance is partially a result of the multiple motivations at work in an individual's decision. Undoubtedly some compliance is the result of coercion or other sanctions and incentives, but at least some compliance expresses a confirmation of a belief in the rightness of the policies and of the trustworthiness of the government actors implementing them. To understand the implications of citizen behavior in democracies demands a capacity to "read" when citizen compliance and noncompliance are political statements, expressing content and discontent with government policies. To develop this capacity requires an explanatory framework to account for the behaviors observed.

Compliance and noncompliance are behavioral variables on which it is possible to collect data. However, for both the negative and positive versions of these variables, there are at least four possible readings or interpretations of what the behavior means (Table 2.1). These interpretations can be transformed into four simplified empirical models of compliance. In each model the cause of compliance is different, and thus the hypotheses accounting for its variation will also differ. Only the second and fourth models involve consent, and only the third and fourth involve rational choices. Neither the model of customary obedience nor of opportunistic obedience assumes a reflective evaluation of government or its policies in the decision to comply. A perception that government is trustworthy or that policies are worthy of support are compatible with the nonconsent compliance models, but they are not the motivating factors. Neither the model of customary obedience nor of ideological

---

[2] Far more extreme examples are offered by others, such as Franz Fanon or Eldridge Cleaver when they claim that even theft, murder, and rape can be understood as weapons in a war by the oppressed against oppressors.

Model of contingent consent: Compliance

Table 2.1. *Possible readings of behavior*

COMPLIANCE			
Habitual obedience	Ideological consent	Opportunistic obedience[a]	Contingent consent
Conformity to habit of obedience	Supportive ideology	MB > MC	Trusts government
			Ethical reciprocity

NONCOMPLIANCE			
Habitual disobedience	Ideological dissent	Opportunistic disobedience	Contingent refusal to consent
Conformity to habit of disobedience	Oppositional ideology	MC > MB	Distrusts government
			Little ethical reciprocity

[a] MB = marginal benefits of compliance; MC = marginal costs of compliance

consent require actors to be rational. The reasons for conforming or acting ideologically derive from habits or emotions rather than from calculations about how best to achieve desired ends.

The model of contingent consent (Figure 2.1) can account for when individuals will be compliant even when their individual material costs exceed their individual material benefits and even in the absence of strong ideological convictions that make costs totally irrelevant. Contingent consent is a citizen's decision to comply or volunteer in response to demands from a government only if she perceives government as trustworthy and she is satisfied other citizens are also engaging in ethical reciprocity. A trustworthy government is a necessary but insufficient condition for large-scale contingent consent. Although the perception of a trustworthy government might explain the choices of some individuals, its effects will be significantly enhanced by the additional presence of ethical reciprocity. If most other citizens are nonreciprocal, even though government appears trustworthy, then the possibility of contingent consent is remote.

An assessment of costs and benefits also influences the decision to comply, but they are not the only consideration of contingent consenters. Even when short-term material self-interest would make free-riding the individually best option, the contingently consenting citizen still prefers

19

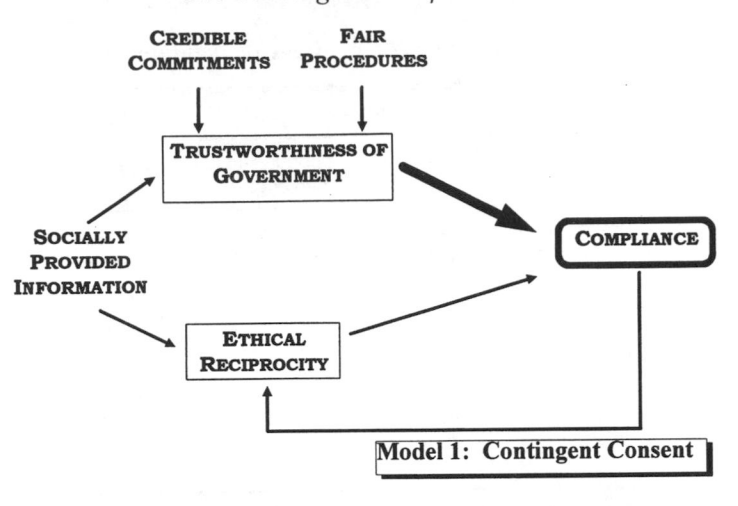

Figure 2.1. Models of compliance: contingent consent.

to cooperate.[3] However, if the costs of compliance become too high, then a cost–benefit calculation will probably trump other considerations.

Contingent consent encompasses quasi-voluntary compliance, which involves compliance with a law when the actor chooses to comply but faces punishment if caught not complying (Levi 1988: 52–5), for example, tax paying or complying with conscription. However, contingent consent is a broader category, for it also includes compliance and volunteering not required by law, for example, voluntary military service or donations of blood. Contingent consent is reducible to neither material self-interest nor normative and moral considerations. Contingent consenters fit Laura Stoker's account of "citizens as ethical actors" with "each citizen as an individual with her own unique hopes and desires who is at the same time joined with others, part of and continually giving shape to a common social and political life" (1992: 376). Given a set of ethical standards about what makes a government just and what is involved in being fair, contingent consenters are those individuals who want to act ethically, who would like to contribute to the collective good, all things being equal, but who will do so only under certain contingencies.

The model of contingent consent implies a relationship that requires

[3] I am purposely avoiding the debate about whether such actors are "quasi-rational (Thaler 1991) or acting out of enlightened self-interest (see, e.g., Binmore 1994: 24 and *passim*). Clearly, however, I am dealing with issues in which moral choice and egoistic choice sometimes conflict (see esp., Hardin 1988: 11 and *passim*).

ongoing sustenance. It involves give and take, trust, and knowledge between those being asked to consent and those doing the asking. It is both fragile and resilient. Consent withers easily, but it sometimes withstands gale force winds. The strength of ethical reciprocity among citizens and their confidence and trust in government determine the durability of consent.

From the model of contingent consent emerge the following hypotheses to explain variation in compliance:

(1) *The more trustworthy citizens perceive government to be, the more likely they are to contingently consent to its policies and, therefore, comply.*

(2) *The larger the proportion of citizens contributing from a given population, the more likely others from that population will also contribute.*

(3) *Government policymakers, their supporters, and their opposition will devote resources to disseminating information about the trustworthiness of government and the probability of ethical reciprocity among the relevant population.*

The following sections elaborate the reasoning behind these hypotheses.

Government trustworthiness

To make an evaluation of government trustworthiness, citizens consider, one, the history of and present capacity of government actors to make credible commitments about the use of their contributions and, two, government's procedures for making and implementing policy. The more a government is capable of credible commitments and the more its procedures meet prevailing standards of fairness, the more trustworthy that government will seem.

Both credible commitments and procedures are largely functions of institutional arrangements. Institutions are composites of rules and incentives that structure social interactions and whose existence and applicability are commonly known within the relevant community. Institutions, so defined, structure the individual choices of strategic actors so as to produce equilibrium outcomes, that is, outcomes that no one has an incentive to alter. The rules have this effect because they convey expectations about sanctions, opportunities, and the behavior of others. This information then enables each actor to make an informed strategy choice.

In principle institutions are distinct from organizations. Institutions are the rules of the game and organizations the players and their strategies.[4] All institutions are embodiments of rules, all have a legalistic aspect, and all possess enforcement mechanisms. They are considered political institutions when the state enforces the rules, social institutions when enforcement is through mechanisms such as approval and shunning, and economic institutions when enforcement is by means of profit and loss.[5]

Institutional arrangements for promoting credible commitments

Credible commitments depend on institutions that ensure that transgressors will be punished. In polities under rule of law, government use of public coffers or citizen armies for illicit purposes can lead to jail sentences, fines, and other direct and tangible penalties. Corrupt governments are certainly likely to undermine contingent consent (Levi and Sherman in press), but an even more common problem for democracies is creating institutions that ensure the credible commitments of government officials to protect minority interests. Elected government officials may face the punishment of defeat in the next election if they break promises to the majority,[6] but the threat of electoral reprisal seldom safeguards a minority, especially if they are in a different political party or not an active part of the electorate.

Another source of credible commitments is reputational mechanisms, both bilateral and multilateral, that create relatively reliable expectations about the behavior of others (see, e.g., Greif 1989, 1994a; North and Weingast 1989; Milgrom, North, and Weingast 1990; Greif, Milgrom, and Weingast 1994). They can be very important in accounting for cooperation within large democracies. Legislative institutions structure the relations among the legislators and between legislators and the executive so that they become repeat transactions among individuals who bargain with each other over a variety of quite distinct issues. This creates the possibility of long-term interactions that depend on contin-

---

[4] Organizations are "groups of individuals bound by some common purpose to achieve objectives" (North 1990: 5) or, what is essentially the same thing, "collective actors who might be subject to institutional constraint" (Knight 1992: 3). Institutions and organization are closely intertwined, and often the same term is used to describe a particular example of both, e.g. firm, Congress, family. The legal institution of the firm is not exactly the same as the actual shareholders, managers, and employees who people the firm. Nor are the informal societal rules that guide family behavior in complete identity with the choices made by the actual family. The institution regulates behavior but cannot totally determine it. The organization, that is the individuals whose fates are tightly interwoven by an overarching common purpose, may not always be regulated.

[5] Michael Lipsky helped me to perceive this distinction.

[6] However, see recent research by Stokes (1996) about how little the effect is on the electorate of policy shifts from campaign promises concerning economic reform.

ued confidence that one's bargaining partner is trustworthy. The relations between street-level bureaucrats (Lipsky 1980) and clients can take on similar characteristics. Corporatist relations among unions, employer groups, and government agencies can also promote cooperation, at least for a time. However, even among those for whom a reputational mechanism would suffice and especially for those for whom it would not, there may still need to be enough common knowledge to produce sufficient trust and confidence for individuals to undertake the risk of cooperation. Common knowledge can result from a preliminary game or set of communications, from shared values, or from networks of social embeddedness (Granovetter 1985).

Punishment cannot occur unless the offense is evident, however. Monitoring of government officials is sometimes difficult, and even more difficult is citizen determination of the appropriateness of official behavior in the face of problems citizens may not adequately understand. Thus, the next problem is credible information. Within contemporary democracies, institutional arrangements that ensure credible information require the establishment or protection of third parties for whom the incentives are to monitor government actors and citizens and then to reveal all. Such are the institutions of the independent judiciary, legislative oversight committees, public hearings, and free press. Together, they provide more reason for faith that commitments will be kept or, at least, that transgressions will be discovered and punished. On the other hand, the easy availability of information may make it harder to maintain contingent consent over time. For example, media revelations of government corruption or secrecy, public debates and inquiries, and regulations affecting accountability have made the normal behaviors of government officials a matter of public and moral concern. It has also become more difficult to prevent one group of actors from knowing about the behavior of another group of actors. So, taxpayers soon enough learn about tax evaders. Those playing by the official rules of the welfare system soon learn how "to play the game." The effect is to undermine the credibility of government in its commitment to enforce contributions.

Fair policy-making and implementation processes

In both contingent consent and contingent refusal to consent, the assessment of the actual policy can make a difference. However, in most cases citizens are willing to go along with a policy they do not prefer as long as it is made according to a process they deem legitimate, and they are less willing to comply with a policy they like if the process was problematic (see, e.g., Lind and Tyler 1988; Tyler 1990).

Contingent consent in modern democracies is constructed around three possible criteria of fairness. The first concerns an equitable principle of participation in the making of the policy. If a group perceives that its voice is systematically ignored, it will not accept the policy-making process as fair. The second has to do with outcomes and equity. A policy that some of the population perceives as discriminatorily harmful is likely to be considered unfair and unjust. The third emphasizes procedural justice as a universalistic principle. A policy that is enforced discriminatorily is likely to be considered unfair. These are not universal norms, however. What is understood as inequitable participation, discriminatorily harmful, procedurally unjust, or nonreciprocal varies across time, place, and group.

The process by which policy is made, the collective good to be achieved, the anticipated contributions of government actors and citizens, and the estimate of any private benefits are all part of citizen considerations of what it means for a policy to be fair. The crucial ingredients, however, are the extent to which citizens feel that their arguments are considered in the policy debate; the delineation of circumstances under which citizens are willing to contribute lives, labor, goods, and money to government or in some other way cede power to government over their persons and purses; and the belief in the relative evenhandedness of government administration of those obligations.

Much of the history of democratic and responsible governance is the history of the search for institutions that provide voting minorities with a means to block majoritarian policies that harm them. Institutions and government actions may prove insufficient, however, to overcome distrust based on recent experiences of government untrustworthiness or on cultural beliefs (Greif 1994a), expectations about the credibility or trustworthiness of others based on group membership. Culturally based distrust does not constitute a freestanding ideology. It draws on concrete historical events to differentiate in-group from out-group members (see, e.g., Petersen 1989), the trustworthy from the untrustworthy. When a cultural identity is triggered, it usually generates an important and nonuniversalistic set of views concerning appropriate collective goods and standards of fairness.

Ethical reciprocity

Ethical reciprocity is a norm requiring that individuals in a given population cooperate with government demands but only as long as others are also contributing. Key to ethical reciprocity is a definition of the population of those to whom each member should behave fairly. This population may encompass all citizens in the country (or even world), or it may encompass only those with certain shared attributes, such as religion, race, or political ideology. Sometimes ethical reciprocity evokes mutual cooperation in support of the government, and sometimes it evokes mutual cooperation in opposition to the government, reducing the likelihood of compliance. When there is no ethical reciprocity, there is less likelihood of contingent consent and compliance. When some members of a population feel ethical obligations only to a small subset of the others or when there is conflict about whether to cooperate with the government, compliance is correspondingly reduced.

Contingent consent is not possible without confidence that other citizens will keep their side of the agreement. Once such confidence in others breaks down, so does contingent consent. Contingent consenters are strategic but ethical actors; they want to cooperate if others are also cooperating. They have a prior commitment to an ethical position of fair play combined with a perception of the extent to which others who presumably share that position are cooperating with each other or free-riding. Thus, ethical reciprocity is distinct from both reciprocity for mutual advantage, a matter only of tit for tat, and social pressure, a question of selective incentives. Ethical reciprocity rests on a desire to behave fairly and is reinforced by evidence that others are doing their part. It has more of the structure of an assurance than a prisoner dilemma's game.[7]

Small communities are arguably the best locus of mechanisms that provide information and assurances at the lowest cost. The relationships of a community produce the long time horizons, cross-cutting and repeat interactions, and mutual knowledge that in turn promote conditional cooperation (Taylor 1987 [1976], 1982) or "nice" tit for tat. Dependence on the community and fear of possible exclusion from its benefits encourages cooperation (Hechter 1987). Such sanctions are relatively inexpensive and endogenous to the community, requiring no construction of a centralized state apparatus.

In large polities, however, individuals often find themselves in situations where they would benefit from cooperation with those about whom they have very imperfect information. This is possible only to the extent that they can have confidence that they will not be exploited by those they trust. One response, of course, is to refrain from taking the risk and to trust only those within a relatively small network.[8] Others

---

[7] Barry (1995: 51) also makes this point and, further, argues that a motivation based on the desire to behave fairly creates greater stability than a motivation based on mutual advantage. The conception of reciprocity as mutual advantage has as its analogue for tit-for-tat strategy in the prisoner's dilemma game. See, e.g., Ullman-Margalit (1977), Axelrod (1986), Elster (1989), and Klosko (1987, 1992).

[8] Yamagishi and Yamagishi (1994) argue that this has been the strategy of most Japanese, and Fukuyama (1995) claims that Chinese familism plays this role. In both cases, the authors argue that the effect is to limit economic growth.

search for mechanisms that will enable them to cooperate with people outside their group. Community accountability and reputational mechanisms, both bilateral and multilateral, produce institutions that can solve this dilemma.

Community accountability was a common practice in Republican Rome, which relied on the *gens* to collect taxes (Levi 1988: 79) and in medieval England, where villages were held responsible for contracts made by any of their members (Greif in press). Community accountability is also quite viable for citizens with strong religious or ethnic ties; the social pressures on them to conform can be quite strong.[9]

However, as distinct villages and regions with distinct laws and traditions evolve into a nation, the salient reference group for ethical reciprocity increasingly becomes the whole society rather than the particular cultural group of birth. Not all agree, of course, but a generalized ethical reciprocity has increasingly become the norm in democratic nation-states, at least when it comes to paying taxes or going to war.

Governmental institutional arrangements designed to provide incentives and to facilitate monitoring and enforcement can also promote contingent consent. Under some circumstances institutional arrangements exist that make normative and instrumental motivations operate in the same direction (see, e.g., Margolis 1990a, b; Ostrom 1990: 94–100; Mansbridge 1990b); government enforcement of compliance assures those considering contingent consent that they will not be suckers. To the extent such institutions affect behavior by influencing the relative costs and benefits of compliance, they contribute to opportunistic obedience. To the extent government coercive capacity assures potentially supportive citizens that there will, in fact, be relative equality of sacrifice, governmental institutions contribute to contingent consent.

Socially provided information

Citizen compliance is in response to government actions; a government demand for contributions, cooperation, or obedience engenders the choice to comply. However, the decision to contingently consent does not occur in a social and political vacuum. Estimates of government trustworthiness and the likely behavior of other citizens derive from

[9] Hechter (1987) develops an argument to account for the ability of a group to exercise that kind of social pressure. Also, see Greif (1989, 1993). In a recent paper, Fearon and Laitin (1996) make a powerful argument that a form of community accountability, which they label "in-group policing," is even more effective for inhibiting interethnic conflict than is punitive action against all members of the ethnic group for the defection of one. In another context, Petersen (1989) demonstrates the role of ethnic group pressure in encouraging or discouraging compliance with military service.

a combination of personal observations and information provided by acquaintances, media, and organizations.

Although government actors may be aware that the behavior of each depends on evidence that others are complying or volunteering, this does not necessarily lead to suppression of information about noncompliance. The state might reveal widespread citizen (or corporate) noncompliance as a side effect of its efforts to demonstrate its enforcement power. Or the press might make revelations as the side effect of getting a "story." Moreover, the media has incentives to uncover government corruption or secret policies and to report public inquiries and debates; libel and other laws make it increasingly difficult to turn pure fiction into fact. We live in a relatively high information society in which it is hard not to know about the behavior of government officials and other citizens. So taxpayers soon enough learn about tax evaders and conscripts about draft dodgers.

Political and cultural organizations can also affect perceptions of the trustworthiness of government and of the extent of ethical reciprocity. Churches, mosques, and other places of worship can provide assurances about the behavior of others and, at the same time, influence evaluations of government policy-making. Charismatic leaders, nationalists, and self-serving entrepreneurs can also serve that role. Often, the individuals who distrust government or other groups in their society are not the same individuals who had the relevant experiences. The Bosnians, Serbs, and Croats who are slaughtering each other in the twentieth century inhabit a material and political world quite different from that of the ancestors upon whose history they draw. Crucial to the political salience of their beliefs are, first, restimulation of past grievances by the experience of new grievances; second, organizations and entrepreneurs who mobilize people around those cultural memories, long past and recent; and, third, the absence (or destruction) of institutions that protected their particular interests. Of course, the interpretation of cultural experiences and events is colored by the teller of the tales. Indeed, tellers of the tales are crucial for effectively activating cultural identity and consequent antagonism to the government and other sets of citizens.

ALTERNATIVE MODELS OF COMPLIANCE

There are three alternative models of compliance (Figure 2.2). In each, institutions and organizations provide information, but the salient information is different.

From these models are derived alternative hypotheses for explaining consent:

27

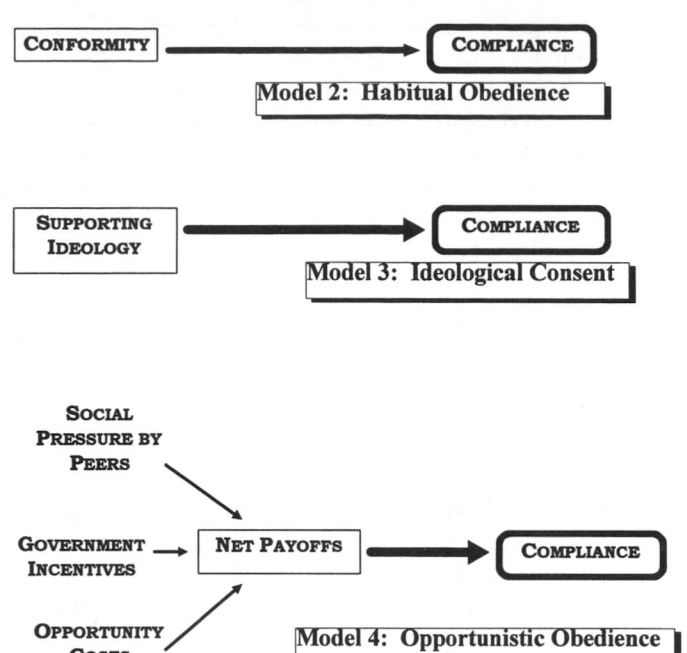

Figure 2.2. Models of compliance: alternative models.

(alt. 1) *The more developed the habits of conformity, the more compliance.*

(alt. 2) *The more strongly and widely held are ideological positions in support of a particular policy, the more compliance.*

(alt. 3) *The greater the marginal benefit to each individual from compliance, the more compliance.*

Habitual obedience

A custom is a regular and normatively acceptable course of action, which may become consensual but was not necessarily established by conscious voluntary agreement.[10] Adam Smith, Max Weber, and many others perceive custom as a major motivation for behavior. Weber (1968: 327) notes, "It cannot be overstressed that the mere habituation to a mode of action, the inclination to preserve this habituation, and

---

[10] This definition borrows from that offered by Weber (1968: 326–7) of tradition and by Opp (1990: 119) of custom.

28

much more so, tradition, have a formidable influence in favor of a habituated legal order."

Customary obedience may be a consequence of tradition, habits of obedience, or following the crowd, but even the most traditional, habit-bound, or fashion-sensitive actor might change with new stimuli or information. If what appears to be customary obedience is actually a response to social pressure or legal coercion (Weber 1968: 327), customary obedience is actually incentive-based behavior. If customary obedience is in response to reinforcement (Herrnstein 1993), it becomes obedience to a social norm, that is, a rule that regulates behavior by means of sanctions. Reliance on norms may enable an individual to avoid excessive calculations; nonetheless, such reliance renders the model of customary obedience consistent with models derived from rational choice and most particularly the model of opportunistic obedience described below. To the extent that this is the case, customary obedience will be subsumed by opportunistic obedience.

Customary obedience is not readily susceptible to investigation through historical case studies. Thus, it will not be directly subject to falsification. To the extent that the other hypotheses fail to account for compliance and to the extent that a story of conformity appears to fit the facts, then custom or habit will emerge as the explanation.

Ideological consent

The second alternative model posits that the causes of compliance are ideological or moral principles that motivate people to comply with – or resist – government demands with little regard to individual selective incentives. At its most extreme, a principled commitment is not affected by what others do; it is a personal moral code that drives behavior (Monroe 1996).

The nature of the collective good is usually what matters, but for some ideological consenters or refusers the evaluation of the nature of the government itself may be important. For example, both the Black Panthers and the Freemen reject the laws of the United States as emanating from an illegitimate government. American Quakers, on the other hand, believe they have political obligations to uphold U.S. law in general, but in the case of war their political obligation is outweighed by the moral obligation to refrain from killing. Thus, they will not comply with conscription, but they will pay their taxes, respect the police and courts, and even serve in dangerous wartime positions.

The only factors that cause behavioral change are changes in the definition of what constitutes moral duty or in the policies of the government to more closely approximate what the ideologically motivated actor believes is right. For example, a change in religious or political identity may affect compliance; thus, joining the Klu Klux Klan in the 1940s, the Weathermen in the 1960s, or one of the militant militias in the 1990s bolsters tendencies toward noncompliance and even terrorism. On the other hand, the abolitionist, suffragist, and anti-apartheid movements lost their raisons d'être with the elimination of policies to which they objected.

The most parsimonious explanation of variation in compliance is variation in ideological or principled commitment to a particular policy. This is a hard variable to measure since it is an internal motivation; attitudes and values, even when captured by surveys and the like, do not always correlate with behavior. Thus, ideology, as in the case of habit, is often a residual. However, patriotism, pacifism, anarchism, and many other -isms are powerful motivators for some people in some places and at some times.

Opportunistic obedience

Incentives also provide a parsimonious explanation. The costs and benefits of actions are usually both observable and measurable and thus are the most straightforward source of explanation for behavioral variation. Indeed, the usual rational choice expectation is that aggregate compliance will vary with individual costs and benefits. This is the Olson model (1965). Opportunistic obedience is compliance due to fear of sanctions or promise of inducements. Opportunistic disobedience is noncompliance motivated by expectations of net gains from law-breaking. Variations in obedience and disobedience are a function of the combination of selective incentives and mechanisms of monitoring and enforcement.[11] They are the effect of material self-interest, that is, a utility function that includes only tangible benefits and costs to oneself and, possibly, a small group of significant others such as family and close friends.

Opportunistically obedient and disobedient citizens are indifferent to the collective good to which they are being asked to contribute, and neither ethical nor strategic considerations influence their behavioral choices.

THE MODEL OF CONTINGENT CONSENT: POLICY-MAKING

The models of compliance suggest the factors influencing variation in citizen behavioral compliance and consent. The next step is to model

---

[11] This is a much narrower definition than Etzioni's (1961). He includes both unconditional and contingent consent under the rubric of compliance. I distinguish consent from compliance.

how citizen compliance and consent influence the making of policy. One of the major punitive actions available to citizens against their governments is the withdrawal of consent if their interests are neglected or ignored. If a set of individuals share an antagonism to government, then, the argument goes, each person in that set is more likely to refuse her consent to the extent she perceives others also refusing consent. This produces the kind of snowballing that characterizes social movements. In all regimes, democratic or not, government actors weigh the likelihood and cost of noncompliance to their proposals, and they weigh the capacity of opponents to topple them. In countries where some segment of the population is enfranchised, government actors calculate the probability of losing elections for imposing unpopular policies.

The analysis begins with a simple decision tree of the interaction between government policy proposers and citizens[12] (Figure 2.3). There are actually two different decisions at issue. The first is the introduction of a legal obligation, and the second is the form that obligation will take, for instance, who will be subject to the legal requirements, who can be exempted, and how exemptions are achieved. Given political opposition by citizens likely to impose a cost if their views are ignored, a government has three options: withdraw its proposal to introduce the policy, introduce the kinds of exceptions that make it palatable to those who may impose the costs, or introduce a universal requirement.

The government policymaker moves first to demand voluntary contributions. Citizens respond to produce either enough voluntary contributions or too few to meet government's goals. The government policymaker then decides whether or not to introduce legal requirements. If citizens continue to evade or resist in large numbers, the government policymaker, given his demand for contributions and the amount of resistance, then decides how many resisters to prosecute. Both government and citizen players are strategic actors. The government policymakers take into account the probability of achieving enough voluntary contributions and of provoking resistance with the imposition of coerced contributions. The citizens take into account both how many others have voluntarily contributed and the likelihood of the government imposing coercion if contributions do not suffice.

There are several possible policy outcomes: reliance only on voluntary contributions (P1), selective enforcement of legally obligated compliance (P2 and P3), and universally implemented legal obligations (P4). The decision tree can be transformed in a simple stylized game (Figure 2.4). However, elucidation of the actual policies and payoffs requires

---

[12] The prototype for this decision tree comes from a paper by Gardner (1991) in which he models draft resistance as an extensive form game. I have altered his decision tree slightly to make it more general.

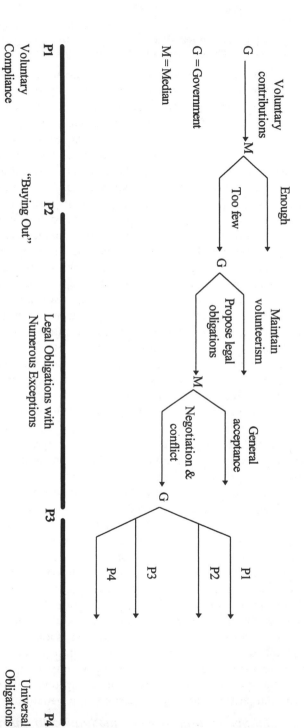

Figure 2.3. Government policy decision tree.

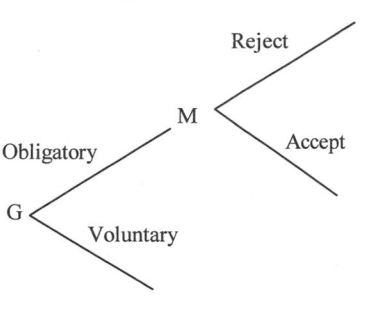

Figure 2.4. Stylized military service policy game.

sufficient knowledge of the actual cases so that they can approach reality.

What the tree and game do clarify, however, is both the demand and supply sides of government policy-making. Government demand is a function of the number of the contributions government believes it requires. Supply is a function of the probable extent of effective opposition and compliance. To the extent that citizens are organized resisters, and especially if they are territorially distinct groups contemplating secession, their threats of noncompliance are more credible and their demands carry more clout. However, even individual acts of noncompliance can have major consequences for the success of government policy. While such individual acts are "weapons of the weak" (Scott 1985), they can nonetheless lead to changes in policy and in institutional arrangements (Levi 1990; Levi and Singleton 1991). Delimiting the decisions of government actors are the electoral, protest, and compliance costs that unhappy citizens can impose on them. Citizen action, both actual and potential, constrains the policy choices and influences what is on and off the equilibrium policy path.

MILITARY SERVICE POLICY

The substantive policy question addressed in this book is the explanation for the military service requirements imposed by different democratic polities at different times in the nineteenth and twentieth centuries. The military service policy bargain is a metaphor for the set of mutual expectations that government actors and citizens have of each other. The process by which policy is made, the collective good to be achieved, the anticipated contributions of government actors and citizens, and the estimate of any private benefits are all part of the bargain. The crucial ingredient, however, is the delineation of circumstances under which, first, citizens are willing to contribute lives, labor, goods, and money to

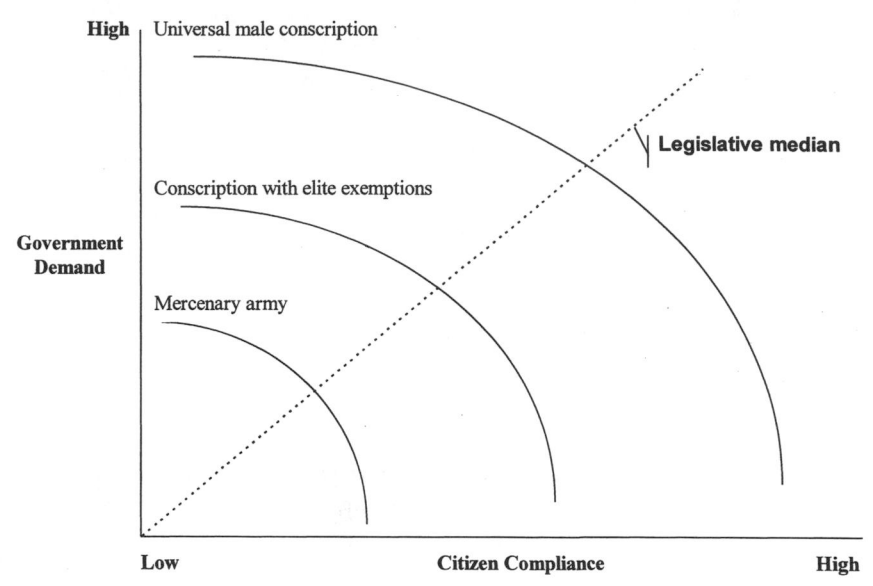

Figure 2.5. Legislative median on military service policies for government and citizens.

government or in some other way cede power to government over their persons and purses; and, second, government can use coercion to enforce contributions and compliance.

There is seldom one unique set of laws and regulations that will meet the negotiated goals of citizens, legislators, and government policymakers. Rather, there is a menu of policies from which governments must choose. For example, in the case of aiding the poor, the U.S. Congress is considering bloc grants to states, job training requirements, and so on. There are alternatives, such as negative income taxes or other forms of a federally provided floor that do not even receive discussion. In the case of conscription, governments can rely on volunteers or conscripts, they can permit widespread exemptions, mechanisms for buying one's way out, or alternative forms of national service to donning a uniform. Thus, to establish an equilibrium policy, government actors must consider not only which policy they prefer but also which is likely to be accepted by the relevant population.

In the historical cases that are the subject of this book, the policy outcome reflects a game between policymakers and the median legislator, the representative of the citizen. The median position is a function of government demand for troops and the extent of citizen compliance with government's demands (Figure 2.5).

Military service policy

Government demand increases with an increase in military threat. In situations in which numerous troops are necessary, government actors, desirous of being able to allocate all potential recruits to their best use in the military or civilian labor force, will seek conscription.

(4) *The more troops government needs, the greater the likelihood government policymakers will try to institute conscription.*

There is no assumption here that all military actions are defensive. Policymakers demand troops because they are under attack, because they are imperialistic, creating the military threat to others, or because they use the military as a means of domestic control and pacification.

An alternative hypothesis derives from the view that the military is a means to forge a national identity out of numerous regional and ethnic groups. If this is the case, government will attempt to introduce conscription even in the absence of a military motivation.

(alt. 4) *The more committed the regime is to nation building, the more government policymakers will try to institute conscription.*

If, in fact, the ability of government policymakers to shift to a new policy depends on supply as well as demand, and if supply is determined by the political and economic costs of achieving compliance, then there are several possible sources of costs. The argument here is that the major obstacle to compliance is the absence or withdrawal of contingent consent. From this follows the argument that as government becomes more democratic in its processes and as the content and implementation of its law become more universalistic, this will signal to citizens that it is a trustworthy government and, thus, induce more contingent consent.

(5) *The more democratic the regime and the more universalistic its laws, the more likely it is that citizens will comply with a policy of universal conscription.*

There are two possible reasons, however, that citizens might perceive such practices as indicative of a more trustworthy government. One is that institutional change, particularly extension of the franchise, gives more citizens the capacity to exercise influence over legislators to block policies these citizens perceive as disadvantageous to them.

(5a) *As the franchise includes more of the population, the more likely it is that citizens will comply with universal conscription.*

In other words, political institutions alter who has relative bargaining power and whose interests the median legislator will attempt to serve.

35

Hypothesis 5 assumes that the nonelites prefer a more universalistic system since it is less certain to disadvantage them. Thus, expanding the franchise changes the identity of both the pivotal legislator and the pivotal voter. An electorate composed only of nobles has a different range of preferences and values than does an electorate that also includes the bourgeoisie, which is different again from an electorate composed of the entire set of adult citizens.

A second possibility is a normative change that transforms the standard of fairness citizens apply:

> *(5b) As the norms of citizens change toward more democratic norms, the more likely it is that citizens will comply with universal conscription.*

The sources of this normative shift may be republican ideology, democratic practice, or experience with the harms caused by previously tried forms of exemption.

Other costs can also affect compliance, however. Development of efficient bureaucratic capacity to register, examine, and muster soldiers may augment government costs in the short run, but an efficient extractive bureaucracy increases compliance and reduces costs in the long run. Citizen compliance may also increase with the benefits (economic or ideological) from compliance. Government actions and institutions affect the monetary costs and benefits for compliance through the pay and bounties offered enlistees and the punitive sanctions imposed on draft evaders.

> *(alt. 5) The greater the capacity of government to offer selective rewards and sanctions to citizens, the more likely it is that citizens will comply with a policy of universal conscription.*

Under standard rational choice assumptions, the government policymaker will prefer the military service policy that most efficiently allocates labor to its best use as producers or soldiers and in the proportions dictated by military needs. When the demand for troops is very low, a mercenary or volunteer army will do. When the demand for troops is very high, government policymakers will prefer a form of conscription which is universal in the sense that all young men of a certain age are eligible and that exemptions are given on grounds of national needs. In other words, government policymakers will prefer what the United States calls "selective service."

Ceteris paribus, the pivotal legislator will prefer a mercenary or all-volunteer army so as to maximize the choices of constituents. However, when the government argues that it must rely on legal compulsion, the

Applying the model

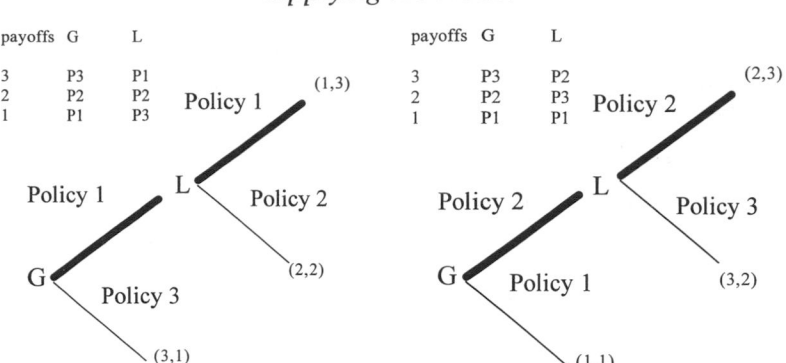

Figure 2.6. Small demand game.   Figure 2.7. Large demand game.

preferences of the legislator over the form of conscription will reflect the pressures of influential constituents, and most citizens will seek ways to free-ride on the service of others.

The actual conscription game involves a sequence of moves in which each legislative rejection leads to a new set of proposals by policymakers until they reach a bargain. There are actually two versions of the game, a small and a large demand game (Figures 2.6 and 2.7). In the first, the median legislator will reject conscription in favor of an all-volunteer or mercenary army. In the second, the median legislator prefers conscription but with special privileges and exemptions for powerful constituents.

Demand transforms the game. Acceptance of policy 1, the earlier equilibrium, is now off the equilibrium path, and rejection of policy 3, once off the equilibrium path, is now on. However, the standard institution for democracies during large-scale wars is universal conscription, or at least a relatively impartial form of selective service. What made this possible? Is demand in and of itself a sufficient explanation, or are there other equally important factors that account for the shift in the median position of legislators from opposition to support of universal conscription?

APPLYING THE MODEL

The case studies provide means to consider the plausibility of the hypotheses generated by the model of contingent consent and the alternative models. Table 2.2 lists the hypotheses.

The cases vary government demand for troops due to the needs of

The contingencies of consent

Table 2.2. *Summary of hypotheses*

Explanations for compliance

(1) The more trustworthy citizens perceive government to be, the more likely they are to contingently consent with its policies and, therefore, comply.

(2) The larger the proportion of citizens contributing from a given population, the more likely others from that population will also contribute.

(3) Government policymakers, their supporters, and their opposition will devote resources to disseminating information about the trustworthiness of government and the probability of ethical reciprocity among the relevant population.

Alternative explanations for compliance

(alternative 1) The more developed the habits of conformity, the more compliance.

(alternative 2) The more strongly and widely held are ideological positions in support of a particular policy, the more compliance.

(alternative 3) The greater the marginal benefit to each individual from compliance, the more compliance.

Explanations for the form of military service policy

Demand

(4) The more troops government needs, the greater the likelihood government policymakers will try to institute conscription.

Supply

(5) The more democratic the regime and the more universalistic its laws, the more likely it is that citizens will comply with a policy of universal conscription.

Table 2.2 *(cont.)*

(a) As the franchise includes more of the population, the more likely

it is that citizens will comply with universal conscription.

(b) As the norms of citizens change toward more democratic norms,

the more likely it is that citizens will comply with universal

conscription.

Alternative explanations for the form of military service policy

Demand

(alternative 4) The more committed the regime is to nation building, the

more government policymakers will try to institute conscription.

Supply

(alternative 5) The greater capacity of government to offer selective

rewards and sanctions to citizens, the more likely it is that citizens will

comply with a policy of universal conscription.

---

defense and war and the extent of citizen compliance. The matrix of case studies (Table 2.3) lays out where each of the cases fit. There are several examples for most cells, and only one cell (high demand, medium compliance) is null. Moreover, in each cell, there is significant variation in the military service policies, defined as voluntary service, obligatory service with socially discriminatory exemptions, and obligatory service with relatively impartial exemptions.

All of the case studies emphasize government design of military service institutions against a backdrop of variation in likely contingent consent. Chapter 3 documents the nineteenth-century history of military service in all six countries considered in this book. Chapter 4 traces the transformation of socially selective exemptions to a policy of more impartial exemptions. The major empirical example is the elimination of various forms of "buying out" of the draft in France and the United States. Chapter 5 is a broad comparison of the introduction of conscription in the five Anglo-Saxon democracies during World War I. The focus is on the variation in the timing and in the level of opposition to universal male conscription. This chapter considers the ways in which

Table 2.3. *The matrix of case studies*

Government demands	Citizen compliance		
	High[a]	Medium[a]	Low[a]

High	WWI
	  U.S. (P3)
	  U.K. (P2)
	  France (P3)
	  New Zealand (P3)
	  Anglophone Canada (P3)
	WWII
	  U.S. (P3)
	  France (P3)
	  Anglophone Canada
	  (P1-P3)
		Napoleonic Wars (P2)
		U.S. Civil War (P2)
		WWI
		  Australia (P1)
		WWII
		  Australia (P1)
			WWI
			  Francophone
			  Canada (P3)
			  Catholic Irish (P2)
			WWII
			  Francophone Irish
			  (P1-P3)

Medium		19th-century wars,
		  France (P2-P3)
			New Zealand wars (P1)
			19th-century wars,
			  Britain (P1)

Low	Vietnam
	  France (P3)
		Vietnam
		  U.S. (P2)
		  Australia (P3)
			19th-century U.S. (P2)
			19th-century Canada
			  (P3)
			19th-century Australia
			  (P1)

[a] P1 = voluntary enlistments; P2 = exemptions by socially discriminatory devices; P3 = selective service.

governments achieve the construction of contingent consent and the circumstances that lead citizens to vote against conscription, protest it, or otherwise refuse to give their consent.

Whereas Chapters 3, 4, and 5 focus on policy-making and the precipitants to reform of military service policy, Chapters 6 and 7 consider several possible citizen choices in response to government requests for volunteers and demands for conscripts:[13] (1) to enlist in the military in the absence of conscription; (2) to protest or support the introduction of conscription; and, (3) when conscripted, to comply or conscientiously object. Chapter 6, based on a paper written in collaboration with Shane Fricks (Levi and Fricks 1992), analyzes francophone opposition to and anglophone support of conscription in Canada during both world wars. Why did individuals from one group tend to refuse their behavioral consent and why did those from the other tend to give theirs? Chapter 7, based on an earlier joint article with Stephen DeTray (Levi and DeTray 1993), considers the variation in reliance on conscientious objection over time as a form of refusing consent in the United States, Australia, and France. Here the explicit contrast is between a model derived from contingent consent and one that privileges ideology.

[13] James Alt pointed out the underlying typology to me.

Applying the model

Although the case studies do not cover the whole range of possible choices by citizens[14] or decisions by legislators, they represent many of the most important choices and decisions. These cases are far from natural experiments, but if the findings prove consistent with the model, the diversity in time, place, and variables lends plausibility to the model of contingent consent.

[14] I was unable, for example, to study draft evasion because of the impossibility of sorting out exemptions granted for real health versus manufactured health problems, for real versus paper marriages, etc. Nor do I deal with desertion, about which there are data; I confined my researches to choices around joining military service rather than the choices made once a man puts on a uniform.

3

Gone for a soldier

"It's now, my brave fellows, if you
    want to enlist,
It's five golden guineas I'll clap in
    your fist;
Besides, there's five shillings to kick
    up a dust
As you go to the fair in the
    morning.

"It's then you will also go decent
    and clean
While all other fellows go dirty
    and mean;
While all other fellows go dirty
    and mean,
And sup their bugoo in the
    morning."

"Och, you need not be talking
    about your fine pay,
For all you have got is one shilling
    a day;
And as for your debt, the drums
    pay your way
As you march through the town in
    the morning.

"And you need not be talking
    about your fine clothes,
For you've just got the loan of
    them, as I do suppose;
And you dare not sell them in spite
    of your nose,
Or you would get flogged in the
    morning."

       "The Recruiting Sergeant," traditional Irish, English,
    and Scottish ballad

Throughout the eighteenth century (and into the nineteenth), a single shilling pressed into the hand of a drunken man in a public house by a recruiting sergeant constituted the enlistment of a soldier in the British army. In France, the dreaded *milice royale* relied on a lottery to choose which peasants would be forced into the King's service. The army was not a popular institution, at least not for those who had to serve in its rank and file. Some joined because they liked the life, but most did so because they were coerced or needed the work or were fleeing from something worse. Those who refused did so because being in the army was inconvenient or actively repugnant. National patriotism is a relatively modern basis for service. It requires a sense of one's country as an entity that can legitimately demand contributions and to which loyalty should be given. Principled refusal to comply on the grounds of dissatisfaction with government is also relatively modern; such a basis of refusal depends on a belief that there are reciprocal obligations between citizens and their governments.

It was only with the American and French revolutions that national patriotic feeling began to take root, but it took root very slowly. In the nineteenth century the countries of Europe and North America developed modern national states, and those in the Antipodes began the process. State building involved the creation of a military adequate to the new demands of relatively centralized government, the exigencies of international politics, and the requirements of increased democratization. The mass mobilization of the French Revolution and the Napoleonic Wars marked the beginning of the period in Europe, and the Austro-Prussian and Franco-Prussian Wars of 1866 and 1870–1 marked its significant turning point. The American Revolution and the Civil War were critical moments for the United States. The process of state building that commenced in the late eighteenth century culminated in the early twentieth, with the guns of August 1914.

With the exception of the Civil War in the United States, however, there were no military conflagrations on the scale of the Napoleonic Wars. Even so, the countries of Europe, North America, and Australasia had to have armies. Nationalism, industrialization, the end of slavery, the growth of labor organization and capitalist counterorganization, and international conflicts over boundaries and markets resulted in numerous disturbances in the body politic during this period. The Pax Britannica was, despite its label, not particularly peaceful or secure.

The problem was how to develop a military service system that was compatible with increasing universalism of law and democratization of governance. Britain replaced impressment with a more regulated recruitment of volunteers, France evolved a system of selective conscription, and the United States (except during the exceptional time of the Civil War) relied on a small volunteer army supplemented by local militias and state-based national guards. Canada, Australia, and New Zealand also had relatively small national volunteer armies and some form of local militias and volunteers, but Australia and New Zealand both experimented with compulsory training schemes during the years prior to World War I.

The transformation of the military that accompanied industrialization, democratization, and the new state forms of the nineteenth and early twentieth centuries has received considerable analytic and historical attention. Otto Hintze (1994), Samuel Finer (1975), Victor Kiernan (1973), and Michael Mann (1993) are just a few among the many social theorists who have noted the effects of technological, social, and political change on military organization. Monographs of military organization and reform are legion. The purpose here, however, is not to rehearse these developments or to produce a better historical account. Rather, the aim of this chapter is to provide a narrative of the factors influencing the form of government demands for military service and citizen responses from the late eighteenth century through the early twentieth. The emphasis will be on those historical moments in which government officials reconsider their military service requirements.

In particular, this chapter evaluates the following hypotheses delineated in the preceding chapter:

(4) The more troops government needs, the greater the likelihood government policymakers will try to institute conscription.

(5) The more democratic the regime and the more universalistic its laws, the more likely it is that citizens will comply with a policy of universal conscription.

The alternative hypotheses are:

(alt. 4) The more committed the regime is to nation building, the more government policymakers will try to institute conscription.

(alt. 5) The greater the capacity of government to offer selective rewards and sanctions to citizens, the more likely it is that citizens will comply with a policy of universal conscription.

The cases permit exploration of the relationship between government demand for troops, noncompliance – anticipated and actual – and military service format. They also offer instances in which changes in compliance may arguably have reflected changes in contingent consent. Finally, they present the available evidence on conscription as a policy meant to build a nation as well as defend it.

FRANCE

France is the only country in this sample that relied on a form of national conscription in the absence of full-scale war. The history of the French military in the eighteenth and nineteenth centuries is the history of changing practices in keeping with transformations in political regimes, changing demands on the military, and changing views of the role of the military in society. Transformations in political regimes gave political clout to different sets of actors and affected the relative bargaining power of the army's officers. War, peace, threats to security from other countries, and threats to domestic stability all affected the organization of the army. Of increasing importance were the debates over the role of the military as a means to protect the general population from an authoritarian state, to protect the propertied and privileged from the masses, and to promote both adequate defense and a patriotic citizenry. France is a case in which the demands for troops were high, and policymakers had to adjust their policies to shifts in the likelihood of compliance.

The army of the Revolution and of Napoleon Bonaparte

The *Ancien Régime* had two armies. The regular, standing army recruited approximately one in twenty men under Louis XV (Forrest 1989: 8), and they served in local regiments whose noble officers had purchased their commissions. Desertion was endemic and a major problem for an army that made so considerable an investment in training its men. However, desertion seemed to have had more to do with the conditions in the military itself than with defiance of the state or antagonism to recruitment practices (Forrest 1989: 6–7; for a different view, see Auvray 1983). The *milice royale,* on the other hand, did generate resistance in the forms of violence, rioting, draft dodging, desertion, and even self-mutilation. Although the *milice* only called up approximately one out of forty eligibles (Forrest 1989: 11), its impact was uneven and arbitrary. It chose recruits through a lottery, the *tirage au sort,* with its *bons numéros* and *mauvais numéros,* but some towns and most of the rich (and their servants) were exempt or could purchase replacements (Forrest 1989: 10–11). Certain regions, particularly those "remote and mountainous areas where modern government and the assumptions on which it is based had little opportunity to penetrate," were particularly hostile to the *milice* (Forrest 1989: 13).

In 1789 the National Assembly began the process of transforming the army. It had to. First, many of the noble officers had emigrated. Second, the rank and file were increasingly insubordinate, making it difficult for the government to use them either as an army or as police. They tended to side more with the protesters than with the government. Third, the soldiers were as affected by revolutionary ideology as the mass of the population. They began to think of themselves as citizens and to express their grievances openly. Fourth, the existing system of recruitment was inadequate to the task of attracting sufficient numbers of men.

Consequently, the National Assembly abolished the detested militia and introduced a national guard whose officers were elected and whose members served with others from their locality. In 1790 the Assembly began reforming the professional army. Commissions were open to talent rather than purchase. The Assembly amended recruitment, pay, and the system of military justice in line with soldier demands. Desertion went down, and volunteering went up. By 1792 the army was less experienced, but it was also younger, more heterogeneous, and probably more patriotic (Woloch 1994: 383). Recruitment still depended on and encouraged the collective solidarities of communes; there was, as yet, no unmediated relationship between citizen and central state (Birnbaum 1988: 58–9). This was to change fundamentally with the *levée en masse* of 1793.

Despite considerable response to the calls for soldiers for the war that began in 1792, the numbers were insufficient to meet the increased military threat. The *levée des 300,000* in the spring of 1793 was an attempt to meet the challenge through centrally determined departmental assessments and local implementation, supported by public opinion. Some communities elected those they disliked to serve; others used the lottery, still closely associated with the *Ancien Régime*. The law permitted the purchase of replacements, which contributed to the fairly general belief that some, particularly the rich, were escaping altogether and which fueled perceptions of inequality of sacrifice. Riots and evasion were widespread; the rebellion in the Vendée was one famous consequence (Forrest 1989: 27–8; Woloch 1994: 384–5). By autumn, the Convention introduced the *levée en masse*. It eradicated the practice of replacement, was "by far the most equitable draft of the Revolutionary years" (Forrest 1989: 32), and produced relatively high compliance in the short run. However, it was a one-time mobilization, and the recruits faced unlimited service. After a few years and a few victories, recruits began to desert, usually by not returning after a temporary leave. In reaction the government hunted down draft evaders and reviewed previous exemptions and temporary leaves. The government soon realized that the economy as well as the army needed manpower. The next, and far more radical step, was the creation of permanent and regularized conscription.

The *loi Jourdan de 19 fructidor VI* (1798) established the principle of wartime conscription. Unmarried men between ages 20 and 25 were eligible for the draft, which would be enacted during war. Each birth cohort formed a class, and the legislature annually determined how many men the army could enlist, starting with the youngest class. If a man was not called by the time he was 25, he was permanently discharged. There were to be no replacements. Administration was through the *départements* rather than the communes. Efficient and equitable implementation of the law required an accurate census of all the eligibles, a formidable task for a small national bureaucracy.

The first reports were of an enthusiastic response, and public opinion seemed strongly in support of governmental policy. Later reports suggested considerable draft evasion and desertion. Concerns about the equity of the draft seems to have increased resistance to it. There was considerable variation in procedures and favoritism from one local jurisdiction to another, which raised questions about how random the lottery really was. Many mayors tried to appear to increase the pool of eligibles in the lottery through the inclusions of unfit and underheight men, who would be later rejected. The prefect of Isère, for example, ". . . observed that the conscripts themselves insisted on such ruses, for they could not bear to see the pool reduced and their chance of drawing a low number increased" (Woloch 1994: 392). However, the real effect was to increase the number of times eligibles had to submit to a lottery, and this in turn increased their resentment of the system.

The major response of the government in its efforts to enhance compliance and reduce evasion and desertion was to tighten its laws and increasingly to take discretion for selection and medical exemptions out of the hands of local authorities. By Year XI (1803), *tirage au sort* was mandatory. By 1806, conscription had become routinized and bureaucratic, "the real breakthrough of the Napoleonic regime, the ultimate form of state penetration" (Woloch 1994: 393).

Several legal procedures for avoiding military service were available. Replacement, to be discussed in the next chapter, was one. Marriage was another and very popular ploy. Insufficient height was a primary reason for being deemed unfit. Medical exemptions probably provoked the most resentment among the population, given a perception of rampant favoritism and the reality of significant local variation in the interpretation and implementation of rules. Medical exemptions were also a major source of conscription fraud by local officials who accepted bribes to disqualify a recruit and by paid, private agents who claimed, often ingenuously, that they could procure exemptions and even good numbers. Cutting off toes and other acts of disqualification were another means to gain an exemption.

The overall effect of the legal procedures was to make some men's chances of serving considerably greater than that of others. Medical exemptions increased the probability of being called up or of drawing a bad number in a subsequent lottery made necessary by the number of people previously excused (Forrest 1989: 407–8). Height requirements had differential effects in different areas of the country, forcing certain draft boards to go further down their lists. Fraud made even more likely the selection of tall, healthy men who either could not afford or did not choose to pay a bribe or lose a digit.

There were, in addition, various illegal means of avoiding military service, that is, draft dodging and desertion. In Years IX-XIII certain regions, the west of France, Massif Central, and the southwest (especially Aquitaine), were particularly prone to evasion and other forms of noncompliance; others, the area around Paris, the east, and especially the Vosge, tended toward compliance (Forrest 1989: 71–2; also see Woloch 1994: 391, 412). Forrest (1989, esp. chs. 4–5) argues that the extent of evasion, draft dodging, and desertion suggests a social environment of resistance to the central state's demands for soldiers and to the conscription system:

In large measure those electing to desert or avoid service did so in a climate that favored their actions, where they could be assured of a degree of support or at least of understanding from their own communities. (Forrest 1989: 97)

The government responded with coercion, manhunts for the law-breakers, and extreme punishment, including large fines and civil death, often for the fathers as well as the recalcitrant sons. However, the task was staggering for a state in the process of developing a centralized administrative capacity capable of penetrating deep into the countryside of France. In 1802 there was an amnesty to which an estimated 155,000 fugitives and 17,000 draft dodgers responded (Woloch 1994: 413). This did not prevent a new tide of draft evasion. In 1806 the government enhanced its enforcement capacity by two means. The first was the imposition of community responsibility in the form of *garnisaires,* penalties against the communes often extracted from the wealthiest taxpayers, who then had to get compensation from the others (Woloch 1994: 416). The second involved reliance on mobile columns instead of the gendarmerie for enforcement; these swooped on communities and were sufficiently feared to induce some communities to begin to police draft dodging themselves (Woloch 1994: 417). In 1810–11, the combination of an amnesty, *garnisaires,* and the threat of mobile columns resulted in the capture or surrender of approximately 136,000 *insoumis,* that is, those engaged in draft dodging or desertion (Woloch 1994: 417). Desertion continued to be a problem and even to rise, but draft evasion was never a major issue again, even in some of the previously most recalcitrant sections of France and even as levies increased in frequency and size (Woloch 1994: 417–21).

Conscription served the military ends of the Revolution, but it also was essential for state building. Birnbaum (1988: 59–61) characterizes the *levée en masse* as a major blow against regionalism and notes the increasing use of mobilization techniques that replaced particularistic loyalties with the defense of the nation, an ideological commitment. As Forrest argues (1989: 218):

Whatever else it achieved, the government's recruitment policy brought the people of villages and *bourgs* face to face with the law as never before. It brought the enforcers of the law into every hamlet in the land. It was, par excellence, the area of government activity that brought the police and the people into direct contact, and often into confrontation, over a period of nearly a quarter of a century.

The Restoration, the monarchy, the Second Empire, and the Second Republic

The Napoleonic army was a considerable achievement, but by 1814 conscription was so detested that its abolition became a political necessity. However, an army of volunteers proved inadequate to the demands upon it. Dominant French military theory of that period emphasized the superiority of a professional over a volunteer army; the officers preferred men who would serve for a long time and thus receive both adequate training and socialization. By 1818 the second Restoration's Minister of War, Marshall Gouvion Saint-Cyr, succeeded in shepherding in a law that established the principles that would underlie military service until 1872.

Saint-Cyr deemphasized the reserves in favor of patriotic volunteerism as the means to produce sufficient men during major crises. There was to be an annual contingent allocated proportionately among the cantons and whose members were drawn by lots, that is, the old *tirage au sort*. Parliament annually determined the size of the contingent and those subject to call up in the reserves, and civilian medical examining boards determined fitness. Those who received a good number in the lottery were definitively released from service as were all of those still on the cantonal list once the medical examiners approved the last person to meet the allotment of their particular canton. Over the years, there were changes in the size of the contingent, the required years of service if selected (initially seven years), and eligibility for the reserves. However, the law remained relatively unchanged in regard to the inequities produced by the uneven geographical distribution of fit men,[1] the use of a lottery, and the acceptance of substitution and replacement.

Regional variation in response also persisted. In the 1820s, certain regions, especially Corsica, Manche, Gironde, and parts of *Occitane* were particularly prone to nonappearance of those whose numbers were drawn (Ladurie and Dumont 1972: Tables 5–6, 78–81). They were also among the regions most prone to exemptions as a result of loss of fingers, often a form of self-mutilation as a form of evasion (Ladurie and Dumont 1972: 26, and Table 34, 138–139). The regions on the border with Germany and the Low Countries were among those with the highest voluntary enrollments (Ladurie and Dumont 1972: 30–1, and Table 1: 70–1). Ladurie and Dumont (1972: 28–35) conclude that the

---

[1] Height remained an issue. Some areas had significantly shorter men than others, and in time there was a reduction in the height requirement to reflect this.

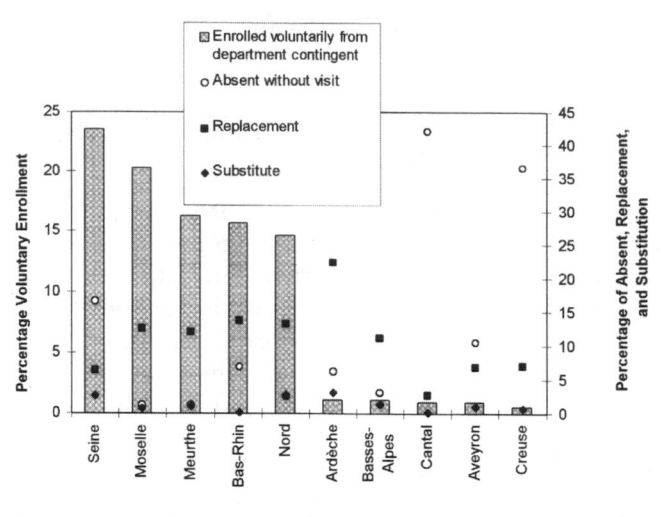

Figure 3.1. France 1818–26: regional variations in response to military service requirements (Ladurie and Dumont 1972: 70–1, 78–85).

regional variation, at least between 1818 and 1826, the period of their study, had multiple sources: the relative height and health of the residents, relative development and poverty of the area, location on a border or a sea, and linguistic status, among others. A comparison of the five regions with the highest voluntary enrollment with the five with the lowest voluntary enrollment illustrates some of the complexity of the correlations (Figure 3.1); regions with large numbers of volunteers might also have large numbers who failed to register or otherwise appear. This and other data (esp. Schnapper 1968) suggest long-term patterns of evasion and even resistance in certain parts of the country.

From 1872 to World War I

Revision of French military organization became a major issue in the early 1870s, in response largely to military defeats by Prussia in 1870–1. The spirit of reform generated by the Paris Commune of 1871 also contributed to the demand for change, and the Jacobin view of a nation in arms was once more on the political agenda. The right wanted universal military service as a means of social control, to instill discipline and respect for authority among the masses and to enhance the role of the military generally. The left sought universal military service as a means to promote democracy and the citizen soldier. An apparently more equitable conscription law passed in 1872. However, Adolphe Thiers, the leader of the Third Republic, preferred a long-service, professional army to one based on universal and personal obligation, and he ensured that the new conscription system maintained and even renewed class biases. Although in principle, all draft-age men had to serve as much as five years, either an exemption or a "good number" in a lottery at the end of six to twelve months could release one from active service. Exemptions were for those who volunteered, at the cost of 1,500 francs, for one year for officer training, those in certain schools, and those in the Church. It did not take long for republicans to seek a more universalistic system without special advantages for those already privileged by wealth or status (see esp. Challener 1955: 33–52; and Ralston 1967: 22–48).

Legislation reduced the obligation from five years to three in 1889 and from three years to two in 1905 and back up to three in 1913, as fear of war increased. However, the 1889 law may have done more to enhance privilege than reduce it, since educational exemptions were more widely available, and, at least according to Ralston (1967: 303), the effect was a flooding of educational institutions.

The first decade of the twentieth century was one of increasing popular antagonism to and distrust of the military, fueled by the Dreyfus Affair, the use of the army in breaking strikes (Horne 1984: 27–8), and growth of republican and socialist sentiment. Increasingly, the effect was to reduce the advantages of privilege in the military.

BRITAIN

British might in the eighteenth and nineteenth centuries was the result of the development of an increasingly powerful central state with a sophisticated fiscal extractive capacity (Brewer 1988; Levi 1988: 122–43; Daunton 1996). The fiscal-military state supported both an army and a navy adequate to meet Britain's foreign commitments in war and peace. The degree of compliance and even active consent necessary to extract sufficient soldiers and money from the population framed British military policy in this period.

The army and the navy bore responsibility for fighting wars abroad, but in the late eighteenth century, the major form of home defense was the militia. Reformed in 1757, the militia law required all English and Welsh counties to provide a quota of Protestant men chosen by lottery and to be given a month's training each year under the leadership of local gentry (Brewer 1988: 32–3; Colley 1992: 287). By 1797 the threat of Napoleon's Army of England compelled government officials to put its fear of the French before its fear of an armed people (and the Scots) and to transform the militia from a domestic police force controlled by the propertied to a fighting force composed of the masses. The first British census in 1800 and the earlier questionnaires required by the

Gone for a soldier

Defense of the Realm Act of 1798 enabled government officials to locate those both eligible and willing to join a defense force. The surprising findings were that the propertied, those believed to have something to defend, were not necessarily the most willing volunteers, nor were the supposedly deferential rural inhabitants. Enthusiasm for the war effort was highest in the towns, the residence of the laboring masses and traders (Colley 1992: 287–300). Recruitment success varied significantly among the counties (Colley 1992: 378–81), but by 1804 approximately 176,000 men were in uniform and another 482,000 said they were willing to join (Colley 1992: 293).

The widespread mobilization of young men to fight World War I was the culmination of the process that began with the widespread mobilization of young men to fight Napoleon. In the intervening years, the British masses gained voting and other citizenship rights, and the regular army and militia were transformed from institutions run for and by the elite to an institution run for and by the central state, presumably on behalf of the British population as a whole. Colley (1992: 312) argues that the experience of civil defense in the Napoleonic Wars

had a transforming effect upon British society that has hardly begun to be explored . . . it was training in arms under the auspices of the state that was the most common working-class experience in the late eighteenth and early nineteenth centuries, not labour in a factory, or membership of a radical political organization or an illegal trade union.

Men from different parts of Britain and different social classes served together and began the process of establishing a common British identity. Moreover, the poor and the workers, and not just the propertied and the owners, were willing to serve in part because they "did not feel that they alone had to bear the brunt of military mobilization" (Colley 1992: 304).

Throughout most of the nineteenth century, the British really maintained four military apparatuses. Of central interest here are the British Army, which fought the many land wars of the period, and the militia, mobilized for home defense. In addition, a large mercenary army, the East India Army,[2] and, of course, the British Navy protected British interests, particularly commercial interests, abroad. The East India Army recruited heavily both within Britain, particularly among the Irish, and among specific ethnic groups within India, especially after the Mutiny of 1857 (see esp. Omissi 1994; Mokyr and O Gráda 1996). The Navy, to which Britain devoted a disproportionate share of its fiscal–military

---

[2] Thomson (1995) thoroughly and thoughtfully analyzes the development of sovereignty in the international state system through the elimination of mercenaries and armies run by mercantile companies.

resources from the late seventeenth century on (Brewer 1988: 29–51, esp. Table 2.1), fought pirates, engaged in privateering, and impressed its sailors at the beginning of the century but had helped eliminate all these practices by the end of the century (Thomson 1995).

Enlistments in the British Army during the Napoleonic era were high, but afterwards the Army rarely met its recruiting targets (Spiers 1980: 35–40 and Skelley 1977: 236–7). The army had an unsavory reputation, the conditions of army life were hard, service was long, pay was low, and the treatment of veterans was an occasional source of scandal. Pressure for reform increased in the late 1850s following the Crimean War (1854–6) and the decline in Scottish and, especially, Irish participation in the rank and file. Two other factors also contributed to the debate over reform: conflicting views among the ministers, legislators, and army officials about how to structure the army so that its recruits formed an efficient fighting force but not a threat to domestic governance; and political changes, including the extension of the franchise in 1850 and the growth of new political movements affected the content and structure of the debate.

Problems commenced at the point of enlistment (Spiers 1980: 35–52; Skelley 1977: 239–99). The traditional ballad quoted at the beginning of this chapter illustrates the contempt and distrust the recruiting sergeant provoked. It was not unusual for a recruiting party, which earned a fee for each man brought in, to seek out the already inebriated or to inebriate potential recruits and then spin a tale of a wondrous life in military service. In some cases, there was also the promise of a bounty, a promise that was occasionally legitimate but just as often false. Because of such recruiting methods, those who had accepted the King's shilling the night before were not always so happy the morning after. Some fled, either immediately if they could escape their guard or after they collected the bounty. Others paid "smart money" of approximately a pound to be excused. The officials who had to examine the recruits were often equally unhappy. Recruiting parties were likely to ignore issues of physical health, family status, or other factors that determined acceptance. Between 1862 and 1910, the army rejected a low of 20.5 percent in 1874 to a high of 55.2 percent in 1910 of those who enlisted, and the rejections were equally high in the earlier part of the century (Spiers 1980: 42–3). Until serious reform commenced in 1867, both the recruiting party and the men they enlisted marked the recruiting system with fraud and deceptions of all sorts.

Nor was soldiering a particularly glorious occupation, especially for the rank and file. Much of the public maintained an image of the soldier as a rough sort and the army as a refuge for those unable to do better work or as an escape from obligations or prison. Of course, this view of military service varied with region and with the form of service. What rarely varied, however, was the observation that army life was unhealthy and unwholesome. It was also long. Enlistment for life or until the receipt of a medical discharge was the practice until 1847, when service could be as short as ten years in the infantry but was more likely to be for the twenty-one or twenty-four years requisite for a pension. Debates about the appropriate length of service raged for decades, exacerbated by the Cardwell reforms begun in 1870 that reduced service to twelve years, only six of which might be with the regular reserve.

Variations in British enlistment

Even so there were many men who chose to enlist. The recruits were disproportionately unemployed or from low paid occupations, but their composition changed over the century on several dimensions: whether they came from England and Wales, Scotland, or Ireland; whether they were urban or rural; and the extent to which they sought to renege on their initial contract. The modal recruit was transformed from a tall, rural fellow who met relatively high physical standards to a shorter, younger, less healthy man, or even boy, from an urban environment.

The Irish and Scots disproportionately provided enlistees for the Victorian army,[3] but the percentage of recruits of Scottish and especially Irish nationality declined significantly over the course of the nineteenth and the early twentieth centuries when measured against the percentage of their populations within the British Isles (Figure 3.2). According to the statistical demographic analysis of Floud, Gregory, and Wachter (1990: 87), the figures on the Scots probably underrepresent their proportions in the army, particularly after about 1830; they feel more confident in their data on the Irish.[4] Other research (Fitzpatrick 1989b: 641) finds that Irish immigrants were a large proportion of the recruits in England and Scotland as late as 1860–1863.

The primary explanation for the decline of Irish participation was the decline in population that resulted from the combination of the potato famine in the 1830s, delayed marriage, and celibacy.[5] Many young Irish

---

[3] This was also true of the East India Army (Mokyr and O Gráda 1996: Table A1)

[4] Floud, Gregory, and Wachter (1990: 87) present a compelling argument about the sampling errors involved in calculating the participation of the Scottish. They found no such bias in the estimation of the proportions of the Irish.

[5] There is a lively and sophisticated literature on nineteenth century Irish population decline. There is some debate about the actual role of the famine and debate about how slack the agricultural labor market actually was, but there is little question that there were fewer young men available for military service. See, for example, Fitzpatrick (1980), Mokyr (1983), Mokyr and O Gráda (1984), and O'Rourke (1991).

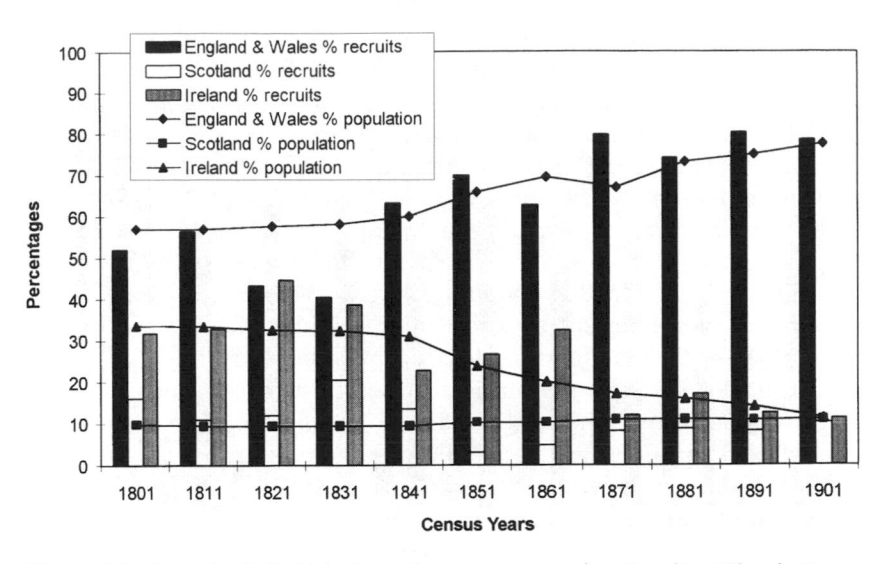

Figure 3.2. Recruits in British Army by percentage of nationality (Floud, Gregory, and Wachter 1990: 91, table 3.4 for 1801–1901; Spiers 1980: 50, table 2.6 for 1830–1912; Great Britain, Army 1901; Great Britain PP 1899: 429; 1908: 101; 1914: 360; 1921).

men emigrated to the United States, Australia, and other countries in search of employment. Moreover, the standard of living went up in Ireland during this period, resulting in a reduction of personal economic incentives.

The decline in Irish participation correlates with a rise in Catholic Irish nationalism. The fact that it also correlates with other factors makes it hard to prove that this was a case of contingent refusal to consent, despite considerable narrative evidence that suggests such an interpretation. There is no denying that the percentage of Irish recruits in the military declined with the decline in the percentage of Irish males in the British male population (Figure 3.3). Fenian encouragement of young men to join the Irish Volunteers as a way to acquire military training and guns confounds the data even more. However, the overall decline in Catholic participation suggests that fewer Irish or at least Catholic Irish enlisted throughout Britain as the century wore on. These figures, too, could of course reflect the decline in Irish population. Unfortunately, there are no statistics on the percentage of Catholics in the general British population during this period. The most confirming evidence for Irish decline as a reflection of contingent refusal to consent was the decision by the British government not to impose conscription on the Irish during World War I; the costs of implementation would

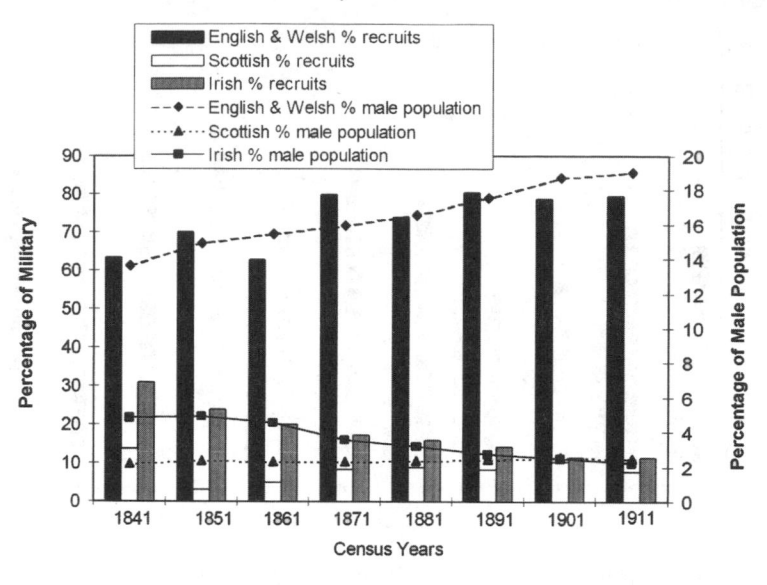

Figure 3.3. Percentage of male population in British military by region of country (Flora, Kraus, and Pfenning 1987: Vol. 1, p. 51; Spiers 1980: 50, table 2.6).

simply be too high (see Chapter 5). No such calculation was made in
reference to the Scots.

The significant decline in the numbers of Irish recruits, whatever its
causes, became a major precipitant to the recruiting crisis of the pre–
World War I army. The number of men willing to enlist fluctuated from
the end of the Crimean War, although the overall trend was up (Figure
3.4). Numerous government reports focused on the problem while the
army, secretary of war, and parliament debated how best to improve the
numbers and quality of recruits. The solutions were generally of two
kinds. The first was to improve the enlistment practices, pay, and conditions of service. The second was to make service in the military more
than a job, to construct it as service to the country. The two were
somewhat linked. Treating enlistees with greater respect and dignity
added to the prestige of the army itself. Reforms did in fact seem to have
a short-term and positive impact on recruitment, but the impact was of
a lesser order and shorter time period than the reformers hoped. What
had an even greater positive impact on recruiting was war and the
mobilizing effects of government and media jingoism. Both were extremely prevalent in Britain in the late nineteenth century, particularly
during the Boer or South African War of 1899–1902.

The serious decline in recruits that followed the South African War,
combined with concerns about the performance of the army there, led to

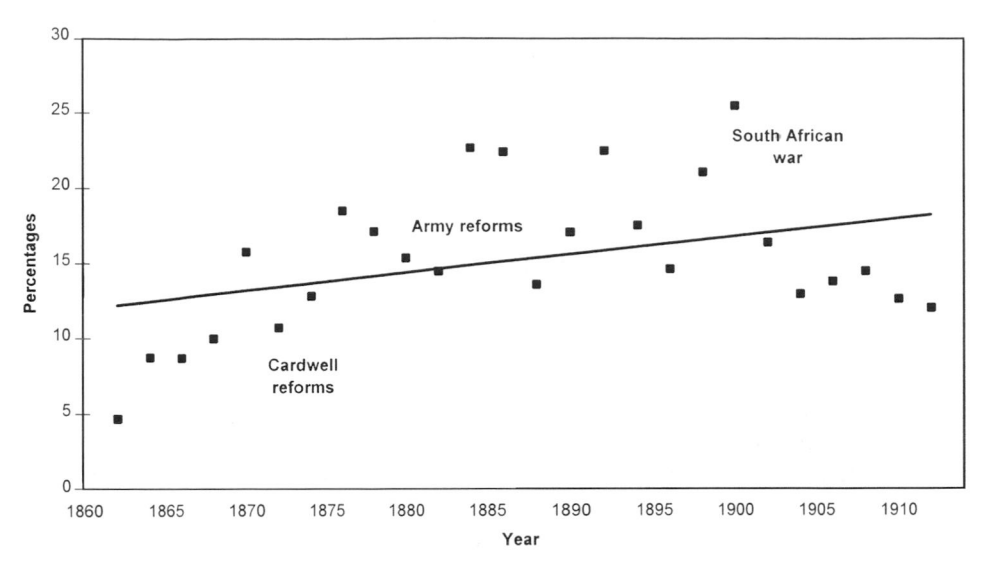

Figure 3.4. Recruits as percentage of effective strength (Spiers 1980: 38–9).

considerable discussion of reform. One consequence was a nationwide preparedness campaign dominated by the National Service League (NSL), an organization founded in 1902 to lobby for compulsory military service (Adams and Poirier 1987: 5–19). The Boy Scouts and the drills at the elite schools and universities were products of the campaign. The second consequence was the important Haldane reforms at the end of the first decade of the twentieth century.

The people of Britain had long prided themselves on their relatively small standing army and continued reliance on their Militia, Volunteers, and Yeomanry. However, the importance of the Militia declined throughout the nineteenth century until it was no more than one source of reinforcements for the regulars (Spiers 1980: 162–71, 179–81; Wilcox 1994). The Boer War (1899–1902) precipitated the twentieth-century debate over conscription. The battles in South Africa made the military command painfully aware of the limitations in the training of nonregulars (Spiers 1980: 236–64; Adams and Poirier 1987: 2–3 ff.). The government responded to its military problems and to the lobby for compulsory military training with a major reform of the army. Following the election of a Liberal Government in 1905, Richard Burton Haldane professionalized the officer corps and reorganized the regular army into two relatively equal parts: a garrison for the Empire and a new Expeditionary Force, for which the Militia, whose members would now be obligated for overseas duty, was to provide a Special Reserve. For home defense and as an additional reserve for the Expeditionary Force, he combined the Yeomanry and Volunteers into a new Territorial Force, based on voluntary enlistees organized locally (Spiers 1980: 265–87; Adams and Poirier 1987: 28–30). This, says Gooch (1980: 138), "was the closest that Britain could hope to get to conscription on the continental model in time of peace."

UNITED STATES

The United States experience seems a marked contrast to that of France and Britain, but in fact many of the same themes pervaded the debate over military organization. Fear of arbitrary, centralized government and of a standing army that could be a tool of tyrannical power was a recurring theme in all of the countries in this sample. However, for the United States the symbol of republicanism was the militia; for France it was the nation in arms in a large-scale and national military organization. Even today in the United States, the militia is a potent symbol of localism, decentralization, and the citizen-soldier.

From the Colonial Era to the Civil War

With the exception of Quaker Pennsylvania, the colonies all had similar laws regarding the militias. They required the mustering and training of freeborn and propertied male members of the community. The men would supply themselves with arms, and they were subject to a draft during times of emergency. Those who wished to avoid this levy could legally do so by payment of a fee or provision of a substitute. In principle, the militia was the dominant, if not only, form of defense in the British North American colonies. In practice, there were at least three varieties of military organizations. In commercial New York, the state relied chiefly on diplomacy and paid soldiers. In New England, the militia thrived. In the South, where men were isolated on plantations and increasingly fearful of slave rebellions, the state hired a small army of regulars. (Shy 1976: 25–7) As Shy (1976: 26) summarizes the critical distinction between the towns of New England and the more isolated settlement patterns of the slave states:

A town could bear the burden of a military draft and still hope to maintain itself against attack, while the loss of a man or two from a single, remote household often meant choosing between abandonment and destruction. . . The meeting-house, large and centrally located, often doubled as the "garrison house," strong point and refuge in case of attack.

The eighteenth century brought changes even to the New England militia. External threats from France changed both military strategy and recruitment practices. So, too, did the transformation from the authority of royal governors to that of legislatures. Consequently, militias increasingly became less military than social organizations, "the hallmarks of full citizenship in the community" (Shy 1976: 29). The actual fighting soldiers volunteered, were impressed, or were hired by contract from among young men seeking adventure and from among those not permitted in the militias: lower class whites, and, sometimes, freed slaves and Native Americans. Chambers labels what emerged as "The Colony Model: minimal local defense and ad hoc, contracted active-service forces" (1987: 15). Despite increasing reliance on paid and usually lower class troops, the colonists maintained their allegiance to the ideal of the citizen-soldier and the community militia as the essential guardians of liberty and as the purveyors of civic virtue (Chambers 1987: 18–9).

When the American Revolution broke out, the Confederation lacked a centralized army. This fact plus the experience of the British with American troops during the Seven Years' War led the British to underestimate American fighting capacity. In spite of numerous obstacles and with the power neither to tax nor conscript, the new central government was nonetheless able to raise an effective Continental Army by relying on state-provided units and longer enlistment periods. As the war persisted, recruiting sufficient soldiers was more difficult. Appeals to patriotism, increased enlistment bounties in money or land, and expansions of eligibility had to be supplemented in some states by drafts (Chambers 1987: 22).

The Continental Army became uncontrollable over time to the point that it was itself a threat to democracy. But for Washington, a military coup would have been the likely outcome of the Revolution (Shy 1986: 14). The militia could also prove unruly and uncontrollable, undermining effectiveness of central government at the local level. Shays's Rebellion in 1786 and the Whiskey Insurrection of 1794 were two of many examples of militia defense of local community versus government interests.

The issue of how best to organize an army suitable to democracy but effective militarily was a principal concern for the new government. The Constitution of 1789 provided for taxation, both national and state roles in developing a military capacity, limited central government, and, most importantly, protection of individual liberties. It granted national government the power to maintain domestic order and to raise an army, but it was silent on means.[6] Fear of a standing army was a leitmotif of the Constitutional Convention, and so was fear of overwhelming power

---

[6] Chambers (1987: 26) argues, "There seems little doubt, however, that most nationalists believed at that time that U.S. Government, like other modern states, would hire its army."

in any one arm of government. Thus, the militia clauses of the Constitution made the president the commander-in-chief of the state militia when called to national service, gave Congress the authority to call forth the state militias and to discipline and arm them when in national service, gave the states the authority to select officers and to train the soldiers, and, with the second amendment, ensured the right of "the people to keep and bear arms" as part of "a well-regulated Militia."

The two-army tradition of the United States involved local militias, whose officers and training the states controlled but which were subject to national standards, and a tiny army of regulars. The Washington administration offered a series of proposals involving enhanced central control of the militia as a basis for an effective national reserve, but Congress rejected the administration plan (Cress 1986: 51–2; Mahon 1983: 51–3). Instead, in May of 1792 it passed "An Act to Provide for Calling Forth the Militia to Execute the Laws of the Union, Suppress Insurrections and Repel Invasions" and, a few days later, "An Act more effectually to provide for the National Defense by establishing an Uniform Militia throughout the United States" (the Uniform Militia Act of 1792). With this legislation, Congress reaffirmed state control of the militia, made the president dependent on governors for troops, and enabled federal intervention into matters the states could not manage while preventing precipitous presidential action. At the same time, Congress reaffirmed that every able-bodied white male between 18 and 45 (with some categorical exemptions) had a military service obligation that required enrollment, training, and self-furnishing of arms. From its founding (and before), the United States was a country whose citizens generally "did not expect to have their careers interrupted to serve in the army" (Chambers 1987: 28). Thus, not surprisingly, the Uniform Militia Act maintained the customary practice of restricting national service to three months in a year.

All fifteen states responded with laws of their owns. All exempted conscientious objectors but varied on whether to exact a commutation fee in return, and "all states reaffirmed the power to draft but without exception permitted a drafted man to procure a substitute" (Mahon 1983: 53).

One of the many debates between the Federalists and the Jeffersonian Republicans was over the nature of military organization. The Federalists argued for a reliable, emergency force and for a specialized and professional army. They claimed such an army would cause less disruption to civilian life than the militia and would produce a better quality soldier. They referred to Adam Smith's logic that a professional army reflected increased social complexity, specialization, and division of labor rather than a move toward absolutism or tyranny (Cress 1986: 55–

7). The Provisional Army Act of 1789 was their first success. Nonetheless, according to John Mahon (1983: 56), "Despite the policy of the Federalists to enlarge the regular services, the era following the American Revolution stands out as a high point in the history of the militia, a time when it was performing particularly well."

Thomas Jefferson began his presidency with a commitment to localism and to retention of the militia as the principal fighting force (Cress 1986: 57–62; Chambers 1987: 30–32; Mahon 1983: 63–77). By the end of his second term, he not only realized the limits of such a decentralized system, he was the first president to obtain authorization for and actually use a small regular army. Nonetheless, he continued to argue that the militia was an effective means to link citizenship with military obligations. In his view and that of other republicans, this was particularly necessary in an age of increasing commercialism, where ties were through exchange rather than duty. Despite this rhetoric, the end of Jefferson's presidency coincided with the creation of a more reliable regular army, the increase in the locally raised but federally controlled Volunteers, and the relative demise of the militia as:

the victim of the localism that had once caused republican theorists to identify it with the preservation of constitutional balance and civil order. It lost its status as a symbol of American republicanism because it had proven to be more often the perpetrator of discord than the guarantor of domestic tranquillity. (Cress 1986: 61)

The War of 1812 sealed this evolution (Coles 1986; Chambers 1987: 32–3). Although the military organization and strategy were chaotic during the war, the nationalism following the peace and the Battle of New Orleans led Congress to establish a regular, if small, permanent army with a permanent General Staff (Coles 1986: 71–89).

The changes in the military brought about by the War of 1812 remained the basis for army organization until the Civil War (Skelton 1986: 91–112). A career officer corps, dominated by graduates of West Point, developed. A bureaucratized, routinized, and centralized staff structure and administration formed. The army steadily grew in numbers but not necessarily in proportion to the growth in population (Chambers 1987: 35). There were still numerous unresolved problems: internal rifts among the officers, a fundamental class cleavage between the enlisted men and the officers, and attacks on the military, particularly during the Jackson era, for the incompatibility of an increasingly professional army with egalitarian and democratic impulses. However, little reform resulted. Fear of arbitrary central power persisted, and President James K. Polk found it easiest to rely on volunteers during the war with Mexico rather than try to increase the size of the standing army.

The major change in the years between 1812 and the Civil War was the decline of the obligatory militia and the proliferation of units of volunteers (Mahon 1983: 78–96; Chambers 1987: 36–9). Many states effectively abandoned compulsory military training for the militias as local conscription became increasingly untenable. Men ceased to show up, preferring to pay fines, or they turned up without enthusiasm or weapons. In sharp contrast was the swelling of the ranks of volunteer units. Volunteer militias often took the form of expensive, private sports clubs with fancy uniforms, but there were also important volunteer units of Irish immigrants, preparing themselves to fight the British (Mahon 1983: 86). Volunteer militias, although privately organized, were eligible for funding and deployment by the states.

Throughout this whole period, national conscription was politically unacceptable to the populace. During the War of 1812, President James Monroe recommended an emergency measure of temporary, direct national conscription, "the boldest assertion of national power yet attempted in America" (Chambers 1987: 33–4). The proposal had few supporters, even in the president's party. The Federalists, already antagonistic to Monroe, were strong in opposition to conscription as a form of Napoleonic despotism. Daniel Webster decried conscription as "the dice of blood." By 1835, Alexis de Tocqueville was to note, "The notions and habits of the people of the United States are so opposed to compulsory recruiting, that I do not think it can ever be sanctioned by the laws" (quoted in Chambers 1987: 37). Some thirty years later, federal conscription was to become a national necessity and reality – but only briefly.

The Civil War

The Civil War revealed the major inadequacy of the military: it was unprepared for large-scale warfare, either organizationally or strategically. When the war began, there were 15,000 men in 198 companies, of which 186 were on frontiers in the West (Symonds 1986: 154). Both the Union and the Confederacy had to build large-scale armies and quickly. By the end of the war, one out of every 1.66 men of military age in the North and one out every 1.2 in the South served in their respective armies (Mahon 1983: 97).

The armies were undersupplied and military life dismal in contrast to the civilian opportunities provided by a wartime economy. Many initial volunteers on both sides planned to depart the service upon completion of their contractual obligations, which ranged from three months to one year. The war was protracted and bloody, discouraging potential recruits. Desertion was endemic.

Conscription became an important tool of policy for both combatants. The Confederacy enacted conscription on May 16, 1862. Relatively short of men, the officials of the Confederate government realized they had to extract as many men as possible. Support for conscription varied, however, among regions and over time. Even in the "solid South" there were many who resisted or evaded the draft and many who deserted (Honey 1994; Bearman 1991).

The Union had four drafts over the course of the war, the first being on March 3, 1863. However, the 1863 Union draft was far from the first step taken to attract soldiers. On April 15, 1861, three days after the shots on Fort Sumter, President Abraham Lincoln called for 75,000 militia to serve the customary three months. On May 3, 1861, Lincoln called for volunteers for three years and increased the regular army by three regiments. The volunteer response was strong but ultimately insufficient. In July 1862 Lincoln appealed to veterans to reenlist and called for 300,000 additional men to volunteer. A second call for 300,000 militia went out in August 1862, this time for nine months of service. The government offered enlistment bonuses or bounties, and it won legislative authority to draft men into the militia of states that had not met their apportioned quotas. This was the first time that the federal government had required members of the militia to serve more than ninety days out of the year while in national service. According to United States Provost Marshall General James B. Fry (U.S. War Department 1866: 11):

This order was the first step taken by the government towards carrying out the maxim upon which the security of republican governments mainly depends, viz.: that every citizen owes his country military service.

Although approximately 520,000 men responded to this call, the demand for reinforcements continued to outstrip the supply of men. Men left after the end of their tour and did not reenlist. Bounty jumping was another serious problem that contributed to the manpower shortage. Volunteers would receive their enrollment bonus and then fail to show up for duty. The volunteer system was failing politically even more than it was failing numerically. (See Table 3.1.) Volunteers were inequitably distributed among the states and among economic groups. Internal dissension and low morale demanded a strong and powerful central counterbalance to the centrifugal forces of regional, ethnic, and class antagonisms.

Congress, acting upon the administration's proposal, took the extraordinary step of passing the Enrollment Act of March 3, 1863, the first national draft in the North and the first draft not done through the militia system. The Enrollment Act signaled a fundamental change in

Table 3.1. *Bounties paid to volunteers*

Period	Number of volunteers	Bounty per man	Total paid
1861–3	905,869	$100	$90,586,900
1863–4	158,507	$400	$63,402,800
1864–5	191,936	$100	$19,193,600
	10,606	$200	$2,121,200
	139,681	$300	$41,904,300
Totals	1,406,599		$217,208,800

Source: U.S. War Department (1866: 213).

traditional recruitment practices, citizen military obligations, and the direct power of central government over the lives of citizens. Indeed, Chambers argues (1987: 48–50) that enhanced national power to prevent disunion was precisely the point of the conscription acts.

It was the job of the new Bureau of the Provost Marshall General to enroll, that is, register, all eligible men, to supervise the actual draft, and to appoint and monitor the medical examiners and enrollment boards. If a community did not meet its quota through volunteers, the Bureau would hold a draft lottery. Hostility to registration was considerable. Fry reports common household resistance as only one of the numerous obstacles to effective enrollment:

Every imaginable artifice was adopted to deceive and defeat the enrolling officers. Open violence was sometimes met with. Several enrollers lost their lives. Some were crippled. The property of others was destroyed to intimidate them, and prevent the enrolment [sic]. In certain mining regions organized bodies of men openly opposed the enrolment, rendering it necessary that the United States authorities should send troops to overcome their opposition. There were secret societies, newspapers, and politicians who fostered and encouraged this widespread opposition. (U.S. War Department 1866: 19)

Thirty-eight employees of the Bureau were killed and sixty wounded between 1863 and 1865 (U.S. War Department 1866: pt. 1: 143; pt. 2: 252; also see Murdock 1971:28, 40–60). The combination of public hostility, the danger of the job, and low pay made it difficult to recruit and retain competent staff, and the widespread use of bribes was a further corrupting influence (Murdock 1971: 30–1).

The institution of the actual draft provoked even greater resistance. The most famous example is the New York Draft Riot of 1863, the largest riot in United States history. However, this was but one among many incidents (see Murdock 1971: 40–60, 84–90). Moreover, there was considerable draft evasion. For the four drafts, 19 percent did not report for their medical examinations, a total of more than 160,000, calculated from the Provost Marshall Report (U.S. War Department 1866: 165–85, 199–200, 211–2). In the first draft, this percentage was 13 percent (calculated from U.S. War Department 1866: 165–75), but by the second it was 24 percent (calculated from U.S. War Department 1866: 176–85).

To appease some opponents of the draft and to buy the full cooperation of important economic and political groups, the initial Enrollment Act included wide scope for exemptions. The exemptions were freely given and susceptible to fraud. Of those drafted 57 percent received exemptions under the 1863 enrollment, and the average for the war was 41 percent. Over time, the Provost Marshall General was able to increase the uniformity and routinization of the exemption system. What remained far more difficult administratively and politically were volunteer bounties and substitutions. These varied considerably.

Conscription proved to be more effective as a means to encourage initial volunteers and voluntary reenlistment than as a device for direct conscription. Mahon believes that many of those who volunteered would have been ashamed to be drafted (1983: 103). In the long run, the reliance on conscription established the right of the central state to use the draft to raise armies when necessary. The ideal of the citizen-soldier obligated to serve his country was insufficient to motivate consent to national conscription, or perhaps it was precisely that ideal that made conscription so problematic. Conscription was a threat by the national government that mobilized states to supply troops through volunteering and their own particular forms of the draft. The numerous forms of exemption reflected continued antipathy to increased governmental power, but it also reflected the fact that the Union Army was attracting sufficient men through other means. What Lincoln and his administration established was the right of federal government to demand service of its citizens unmediated by state militias.

Although the conclusion of the Civil War signaled the end of national conscription, it did not signal the end of the Volunteer movement reconstituted as the National Guard. Governors increasingly called on the National Guard to intervene in industrial disputes, usually on the side of business (Mahon 1983: 112–3, 116–8). The Guard became the alternative to a standing army, at least in the eyes of its proponents (Mahon 1983: 120–4) and particularly in cases of defense. Its detractors, on the other hand, pointed to the lack of training, professionalism, and offensive capability. The pivotal role of the National Guard in the war with Spain (1898–99) demonstrated the value of the National Guard in providing volunteer troops for an overseas war, but the military failures in that war raised serious questions about U.S. military effectiveness. The major manpower concerns were the absence of an efficient reserve and of adequate training. By the turn of the century there was a preparedness campaign, similar to those in Britain, Canada, Australia, and New Zealand.

CANADA

Canada began as two countries, one French and one English, and many of its military service quandaries have their origins in that history. Policies supported by anglophone Canada often provoke opposition in francophone Canada. Its early history, however, was marked not only by the conflict between the British and the French but also by a conflict between the colonists and the British government, a conflict that marked all the British colonies, over the appropriate contributions of money and men to the military.

English settlers migrated to Canada after swearing allegiance to the British Crown. Britain protected the colonists from foreign attack, protected sea trade, and provided some "powder and munition," but it did not actually establish garrisons on Canadian soil until the war with France in the late seventeenth century. The settlers formed militias, similar to those in the United States, Australia, and New Zealand, and these provided the major form of defense against Indian raids When the war with France broke out, however, the British had difficulties coordinating the militia and the Regulars (Stacey 1963 [1936]: 2–4).

The French, on the other hand, already had a garrison in place and a unified military. Compulsory military service was the law of New France and, consequently, its settlers had a strong militia system under local captains selected by the community. The militia weakened significantly after the defeat of the French in 1763. The *Conquête* remains, even to this day, the defining moment in Quebec history. In the resulting Treaty of Paris, the British sovereign pledged that French Canadians, who numbered approximately 60,000, could continue to practice the Roman Catholic religion under the British crown. Despite efforts, albeit half-hearted ones, by the British to protestantize and anglicize the francophone region, French Canada endured. The passage of the 1774 Quebec Act granted French Canadians the right to keep their civil laws, language, and customs. It also reempowered the Catholic Church to collect tithes, reinforcing the organizational power of the Catholic Church in French Canada. The French Canadians had only to accept the British criminal code (Wade 1967: 64).

The American war of 1776 led to the immigration of thousands of British Loyalists from the emerging United States. These Loyalists demanded British institutions and law and received them in the form of the Constitutional Act of 1791. This act and related legislation partitioned the colony into an English-speaking Upper Canada with British laws and customs and a French-speaking Lower Canada, which relied on French civil laws and customs as allowed under the Quebec Act. The social pact, at least from the francophone's perspective, now assured a certain degree of French Canadian autonomy and required the government to consider the effects of policies not only upon individual French Canadians but also on French Canadian institutions and culture. The ground work for a divided Canada was complete (Armstrong 1974 [1937]: 7).

During the American Revolution, the francophones resented the extractions demanded by the Militia Act of 1777, and the British experienced difficulties in enforcing the law in French Canada (Stacey 1963 [1936]: 8–9; Wade 1968: 73). Quebec played little part in the War of 1812, but French Canadians did demonstrate greater loyalty to Canada in this war than they had in 1776 (Wade 1968: 121–3).

The major problem for the British government was extraction of revenues from the colonists to support the British regulars. The colonists so resisted the Revenue Act of 1764 that it was abandoned in 1770 (Stacey 1963 [1936]: 4–7). A rebellion in Canada in 1837 and continuous conflicts with the Americans increased the demands on the British military and led to an enhanced commitment of troops. By the 1840s the British Parliament was discussing how to make the colonists contribute to the expenses of the large colonial armies in Canada, Australia, New Zealand, and elsewhere. When Lord Charles Grey became the colonial secretary in 1846, he advocated reductions of British garrisons where possible, colonial payment for internal policing, and colonial payment for any supplements to the forces under British command. The Canadians, to the extent that they were ever willing to expend their own funds on defense, preferred local forces over which they exercised complete control (Stacey 1963 [1936]: 17–25, 35–51, 64–7, 86).

By the middle of the nineteenth century, Canada depended on a small regular army supplemented by companies of volunteers in times of greater need. The four provinces of anglophone Canada imposed a universal obligation on all military-aged men, who would serve under regimental officers. This proved a cheap way to mobilize the population in 1812, but the militia were poorly trained in comparison to the Regulars, who were the more effective fighters. Nonetheless, according to Stacey (1963 [1936]: 12) Canadians had "an overweening confidence in the military virtue of mere courage and patriotic feeling, and an almost complete lack of appreciation of the value of the trained professional soldier." The Militia Act of 1868 reinforced the voluntary principle.

The debate over Confederation in 1867 resulted in English Canada making numerous promises to protect the culture, language, and rights of French Canada. The recognition of Quebec as a province was but one, albeit the principal, means to ensure this aim (Linteau 1989: 75). The *théorie du Pacte*[7] obligated the federal government (1) to protect the French Canadian way of life and (2) to refrain from calling upon francophones in the defense of British interests. In return, francophone citizens respected the largely Anglo-Saxon institutions of government and law and were loyal to the federation.

Subsequently, the Canadian military became even more of an anglophone cultural organization in its traditions and practices (Gravel 1974a, b; Morton 1971, 1980; Pariseau and Bernier 1987). By 1914 French Canadian participation in the military had dwindled to a mere formality (Pariseau and Bernier 1987; Morton 1971: 103).[8] There was relatively little volunteering for the military among francophones in peacetime, despite what might appear to be the economic security of being in the armed forces. On the other hand, the Canadian military was relatively small. It did not offer the opportunities of the nineteenth-century British or late twentieth-century American armies. It could afford to be an anglophone club.

Canada did send troops to various British war efforts, most notably the South African or Boer War of 1899–1902, to which Canada sent a small contingent of 7,368 men under British control. The major effect of its participation was the discovery of its relative military unpreparedness, a subject of debate even after Canada's entry into World War I (Stanley 1974 [1954]: 279–89; Miller 1975).

NEW ZEALAND

The major military threat to New Zealand's settlers was from the indigenous Maori population, which had well-organized armies. However, there was actually a three-way political conflict; the settlers and Maoris were pitted not only against each other but also against the administrators of the colony. The Maoris resisted the confiscations of their lands, and the settlers demanded the rights of self-government. The settlers of New Zealand, as did their counterparts in Canada, expected Britain to provide the bulk of the men and monies for the military.

In the late eighteenth and early nineteenth centuries, British military

---

[7] Daniel Latouche pointed out that this is how French Canadian history refers to the political settlement of 1867. Also, see Laurendeau 1962: 25–32.

[8] At the very highest levels, French Canadian participation was superficially more balanced. Governments made efforts to provide political patronage to French Canadian party members by giving them military commands. However, these commands were usually little more than figurehead positions.

presence in New Zealand was minimal. Settlers were formally under the protection of troops stationed in Australia and, on occasion, more informally under the protection of local Maori chiefs (Hill 1986a: 48). In the mid 1820s New Zealand mercantile interests began demanding a British military presence. In the 1830s, to defend themselves against prisoners, the poor, and the native population, the wealthy established private police or "armed associations" (Hill 1986a: 84–6). With the formal annexation of New Zealand in 1840 came British recognition of its responsibility for the colony. Although William Hobson, the first Governor of New Zealand, opposed the armed associations and militia for fear that they would precipitate trouble with the Maori population (Hill 1986a: 91), the Militia Act of 1845 regularized local practices, especially in Auckland, legalized drilling, and authorized the swearing in of all adult males as constables to be on call in case of Maori attack.

The volunteer militias had the same difficulties in mobilizing men as those in Canada and the United States. Even in the midst of the wars with the Maoris, the settlers demanded that the British government pay most of the costs of defense (Dalton 1967: 19; also, see Hill 1986a: 188 *passim*). In 1863, to ensure adequate troops in the increasingly costly wars, first Prime Minister Alfred Dommet and then his successor Sir Charles Grey proposed the establishment of Military Settlements, whose inhabitants were to be paid with some of the lands confiscated from the Maoris (see esp. Harrop 1937: 200–9; Dalton 1967: 181–205; Hill 1986b: 797, 907–8). The remainder of the land would be sold to support the war effort. Grey, who had engaged in a similar enterprise in British Kaffraria (Harrop 1937: 199–200), envisaged an initial enrollment of 2,000, which would increase to 5,000 men. The advocates of the plan argued that it would deal with both the problem of defense and the problem of the military settlers currently being paid by the colony as auxiliary troops (Dalton 1967: 188–192). The opponents argued about the amount of land involved, feared Maori reprisals, or doubted the ability of the military settlers to survive as farmers (Dalton 1967: 192–205; Hill 1986b). Nonetheless the New Zealand Settlements Act or "Confiscation Act" passed in 1864.

The most successful of the military settler schemes produced the Waikato Militia, which attracted men largely from the Otago and Australian gold fields. This militia swelled in size from approximately 300 in September 1863 to approximately 4,000 by early 1864 (Belich 1986: 126). Indeed, they represented the largest proportion of the colonial forces during this period. The Imperial troops numbered nearly 12,000 at their peak (Belich 1986: 126) and the Maoris approximately 4,000 (Belich 1986: 132). The Waikato War (1863–64) was important in determining the outcome of the New Zealand Wars, but even so the

Maoris came closer to winning than the Victorians preferred to admit (Belich 1986).

There is some controversy about the quality of the military settlers as soldiers, but there is little doubt that they were dismal as farmers. The land was not high quality and problems with the Maoris persisted. Consequently, "many of the settlers walked off to more attractive speculations like the Thames goldfield" (Sorrenson 1981: 185). Nor did the sale of lands produce much profit for the government.

New Zealand was an enthusiastic participant in the Boer War, with a contingent of over 6,000 men, most of whom provided their own horses (Baker 1988: 11). The conflict in South Africa affirmed to the New Zealanders the limits of British military might and the need for a better prepared New Zealand army. In 1909 the Liberal Government, under Prime Minister John Ward, introduced compulsory military training (CMT) for males between 12 and 21 and later revised for males between 14 and 25. The vote in Parliament was nearly unanimous.

Not all New Zealanders were supporters of compulsory military training and the 1912 revisions made to it by the Reform Government, under Prime Minister William Massey and Minister of Defence James Allen. The same sectors of the population who would later denounce conscription composed the opposition: pacifists, anti-militarists, and militant labor. They were the minority, but often they and their sons were willing to resist to the point of imprisonment, fines, and military detention for absence from parade (Baker 1988: 12).

AUSTRALIA

Australia's early military experience is unique among the countries surveyed. Created as a penal colony in 1788, its initial immigrants were transported there under chains rather than as an act of free will. There was no question of their supporting the military that was supervising them. Moreover, although there were certainly conflicts between settlers and the aboriginal population, the Australian aboriginals did not possess the military organization or prowess of the indigenous peoples of the United States, Canada, or New Zealand.

When the British government first colonized the continent of Australia, it sent garrisons of Regulars and companies of Royal Marines to accompany the convicts. The major military task was internal policing of the convicts and, to a lesser extent, control of the aboriginal population. Reports of a possible Irish uprising in Sydney prompted the formation of the Sydney and Parramatta Loyal Associations, composed of soldiers raised from the citizenry, but they were soon disbanded (Grey 1990: 9–21).

Australia

After 1840, with the cessation of transportation of convicts, the six Australian colonies came to rely increasingly on volunteer militias. Lord Grey urged the colonies to form militias; his aim was to reduce the fiscal and manpower burden on the British government. His prompting met support from those who perceived the militia as a form of self-government and Australian national expression. However, with the combination of war scares and of unrest created by the gold rush, Britain once again dispatched troops to Australia (Grey 1990: 9–25; Wilcox 1994).

The six colonies of Australia continued to raise local forces, especially in response to the Crimean War in 1853 and to later wars, including the Waikato War in New Zealand. In 1863 the Imperial government demanded a capitation fee for troops stationed in Australia. The colonists resented this demand to pay for troops over whom they had no control and who could be dispatched elsewhere in accordance with British needs. The colonies continued to raise their own troops, using land grants and other remunerations as an incentive to volunteers. The conflict over the division of the fiscal responsibility coincided with a growing Australian nationalism. The culmination was the withdrawal of the last British regiment in 1870 (Grey 1990: 21–3).

By the late 1880s the six colonies of Australia began to discuss a combined defense force. In 1899–1902 they together sent a total of 16,175 men to South Africa to fight in the Boer War, but this was not a particularly strong response given the available population and in comparison to the response of New Zealand (Grey 1990: 56–7).

On January 1, 1901, the six states of Australia officially became confederated into the Commonwealth of Australia, a self-governing dominion within the British Empire. The state defense forces were transferred to the federal government in March after "the Defence Minister, Sir John Forrest, had moved to that portfolio from the more demanding office of Postmaster-General" (Grey 1990: 67). In 1901 Australia's armed services consisted of approximately 29,000 men in the military and 2,000 in the navy, but there were only 1,500 permanent soldiers and 250 full-time sailors. A contingent of nearly 5,000 was still in South Africa, fighting in the Boer War. Duntroon, the military college that was to train the officers of Australia's military, did not accept its first class until 1911. The first commander-in-chief, Sir Edward "Curly" Hutton, recruited from among senior British army officers, did not arrive until 1902. The first Defence Act was not passed until 1903 (Grey 1990: 68–9; Coulthard-Clark 1988: 121–3).

Australia was and is a country with a large land mass and a small population. At Confederation, the total population was 3,750,000, of whom two-thirds lived in New South Wales and Victoria, mostly in

Sydney and Melbourne (Crowley 1974: 261). It was also a relatively poor country, and its initial programs were aimed at economic development. Defense was a secondary and, to some, trivial issue at first. Australia, even the newly self-governing Australia, had no right independent of Britain to declare war or make peace and initially depended on Britain for defense. Given that Australians perceived no significant military threat, this arrangement suited the fiscally conservative government and parliamentary leadership.

As the government attempted to draft and pass its first defense bills, both the nature of the Australian military and the relationship of Australian and British defense policy came under scrutiny. The foremost concerns were rationalization of the military and cost containment. There were two additional, and contradictory, issues that also affected policy. The first was the fear of a standing army, which implied militarism and the creation of a military caste. Hierarchical stratification and impressment were among the facets of British life many Australians had attempted to escape. There was, at the same time, an increasing interest in developing a national, as opposed to an imperial, defense policy. Hutton was clearly not the man for this job; he was more interested in promoting British interests than in constructing a policy based on Australia's particular needs (Grey 1990: 69–74).

The very first federal Defence Act affirmed the government's commitment to use a volunteer army in any engagement beyond Australia's territorial boundaries. Grey (1990: 73) argues that this was one of the means legislators used to ensure against attempts, such as Hutton's, "to enmesh Australia's forces into a system of imperial defence." Positive efforts to augment Australian independence within the British Empire were explicit in the 1903 discussion of ratification of the Naval Agreement that emerged from the Colonial Conference of 1902. Ratification meant an increase in the unpopular subsidy paid to Britain in support of the navy and a decrease in the already tiny amount of control the Australian government had exercised over naval equipment and movements. Although it was decided that Australia could not yet afford ships of its own, criticism of the naval agreement signified citizen and parliamentary unease with continued Australian subservience to Britain (Inglis 1968: 23; Coulthard-Clark 1988: 130–32; Grey 1990: 75–6). By 1914, Australia, alone among the dominions, had established its own navy, albeit, "a navy within a navy" (Senator George Pearce as cited by Coulthard-Clark 1988: 137).

By 1905 the world was heating up, and the Pax Britannica was breaking down. Australians began to feel concern for the security of their continent, especially after the Japanese naval defeat of the Russians. The Pacific was far from secure, and Australians were eager to maintain a white island in an Asian world, a world to which most Australian citizens felt hostile and unreceptive. The media, parliamentarians seeking a larger and better military force, and the Australian National Defence League played on the racialist fears of the citizens and their representatives (Inglis 1968: 25; Robson 1970: 13–4; Barrett 1979: 14–19).

Australia was not exempt from the concerns about preparedness that infected Britain, most of Europe, North America, and New Zealand at the turn of the century. Spearheading the campaign for military preparedness was the Australian National Defence League, started in 1905. Among its founders was W. M. "Billy" Hughes, a Labor MP and the Prime Minister during World War I. Hughes did not share the smugness of some of his countrymen in regard to the performance of the Australians during the Boer War. He feared the outcome for Australia if her young men were not properly trained. At the same time, he was no advocate of militarism. Since the 1901 debate over the first Defence Bill, he had been arguing for compulsory military training on the Swiss model:

. . . there is no kind of security in time of danger, but that which comes from an efficiently drilled, adequately paid, and sufficiently numerous body of men in our own country. This Bill does not provide for that. But there is one thing which I do see . . . It provides for a military establishment on a permanent footing which, while it is wretchedly inadequate to repel a foreign invader, is sufficiently strong to overawe on some occasions – perhaps on many – the citizen in his pursuit of constitutional reform or in the maintenance of civil liberty and right . . . It appears to me that the only remedy, the only sure and certain method of defence is a scheme, if you like to call it so, of a national militia. I believe that every man should do what is done in Switzerland, that particularly favored country, so far as liberty is concerned. (Quoted in Main 1970: 10)

In 1907, Prime Minister Alfred Deakin proposed a scheme for compulsory military training, and his Protectionist government introduced a bill to that effect. The government fell before anything came of the bill, but by that time compulsory military training was a fait accompli. Virtually every major faction now supported one scheme or another (Barrett 1979: 66). In 1909 the Fusion government that Deakin helped form amended the Defence Act to include compulsory training. The scheme awaited implementation until 1911, however, so that it could benefit from the suggestions of Lord Kitchener, who visited in 1910.

On January 1, 1911, compulsory training in the form of "boy conscription" was initiated.[9] The eligible were required to register, and only

[9] Unless otherwise noted, the detailed factual material on the scheme comes from Barrett (1979: 66, 69–75). Also, see Inglis (1968: 27–9). Historians disagree about the reasons for Hughes's support of boy conscription. Jeffrey Grey (1990: 78), for example, claims that "Hughes' motivation was not militaristic; his suspicion of

then would the administrators make a determination whether the boy was deemed exempt on grounds of physical unfitness or geographical inaccessibility to training facilities. There was no exemption, however, for conscientious objection. The amendments to the Defence Act legislated compulsory junior cadet training for males aged 12 to 14, senior cadet training for those 14 to 18, and citizen force training for those 18 to 20. Men ages 20 through 26 were to make up a reserve force but would not undergo training except in time of war. The scheme was to apply only to those males who had not yet turned 18 at the time of its initiation; everyone older was exempt. Effectively, the scheme was compulsory military training for boys who lived in urban areas.

Compliance with and acquiescence to the scheme were by no means universal. By all accounts there were 27,749 prosecutions and 5,732 cases of detention or imprisonment from 1911 to 1912 (Jauncey 1935: 52; Grey 1990: 80). Barrett (1979: 206) revises these numbers to 34,000 and 7,000 if one extends the figures to mid 1915. Nor does anyone deny the existence of organized opponents, most notably among the Quakers and other religious pacifists, some unionists, socialist organizations, and the Australian Freedom League, a coalition drawing largely from these groups (see esp. Barrett 1979: 81–127).

How to interpret this opposition has been the subject of some historiographical contention. In his 1935 book L.C. Jauncey argued that the facts added up to considerable resistance and noncompliance (pp. 52–3). Barrett (1979 *passim*) and Grey (1990: 81) claim that, for the most part, Australians went along with boy conscription. Barrett's recalculations (1979: 206) reduce the percentage of registrants prosecuted from the nearly 25 percent Jauncey figured to about 5 percent; in addition, he notes that many of these prosecutions were for second offenders. Grey (1990: 81) calculates the rate at only about 2 percent of the total per year. Grey adds, "many of those prosecuted were persistent offenders, and further that many of the prosecutions were for minor infringements of the regulations not in themselves symptomatic of an attempt to buck the system" (1990: 81). Noncompliance by eligible youths certainly existed, but it was not in itself particularly significant.

The issue of the extent of organized opposition is more ambiguous. Founded in 1912, the Australian Freedom League had chapters in every

permanent standing forces conformed with good socialist principle. He saw universal service as a means of avoiding the propagation of militarism and threat that armed forces might be used against the workers, while providing for the defense of the nation with minimal disruption to business and civil life." On the other hand, K. S. Inglis argues that Hughes's underlying aim was to preserve the racial purity of white Australia (1968: 23–4). What is uncontested is the essential role Hughes played in convincing Labor members to incorporate and support compulsory military training in 1909 and again in the Defence Act of 1911.

Analysis

capital city, claimed a membership of 55,000 at its peak in 1914, and had built some support in parliament, particularly among Labor members (Barrett 1979: 111–27; Inglis 1968: 28–9). In contrast the membership of the Australian National Defence League was probably not more than 3,000 (Barrett 1979: 116). The Australian Freedom League was a politically important pressure group that organized publications, public meetings, and petition drives. It lashed out at the cost of the scheme, its militarism, the treatment of the detained, and the indifference to conscientious objection. It obtained the active support of 1.2 percent of the population (Barrett 1979: 127) but was unable to stop or even seriously alter the nature of compulsory military training. At the outbreak of World War I, it voluntarily disbanded, claiming no change in its position on training but at the same time a desire "not to hamper the Government in the discharge of the grave responsibility" (quoted in Barrett 1979: 117).

The history of boy conscription is really the history of the establishment of the policy bargain among government officials and between government and the citizenry regarding conscription. Legislative debate set the terms, and citizen reactions generally confirmed consent. Some citizens objected but most acquiesced to compulsory military training. A majority withheld approval, however, of conscription for military service outside the territorial boundaries of Australia.

ANALYSIS

The combined narratives of nineteenth- and early twentieth-century military service in France, Britain, the United States, Canada, Australia, and New Zealand have several common features. First, all of the countries were undergoing the transformation from a series of regions or colonies into a single nation. Second, compliance as well as fiscal costs figured into the determination of the military service format. These similarities did not produce a convergence in military service policy, however.

National conscription occurred only in France and the United States. Britain relied on militia and volunteer corps for civil defense and a professional army for foreign ventures, and it tried to get reluctant colonies to share the burden of its costs in their locale. The United States resisted the formation of a standing army and resorted to popular mobilization in time of war; Canada, Australia, and New Zealand engaged in similar strategies. Despite the construction of national identities during this period, only France used conscription as a means to socialize and integrate its diverse inhabitants. Nation building certainly contributed to the reliance on conscription in France, but nation building in and of itself did not produce centralized conscription elsewhere. Nor did

75

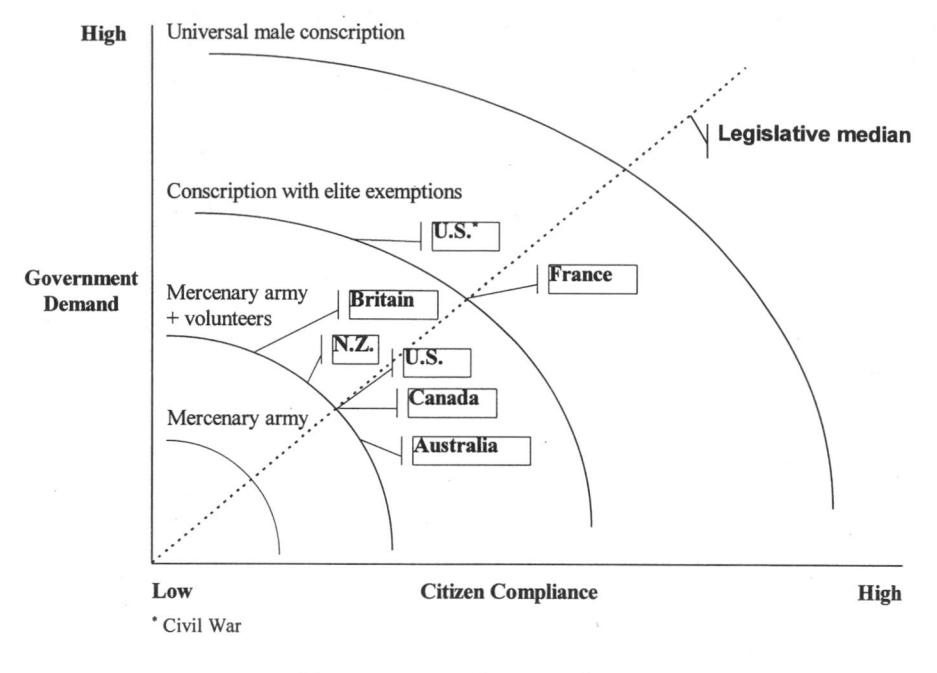

High | Universal male conscription

Legislative median

Conscription with elite exemptions

U.S.*

Government
Demand

France

Mercenary army
+ volunteers

Britain

N.Z.   U.S.

Mercenary army

Canada

Australia

Low   Citizen Compliance   High

* Civil War

Figure 3.5. Legislative median.

it produce in France the elimination of exemptions based on social status or money.

A more plausible explanation of the differences in military service policy is the variation in the level of government demand for troops, on the one hand, and citizen compliance, on the other. Figure 3.5 illustrates the distribution of the countries along these dimensions. The three governments with the highest demand were also the first to institute some form of national conscription: France, the Union, and the Confederacy. The demand of the other governments was below the threshold for consideration of national conscription. The demand of the British government was considerably more moderate but higher than that of the governments of New Zealand, Canada, and Australia in that order. Canada until 1867, Australia until 1901, and New Zealand until 1907 were not independent states but colonies or protectorates of Britain. Although each had a legislature to which citizens elected representatives, colonial administrators had considerable say and Britain was largely responsible for defense. The demand of the central governments of the colonies was generally low.

It is difficult to measure compliance and noncompliance, especially in this period, but several facts stand out. In Britain, between 1862 and

1912 the recruits as a percentage of the effective strength of the British army went up, and between 1882 and 1910 the percentage decreased of those who failed to show up for attestation after they were served with notice papers. In France many young men continued to find ways to avoid the draft, but there was a decline in the problem of *bons absents* and in the loss of fingers and toes, forms of self-mutilation that resulted in a medical rejection from the military. In the United States, willingness to serve in the obligatory local militia declined over the century, but most of those who served in the Union Army during the Civil War were volunteers. Anglophone Canadians were reluctant to contribute to the national army, but the francophones were even more reluctant, a reluctance that did not vanish after Confederation. In New Zealand and Australia, there was relatively little cooperation with the Imperial demands for troops, considerably more with the demands of their local and, later, central governments.

In all of the countries, regional variation in volunteering and draft resistance was the rule. Initially, this probably was an effect largely of the uneven and undeveloped extractive apparatus of the state. However, even when bureaucratic capacities no longer varied greatly among the countries, the likelihood of compliance did. Indeed, the variation seems to correlate with the factors hypothesized to affect contingent consent. Incentives and coercion also affect rates of enlistment, but a cost-benefit approach has difficulty accounting for the groups reluctant to join up despite their relative poverty or for the rapid rise in volunteering at the onset of major and even not so major wars, when the costs to the volunteer go up significantly. Whether contingent consent offers a better explanation will be the subject of later chapters. Suffice it to say here, over the course of the nineteenth century, government actors increasingly appealed to civic obligations and patriotism as a means to attract recruits. They were actively seeking to build consent, not just compliance.

One way to think about this variation is by means of the stylized conscription games introduced in Chapter 2. When there was relatively low demand, government officials preferred conscription but could tolerate a volunteer army, the policy the legislative median most preferred (Figure 3.6). When there was relatively high demand, government officials did not even present a volunteer army as a possibility (or, more likely, withdrew it from consideration after evidence of its failure) and preferred universal conscription over conscription with multiple, politically based exemptions (Figure 3.7). The median legislator, however, would have rejected universal conscription. Through either backward induction or by dint of experience, the government policymakers introduced conscription with exemptions. In both games, the government policymakers get their second choice, but it is a different second choice

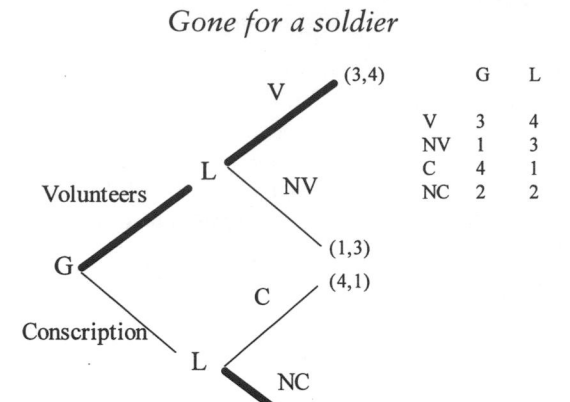

Figure 3.6. Small demand game.

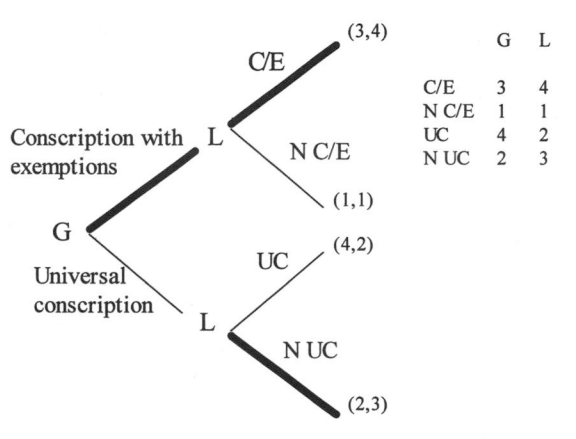

Figure 3.7. Large demand game: France and United States.

given the change in the dimensions of the demand. What influences the preferences of the legislative median is the anticipated level of citizen support.

The games draw on and illustrate the narrative. They emphasize the obvious, that is, the importance of the size of government demand in getting a national conscription policy even considered by a legislature who must answer to the men and fathers of the men who will be called upon to serve. On the other hand, the narrative illuminates the game. Even in the absence of war or active external threat, France maintains national conscription, but Britain and New Zealand seem not even to consider such an option despite a sometimes comparable need for troops. One difference appears to be in the level of anticipated compliance. In France the combination of defense requirements, bureaucratic capacity, and the republican ideology of the "nation in arms" produces both government demand for conscription and widespread citizen compliance. The "nation in arms" represents an egalitarian commitment but also a bulwark against the threat to liberty of the French standing army. The United States, Britain, New Zealand, Canada, and Australia lack a standing army and perceive national conscription as a threat to liberty, a threat that should be resisted.

Only when the demands of war become even greater and their governments more democratic and trustworthy will the citizens of the Anglo-Saxon democracies even consider national conscription. Before turning to this important transformation during World War I, however, it is worth considering the shifts in the nature of national conscription among those countries that relied on some form of national conscription in the nineteenth century: France and the United States.

4

The price of citizenship

We're coming, ancient Abraham, several hundred strong
We hadn't no 300 dollars and so we come along
We hadn't no rich parents to pony up the tin
So we went unto the provost and there were mustered in.
　　　Carl Sandburg, *Abraham Lincoln,* v. 2: 362

Throughout the nineteenth century states enhanced the extent and depth of their coercive capacity while also expanding the privileges and numbers of citizens. Rulers developed increasingly efficient and centralized administrative apparatuses to monitor and extract manpower from the countryside, but they had to appease citizens who were also voters and to ensure the cooperation (or at least avoid the resistance) of those whose services they sought, whether voters or not. Nearly all the European, North American, and Antipodean states – democratic or autocratic – devised new equilibrium policies to define the mutual obligations of citizens and government actors. In terms of military policy, the problem for modernizing states was how to develop an effective fighting force more embedded in national society than the absolutist armies of Europe or the local militias of the new countries of North America and the Antipodes.

The substantive focus of this chapter is on the disappearance of various forms of buying one's way out of military service if conscripted: commutation, a fee paid to government; and substitution and replacement, payment to someone else to take one's place. "Buying out" had its origins in the feudal obligations of subjects to their lord; feudal subjects had the option of paying a fee in lieu of military service. The nineteenth-century defense of medieval practices led to a series of rationales, but all were based on distinctions among classes. Buying out, advocates claimed, protected the sons of the well-off from the greater suffering and costs military service would impose on them than on those more used to the rough life. Further, they pointed to the benefits to society of a system in which those who could serve the country better in other occupations were permitted to do so while also contributing to the government's coffers.

These rationales generally prevailed at the beginning of the nineteenth century. There was some, but relatively little, outcry against either the practices or their justifications. By the end of the nineteenth century, however, buying out was disappearing everywhere. During the debates over military organization in the decade prior to World War I, buying out was no longer on the agenda of possible policy options. The analytic narrative below explores how and why the practices of substitution, commutation, and replacement disappeared from the public agenda.

In exploring the shift in the position of the pivotal legislator from support of buying out to support of more standardized exemptions, the narrative centers on two puzzles. The first is the lack of a precise fit between the number of soldiers required by government and changes in buying out. Although an increased government demand for troops often promotes discussions of military reform, practice changed in France even in the absence of the need for total mobilization. Post-Napoleonic conscription was instituted in peacetime, and the elimination of various forms of commutation often occurred postwar. In the United States, during the Civil War, there was total mobilization, and yet substitution was retained.

The second is the nature of the relationship between ideological and institutional change. Universal manhood suffrage followed rather than preceded the elimination of buying out. Moreover, the norm of equality of sacrifice, enforced by relatively universal and impartial selection procedures, was not simply an artifact of increased democratization. Prussia eliminated buying out long before the extension of the franchise. Even the most republican elements of France and the most democratic in the United States accepted replacement and commutation as fair well into the nineteenth century. Even many who seemed to benefit from replacement and commutation sought the end of these practices by the 1870s.

This history thus permits reconsideration of the two hypotheses explaining the shift in the position of the median legislator:

(5) *The more democratic the regime and the more universalistic its laws, the more likely it is that citizens will comply with a policy of universal conscription.*

(5a) *As the franchise includes more of the population, the more likely it is that citizens will comply with universal conscription.*

The price of citizenship

(5b) As the norms of citizens change toward more democratic norms, the more likely it is that citizens will comply with universal conscription.

The situation of primary interest is one in which a country is under some degree of serious military threat and in which government policymakers prefer some form of conscription to a mercenary army composed of volunteers. The analysis that follows relies on modifications of the conscription games between government policymakers and pivotal legislators first developed in Chapter 2. Government policymakers propose a sequence of policies, which legislators reject or accept and to which citizens comply or not. Legislators express their preferences by voting a proposed policy up or down. Citizens express their preferences through their candidate selections, lobbying, protest, and noncompliance.

To simplify the story, there are four possible policy choices: voluntary compliance, buying out, exemptions based not on purchase but on other forms of special privilege, and a selective service in which all young men are eligible and government agents use impartial criteria to pick among them. In the cases discussed below, government policymakers have eliminated voluntary compliance as an option; their demand for men is too great.

Government policymakers will prefer the military service policy that gives them the most control over selection of recruits, but their choices are constrained by the relative bargaining power of legislators and by the probable compliance of citizens. Legislators will prefer the policy that brings them the most support from powerful constituents and the most compliance with the enacted policy. Most citizens will prefer a policy that either exempts them and their sons or provides adequate compensation in return for service, but they may object to a policy in which some are permitted exemptions they are not or in which policy is made without taking their interests into account.

Citizens are not a single entity, however. They disagree over the best form of exemption or whether there should be exemptions at all. Some have the vote, and some do not. There will be those who evade, those who protest, and those who simply go along. For the purposes of the narrative to follow, the effective constituents of legislators may be only the wealthy, the wealthy plus other propertied citizens, or nearly the entire adult male population. Each of these aggregates has a distinct set of preferences over conscription (Figure 4.1).

As long as only a wealthy elite holds effective power and in the absence of any costly noncompliance by others, the game between government policymakers and the pivotal legislator is a straightforward one

P1	P2	Legal Obligations with	P3	P4
Voluntary Compliance	"Buying Out" (money-based exemptions)	Numerous Exceptions	Lobbied Exemptions	Selective Service

Preferences on Form of Conscription

Policymakers	Wealthy	Propertied but Not Wealthy	Majority of All Citizens
P4	P1	P1	P1
P3	P2	P3	P4
P2	P3	P2	P3
P1	P4	P4	P2

Figure 4.1. Policy choices.

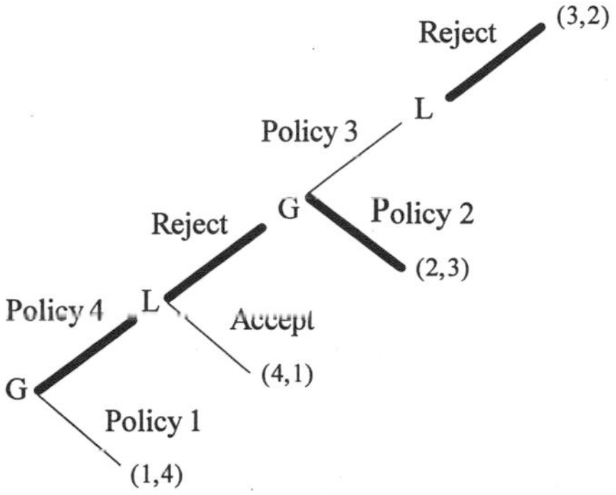

Figure 4.2. Conscription game I: legislator as representative of wealthy elite.

(Figure 4.2). Once the government, which sets the agenda, eliminates Policy 1, voluntary compliance, then Policy 2, buying out, will emerge as the equilibrium policy bargain. Equally straightforward is a game in which the median legislator represents the median position of the whole population. The equilibrium policy is selective service (Figure 4.3).

The problematic game is precisely the one that characterizes the history in France and the United States. The wealthy no longer have clear dominance over the legislature, and the majority of the population have not yet secured the vote or other means to influence legislators directly. The franchise does extend, however, far enough into the social base to include propertied farmers, small businessmen, and others. The

83

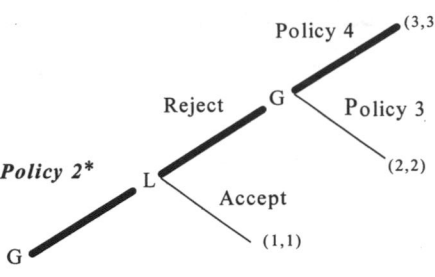

Figure 4.3. Conscription game II: legislator as representative of majority of population.

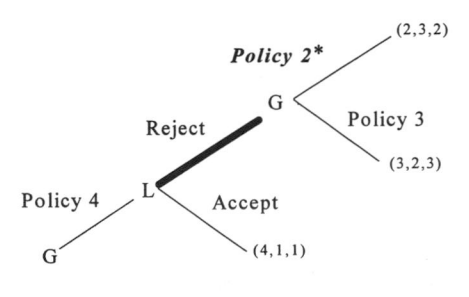

*equilibrium policy from last round

Figure 4.4. Conscription game III: multiple pressures on median legislator.

monetary price of buying out may be too high for them, but they do want to protect their sons and workers. Thus, they will appeal to other bases of exemptions that serve their particular interests. If they split among themselves and with the wealthy about the best form of exemption or if their solutions create protest and noncompliance among the rest of the citizenry, then the game will have no determinant outcome (Figure 4.4).

Relying on detailed accounts of substitution, replacement, and commutation in France and the United States, this chapter recounts the history of buying out, the political debate on the issues, and the response by affected publics to changes in conscription. It then contrasts the experiences of these countries with each other and with others. Finally, it evaluates reigning explanations in light of arguments concerning the relationship between changing standards of fairness and institutional changes in governance.

FRANCE

The French government introduced conscription in 1793 and has been experimenting with its form ever since. Until 1872 replacement or some other form of commutation was almost always available as a legal means to avoid obligatory military service. The percentages using replacement fluctuated (Figure 4.5) and so did the price (Figures 4.6 and 4.7). The practice of replacement began during the French Revolution and ended soon after the Franco-Prussian War and the Commune of Paris.

The French Revolution mobilized large numbers of men (see esp. Forrest 1989; Van Holde 1993; Woloch 1994) and initially permitted replacement. However, the use of replacements contradicted the universalistic ideology of the Revolution and appeared to be one source of resistance to military enlistment by the central state. Consequently, the *levée en masse* of 1793 and the 1798 *loi Jourdan de 19 fructidor VI* prohibited replacement. Napoleon reintroduced the practice with his first conscription law of 1800 for those "who cannot sustain the fatigues of war or who are more useful to the state in continuing their work and their studies rather than in becoming part of the army" (Schnapper 1968: 21, my translation).

Replacements had to meet the physical qualifications of conscripts but could come from any part of the country and be under age. The overall rate of replacements was 16 percent among the 70,000 men incorporated into the service with a rate as high as 30 percent in some districts, even among districts which usually could be relied on for recruits. In 1802 the government sharply restricted replacement but permitted substitution, a practice that permitted men from the same communes to exchange numbers. The laws of 1803, 1804, and 1806 permitted replacements for those in certain occupations of particular value to the state, for those in training in valued professions, and for those who were in the second and third classes and had drawn a bad number (Schnapper 1968: 20). However, replacement was initially a privilege, not a right, and it was closely administered. The replacement had to meet all the qualifying conditions and be among the previously uninducted from the same département as the person who hired him. The purchaser paid an indemnity of at least 100 francs to the state and stayed on the list until his replacement was discharged or died. If the replacement deserted, the purchaser was responsible to fill his shoes. Given the numbers of men called up, the prohibition against intermediaries, and the numerous legal requirements, replacements were relatively expensive (Figure 4.6) and rare. Schnapper (1968: 26–8) estimates that replacements were never more than 4.3 percent of those drafted. He also notes considerable regional variation in price, with the highest at about

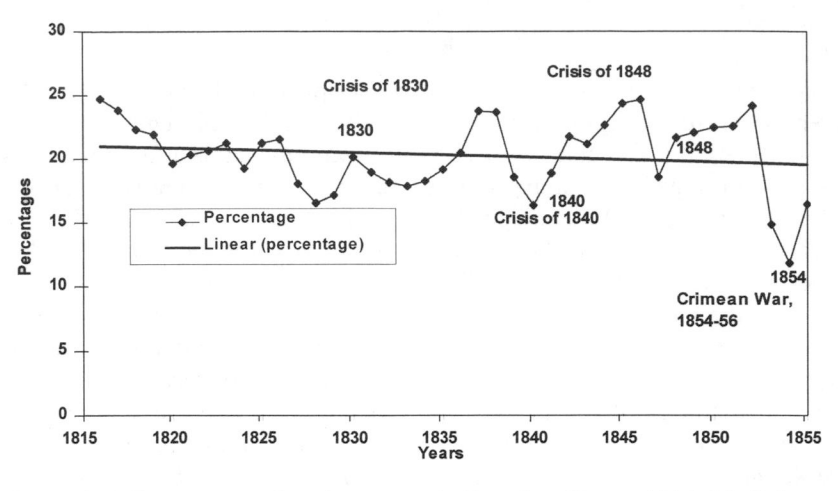

Figure 4.5. Percentages of replacements in French military, 1816–55 (Schnapper 1968: 291–2).

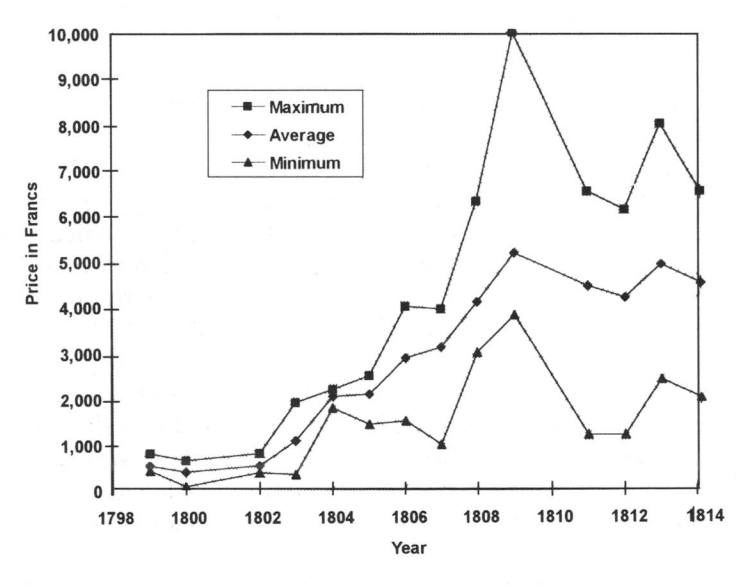

Figure 4.6. Prices of replacements in Avignon, Year VIII–1814 (Forrest 1989: 59).

9,400 francs in 1813 (also see Woloch 1994: 401–3, esp. table XIII-2 on p. 402). Given the cost, contracts developed between the replacement and the purchaser of his service so that the sum could be paid out over time. The abolition of conscription in 1814, therefore, provoked a series

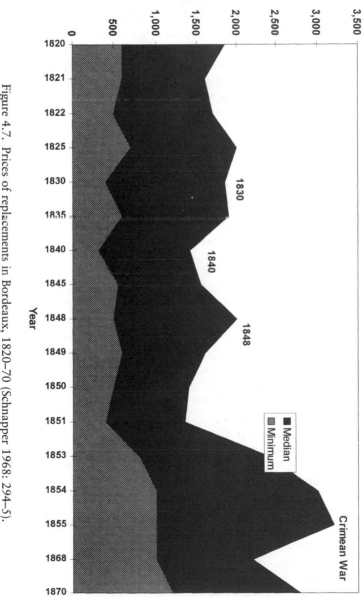

Figure 4.7. Prices of replacements in Bordeaux, 1820–70 (Schnapper 1968: 294–5).

of lawsuits by those who had contracts to receive ongoing payments as replacements against those who were now unwilling to honor those contracts (Schnapper 1968: 33–4).

The use of replacements was not restricted to those of great wealth. Peasant proprietors commonly relied on replacements as a means to retain their sons for work on the family farm even though they had to make large commitments of assets and money, particularly when payments were over time and subject to interest. The advantage to government of this system was that it maintained the complement of soldiers while providing an alternative to propertied citizens who might otherwise resist conscription politically, avoid the draft altogether, or desert. Moreover, the average replacement tended to be more enthusiastic, or at least more resigned, about being in the military than the coerced and reluctant conscript (Forrest 1989: 61). The disadvantage was its potential divisiveness to the extent that the relatively poor perceived replacement as a means for the rich to escape military service.

Those who became replacements tended to reflect a relatively wide cross section of France, both occupationally and geographically (Forrest 1989: 60–1). Veterans were particularly numerous among the replacements. For at least some of the replacements, the law permitted them to receive a bonus for doing what they preferred to do anyway, that is, joining up. The fact that the more wealthy bore this cost alleviated some of the sense of injustice that might otherwise have arisen. Woloch (1994: 403), for one, considers Revolutionary replacement a form of redistribution from the rich to the poor.

Between 1814 and 1818 young French men were not subject to a draft. The law of Saint-Cyr in 1818 reintroduced both conscription and buying out. Replacements had to meet the physical standards of the military and be free of susceptibility to the lottery. In other words, they were veterans, those with good numbers, or those already excused due to the completion of the cantonal allotment. They could come from any region in France (Schnapper 1968: 40–1). Substitutes, on the other hand, were from the same canton; they were those with a good number who were willing to change places with someone with a bad number. Substitutes represented less than 1.8 percent of the military and seldom involved a middleman even when money was involved (Schnapper 1968: 70). The regulations affecting substitutes remained constant until 1855, but the regulation of replacements, for which a market arose, underwent numerous readjustments over time, until the temporary suppression of all replacement in 1855. The regulations were most liberal in 1818 (Schnapper 1968: 41).

Between 1819 and 1826, statistics on military recruitment (Ladurie and Dumont 1972) reveal significant regional variations in percentages of conscripts meeting the physical standards and percentages finding means to evade the draft, often going so far as cutting off fingers or toes. Of particular interest is the large number of evaders from the Midi, the *pays basque,* and linguistic minorities, suggesting a lack of national integration of these groups (Ladurie and Dumont 1972: 25–6).

Those who complied with the law, particularly those with money, resorted to other means to escape from military service. By 1820 a market in replacements developed, and widespread insurance schemes evolved to cover the price of a replacement in case a son was chosen in the lottery. The price of replacements varied principally with the size of the contingent of those called to arms, the geographical area and its success in meeting its allotment, the call-up of the reserves, and, most markedly, war. The state of the economy seemed to matter less than the numbers demanded, which was largely a function of international crises. During most crises (1848 being the exception), replacements decreased as a percentage of the French military (Figure 4.5). The supply went down relative to the demand, in part because of the increased demand and in part because of the increased danger, and the price went up, often quite significantly (Figure 4.7). However, there were certain occupations, particularly leather and textile workers, who seemed particularly affected by economic crises (Schnapper 1968: 124–6); indeed artisans of various sorts disproportionately supplied the ranks of the replacing and were only clearly outnumbered by peasants in the mid 1840s and after (Figure 4.8). Moreover, throughout this period the major demand for replacements was rural, largely by proprietors of family farms wishing to keep their sons on the land.

Always prone to fraud and corruption, the insurance schemes and the actions of agents who offered the insurance and located replacements became even more suspect over time. The regime crisis of 1830, in which the monarchy of Louis Philippe replaced the Restoration, did not seem to have much effect on the price or practice of replacement, but the commercial and international crises of 1840 did. In this year France conflicted with England over Egypt and Syria and faced problems in Turkey while the economy slowed. More reserves were called up. Several insurance companies failed. Families discovered their payments had not purchased a replacement after all, and replacements had difficulties securing pay they were owed by contract. Thus, it is not surprising that there were 11,000 draft resisters in 1840, a high number for this period. The median price of a replacement did not change, but the price fluctuated significantly throughout the country, and increasingly replacements began to demand cash and refuse to serve on credit (Schnapper 1968: 157–9).

The crisis of 1848 and the institution of the Second Republic intensi-

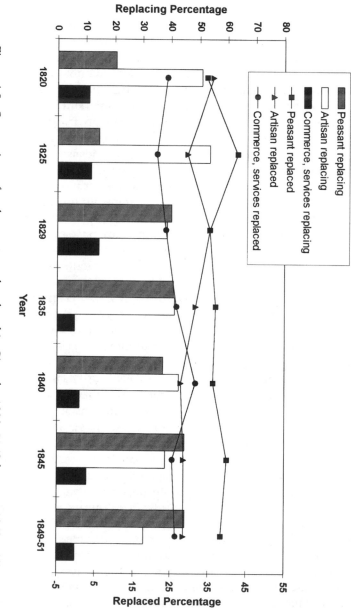

Figure 4.8. Occupations of replacements and replaced in Gironde, 1820–51 (Schnapper 1968: 143).

fied the fears of the propertied voters that they would be unable to secure exemptions for their sons. The coup of 1851 and the rule of Louis Bonaparte under the Second Empire led to a major reconsideration of the military system, propelled further by the Crimean War and the surge in the price of replacements across France (Figure 4.7). Consequently, replacement was suppressed in favor of *exonération,* in which a payment to the government secured a discharge. The payment went into a central fund controlled by the Ministry of War and was used to pay premiums to reenlistees and veteran pensions. The conscript had to pay up within ten days, and there was no credit. Since there were more *exonérations* than reenlistments and since the price of a discharge was higher than the premium for reenlistment, the army soon had a surplus. In return it bore the administrative burden of finding reenlistees (Schnapper 1968: 225–9).

There were to be no intermediaries or need for them. One aim of *exonération* was to cut intermediaries and insurance companies out of the system, but in fact a new kind of insurance company, *mutuelles,* emerged to establish funds to buy exonerations for those who received a bad number (Schnapper 1968: 229–43).

The real beneficiaries of the system – whether intended to be or not – were the very rich, who could afford to buy replacements, and the very poor, who could neither afford to buy nor meet the physical and health requirements for qualifying as replacements (Ladurie et al. 1969; Ladurie and Bernageau 1971). The real losers were the middling and lower income, especially peasants, whose chances of being chosen by lottery may have increased and whose opportunities for receiving a premium by becoming a replacement certainly decreased. The price no longer fluctuated with the regional market, and regional inequalities intensified (Schnapper 1968: 245–9). An increasing number of peasant proprietors who had benefited from the replacement system found it harder to come up with the lump sum required for *exonération,* and even the new insurance was out of the reach of many. The combination of resistance to *exonération,* the enhanced power of the military provided by its surplus funds, and the demands for more men caused by the military disasters of 1866 led to the brief reintroduction of replacement and the consequent reinvigoration of the agents. The temporary suppression of replacement after 1855 and its brief reappearance after 1866 was a response to the needs and complaints of the military. It may have also been an attempt by Thiers to manage the political responses of both the well-off and the rural population who opposed conscription and relied on buying their sons out of the service (Jauffret 1984: 46).

The military defeats of 1870 and the Commune of Paris were to sound the death knell of replacement. The first inspired a desire to emulate the Prussian system of universal military service and the second a spirit of reform. In 1872 a new law passed that moved toward making the military obligation universal and personal for all young men. There was still to be a lottery to divide those who had to serve three years in uniform and those who had to serve but six to twelve months, but replacement and substitution were never again to be acceptable practices.

Sources of change in France

The narrative as presented so far reveals multiple causes for the demise of substitution and replacement and the constitution of a new equilibrium policy: increased government demands for troops; military and market problems that revealed previously hidden costs of the replacement system; and effective political dissatisfaction expressed by those harmed by market failures and rule changes that made it more difficult for them to attain exemptions. In itself, government demand explains little since demand never reached the point of full-scale mobilization, but increased requirements for troops did raise the price of replacements and fuel citizen dissatisfaction with the system.

The costs to government of implementing and using replacement decreased in some ways over time, as central government enlarged its bureaucratic and coercive reach and as private markets did much of the work of finding and allocating replacements. However, increasingly government was called upon to regulate a market quite difficult to regulate. At the same time, the military hierarchy argued that replacement and substitution increased civil interference in determinations of eligibility and tended to produce poor quality soldiers (Schnapper 1968: 47–54, 149, 186–201, 207–8, 226–7, 260). They encouraged reenlistment but perceived that the market in replacements complicated the decision to reenlist and introduced into the process contemptible intermediaries and agents who trafficked in men. They further believed that anything short of a professional army reduced military efficiency. Finally, increased popular antipathy to a form of conscription that privileged the elite threatened to increase the costs to government of achieving compliance.

Perhaps the major reason for the shift away from replacement was increased citizen disaffection. However, further details are necessary to clarify the relative effects of market failures that disadvantaged a segment of the elite, institutional changes that increased the franchise and, thus, the locus of the median effective citizen, or ideological changes that altered the standard of what constituted a fair and just policy. The investigation centers on the legislators, who were the representatives of the citizenry and who did the actual bargaining over policy with government, but also considered are the actions of citizens that indicated opposition to replacement and the reasons they gave for their action. The position of the median legislator shifted in this period from clear support for replacement to opposition; the move was toward more universal military service.

There was a strong belief among some in France – and, as we shall see, in the United States – that the best fighting force constituted citizen soldiers called on as needed to protect their homes and nation. This was in contradistinction to the military view of efficiency. There were also other considerations that made many resistant to the military's arguments. First was the fear of a standing, professional army relatively immune to civilian control. Second, and perhaps equally important, were considerations of political efficiency, in particular the transaction costs of attaining widespread compliance. The influence of the military on policy was fairly minimal, especially in the Second and Third Republics, when fear of army power was high, and their policy proposals went generally unheeded. The military defeats of 1870–71 confirmed the need for reform of both the military and its recruitment system.

By 1870 replacement, substitution, and commutation were sufficiently unpopular with civilians, legislators, and ministers – as well as generals – that their elimination was relatively unopposed. This definitely represented a shift in the median legislative position, caused in some part by the experiences of the propertied classes with the military inefficiencies and market failures of the replacement system that ultimately reduced their support for buying out. Until 1855 the propertied supported and benefited from substitution and replacement. Commercial crises and rises in the price of replacements caused by mass mobilization wars led to a political demand for change. The solution, the institution of *exonération,* served only those with sufficient ready capital to pay the commutation fee. The peasant proprietors could not afford *exonération* and perceived that it enhanced the chances that they or their sons would have to serve by permitting some to buy their way out. They expressed their dissatisfaction politically, and they had clout. Consequently, replacement was reintroduced – briefly.

If this had been all that occurred, the explanation for reform would be the increasing costs to elites of the policy and their decreasing consent to the policy. However, there were other important factors. Additionally affecting policy was the extension of political influence, through organization and votes, to a growing portion of the population. Yet there is little evidence that the nonpropertied opposed replacement throughout much of its history. Why should they? Substitution and replacement contracts were win–win, permitting those who preferred to avoid military service to pay a supplement to someone else who perceived this as a reasonable alternative. In principle, the parties to the contract were better off, and no third party was harmed. The way the system worked meant that few faced increased chances of serving.[1]

Ideological change in the standard of fairness was an additional stimulant to demands for abolition of replacement. Evidence of objections on equity grounds are the working-class riots in Toulouse in March 1868 against the revisions of the draft law; the demonstrators expressed republican sentiments and slogans such as "Down with the rich!" (Aminzade 1993: 106, 133). More indirect evidence comes from the statistics on the class bias in draft evasion and delinquency in the conscript contingent of 1868 (Ladurie et al. 1969; Ladurie and Bernageau 1971).

Other evidence of ideological change occurred among legislators, representatives of those who possessed both property and the vote. Over time more and more began to question the fairness of buying out even when it arguably advantaged their constituents. The debates in the popular assemblies (whose names changed with the regimes) reflect the changing attitudes concerning replacement and substitution.

The relative lack of debate over replacement even during the revolutionary period is indicative of its widespread acceptance at that time. In 1818 only a few ultraroyalists opposed substitution and replacement (Schnapper 1968: 39–42). Well into the 1830s, only the army hierarchy was opposed, for they believed substitution and replacement represented civil interference in the military and tended to produce poor-quality soldiers. They also were offended by the existence and behavior of the intermediaries (Schnapper 1968: 47–8). Replacement, believes Schnapper, fit nicely with the economic liberalism of the era and with an electorate defined by property qualifications (Schnapper 1968: 57; also see Sales de Bohigas 1968).

By the 1840s, however, there began to be debate about whether replacement represented a labor market or a form of white slavery, *la traite des blancs*. Louis Bonaparte was among those who wrote a pamphlet condemning the practice, but he shared the contradictory attitudes of others of his day when he voted to uphold replacement in 1848 (Sales de Bohigas 1968: 266). In the parliamentary debates of 1841, 1843, and 1844–46, there were other expressions of concern about inequities. However, even most of the Republicans seemed to support exemptions and other forms of discharge that released the citizen from obligatory personal service, still regarded as a remnant of the *Ancien Régime* (Schnapper 1968: 46–7).

The first real debate occurred in 1848–49 (Schnapper 1968: 186–

[1] Avner Greif raised this as a possible source of endogenous norm change; however, it seems to fit the logic of exemptions from service in the Korean or Vietnam War in the United States more than the French practices of the nineteenth century.

201), and there was actually a chance replacement might be abolished on democratic principles. It was not. However, the discussion did clarify three distinct ideological positions on the question of replacement and the nature of the army. The first was the Jacobin vision of a nation in arms, in which every male citizen was a soldier sworn to the defense of France. The second position was the democratic and, in some instances, socialist view that advocated equality of sacrifice and was generally antimilitarist. The third was the bourgeois view of social order, in which an armed proletariat was a threat to be permitted only in times of defense; a professional military and provisions for exemption were the best means to build an army that would protect boundaries and property and that could fight foreign wars.

The left was, in fact, badly divided on the military question. All leftists decried the injustices of the current system and the advantages given the rich over the poor. However, some envisioned an army as a means of social reform while others worried about the army as a repressive force. Nonetheless, the members of the *Assemblée constituante* did overwhelmingly declare support of abolition of replacement.

The replacement agents and the right engaged in a formidable public campaign. The arguments of Thiers, in particular a speech he made in parliament in 1848, were widely cited. Thiers argued eloquently against the nation in arms on the grounds that it would promote "barbarism" and "communism." He objected to the personal service it implied and appealed to French nationalism in his hostility to the adoption of the Prussian system. He and others echoed a common sentiment that equality of service is not true equality; the poor are better able to bear the conditions of the camps and sacrifice less in their work lives than do the well-off. The vote of the *Assemblée nationale* was 663 against and 140 in favor of the amendment Thiers opposed.

What ultimately killed off replacement was less the continued opposition of the military than the combination of increased hostility by some of the propertied and of increased republican sentiment for abolition. The interesting question remains the cause of this ideological shift. One possibility is, of course, electoral pressure from nonpropertied citizens who perceived their interests harmed by replacement and substitution. Yet this argument does not seem to have much support given evidence of insufficient popular political clout to affect the median legislator. Since full male democracy was not achieved until 1884, direct political pressure by those who had come to believe themselves most harmed by the inequities of the system cannot explain the change in governmental norms about military service. However, ideological objections to the form of conscription as unfair could have political consequences, nonetheless, in the costs of achieving compliance with the draft.

The political power of the propertied goes a long way to explaining the persistence of replacement, and experience with a variety of its forms is part of the explanation of the change. So, too, is the desire to emulate the success of Prussia. However, at least part of the explanation must be the republican and democratic activation of a revised ideology of an egalitarian army and of a universalistic state. In 1793 the French state lacked an effective centralized administrative capacity for enforcing conscription, and it faced a mobilized populace very self-conscious of its rights and very fearful of central state incursions. By 1870 the French state had the necessary administrative capacity and a citizenry accepting of the principle of the obligation to serve, but it was a citizenry whose behavioral consent was contingent upon their confidence that government would enforce universalistic standards of recruitment and relative equality of sacrifice. By the end of the eighteenth century, the costs of achieving compliance to a policy that produced anything less were too high. Replacement and substitution, symbols of unfairness, were abolished.

UNITED STATES

Substitution was a common and traditional practice in the militias of Colonial times and the early national period. According to Mahon (1983: 37–8), even during the American Revolution:

Masters of indentured servants and owners of slaves could send their laborers as substitutes, and fathers could send their minor sons. In Northampton County, Pennsylvania, 54 percent of the enlisted men were substitutes for actual draftees.

There was not always straightforward commutation, but a series of fines amounted to the same thing. Those willing to pay the fines effectively paid a fee in lieu of participating in the required training.

The Civil War was the first war since the Revolution that required full-scale mobilization. It also was the first time in which the issue of buying out was a subject of political debate. The Confederacy relied on national conscription from 1862 until the end of the war. Initially, its conscription law permitted substitutes, but when the price soared to $600 in gold, making this option unavailable except to the very rich, the Confederacy abolished substitution in favor of occupational exemptions (Chambers 1987: 45–7). The North maintained the practice of substitution throughout the war but eliminated commutation.

For the Union the introduction of conscription was more important in inducing volunteerism by citizens and states than it was in its direct production of men. Only about 2 percent of the Union Army were conscripts; another 6 percent were substitutes furnished by those who

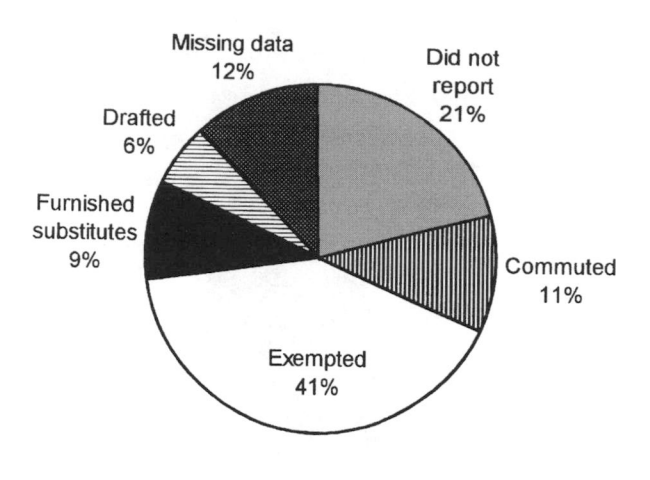

Figure 4.9. Total percentages for all Civil War drafts (U.S. War Department 1866: 184–5, 199–200, 211–12; Murdoch 1971: 356).

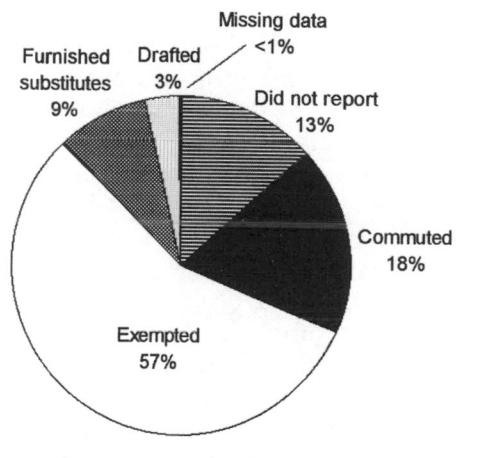

Figure 4.10. U.S. Civil War: Draft 1 (U.S. War Department 1866: 184–5, 199–200, 211–12; Murdoch 1971: 356).

had been drafted (Chambers 1987: 44). Of those who actually were subjected to the draft, the totals were not much greater: 5 percent were actually conscripted, 9 percent furnished substitutes, 12 percent commuted, and a whopping 41 percent were exempted (Figure 4.9). If one considers only the two drafts in which commutation was permitted, those actually drafted composed but 3 percent of the total eligible (Figures 4.10 and 4.11).

Only a tiny percentage of soldiers were obtained through the national

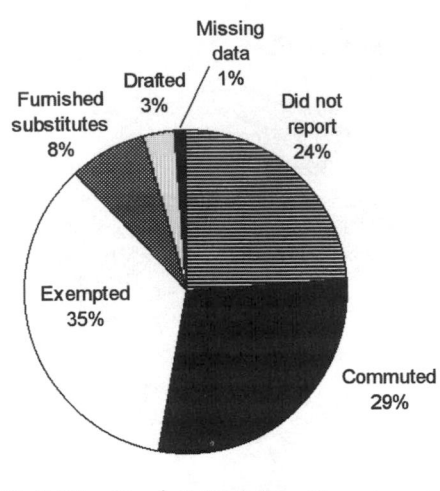

Figure 4.11. U.S. Civil War: Draft 2 (U.S. War Department 1866: 184–5, 199–200, 211–12; Murdoch 1971: 356).

draft. Most came through local and state drafts, and most of those by means of small towns furnishing their allotment of men. Perhaps the most common form of escaping the national draft (but not necessarily military service) was by living in a community that provided sufficient volunteers to meet the centrally established enlistment quotas. Local and state drafts persisted, and communities paid high premiums, called bounties, to attract volunteers they could count on their roles. Murdock estimates that the combined expenditure on bounties by federal, state, and local governments was over $700,000,000, of which approximately $300,000,000 were federal (about half of which was for direct volunteers and the rest for other categories of recruits) and $300,000,000 local (1971: 281). Government maintained the bounty system throughout the war although the price varied with the need for volunteers. The price was largely a function of the incentives needed to obtain sufficient manpower. The local price thus went up with the introduction of the draft and the desire to avoid it.

Substitution was a practice available only to draftees, and it too was maintained throughout the war. Local communities used both bounties and substitution contracts as means to attract volunteers to fill their quotas or replace their own men. However, the supply of substitutes was fairly limited, since substitutes had to be found among those not otherwise eligible for the draft: minors between 18 and 20, alien residents, honorably discharged veterans who had already served at least two years, and, eventually, blacks (Murdock 1971: 179–80). The transaction costs of accepting substitutes was high for the enrollment boards, who had to ensure that the substitute was ineligible for the draft and was not a bounty jumper and that the contract was understood by and acceptable to both parties involved (Murdock 1971: 181–4). A burgeoning market in substitutes and the role played by intermediaries in arranging substitution contracts (as well as finding bounty volunteers) contributed to fraudulent practices and official distrust of those who enrolled for the money (see esp. Murdock 1971: ch. 11).

There were also problems of substitutes who failed to fulfill their contracts, who took the money and ran. This was equally a problem among those who volunteered only to obtain the bounty and among another kind of substitute, not covered by the legislation, those whose services had been purchased by a community in order to meet its quota.[2] This led to various localized devices for withholding full payment until the substitute's term of service was complete and, in December 1864, a General Order from Provost Marshall General Fry that required monies paid to both substitutes and volunteers be taken from them at the rendezvous and banked until they arrived at the front (Murdock 1971: 184–5). As the war progressed punitive measures also became more severe, up to and including the death penalty (Murdock 1971: ch. 10). The aim was to make bounty jumping of any sort far more difficult.

Commutation was another legal device for getting out of the draft (Chambers 1987: 57–61; Murdock 1971: ch. 8). A man could commute his or another's service for a fee of $300. This practice had the advantages of (1) permitting those who did not want to serve, for religious, economic, or some alternative reason, to buy their way out – albeit at a very high price; (2) providing industrialists a way to pay for the retention of their employees; (3) providing additional funds for the administration of the draft; and (4) keeping the price of substitutes low since no one would pay more to a substitute than what it would cost him to commute. In many cases, it was not the draftee who supplied the $300 but his religious community, his town, or his employer.

There were both political and military disadvantages to this system, however. By some accounts commutation stimulated the 1863 draft riots in New York, the largest riots the United States ever experienced. Commutation reduced confidence in government's commitment to ensure equality of sacrifice. Servicemen objected to shirkers, and the Midwestern Congressional delegation was particularly vocal in objecting to its inequitably high contribution of men to the war effort and to the proclivity of other sections of the country to purchase substitutes or pay commutation fees (Chambers 1987: 56–7). Nor was commutation particularly advantageous to the military, for it produced more money

[2] See Murdock (1971, ch. 9) for a more detailed discussion of bounty jumpers.

than men. Especially in the aftermath of the 1863 draft riots, numerous municipalities chose to raise money to cover commutation fees so as to head off the kinds of resistance that might produce a riot in their locality (Murdock 1971: 199).

The combined power of the New England industrialists and the Peace Democrats, who used commutation as a way to escape military service, kept the practice alive for the second draft – although permitting exemption only for the life of a particular draft. However, by the third draft in 1864, the Bureau, the Administration, and more of the Congressional delegation opposed and succeeded in abolishing commutation – albeit the reasons varied among them. At the same time, they retained substitution and increased the bounty for volunteers to $400.

The analytic model presented earlier helps explain the abolition of commutation. Increased government demand for troops goes a long way in explaining the policy change. Total mobilization required men, and commutation produced money instead. The costs to the government, bureaucratically and politically, of administering the draft were high enough without the added costs created by commutation. The refusal of a large proportion of the citizens to consent to commutation and their expression of their disapproval through riots and draft resistance made the change inevitable.

The shift of the pivotal citizen from support of to opposition against conscription has less to do with the extension of the franchise than significant objection to the fairness of the practice. There is little evidence, however, that this view represents a transformation in the standard of fairness citizens applied. Rather, full-scale conscription affected them as conscription never had before, and they reacted. With their riots and other forms of protest, individuals who had not counted in the determination of the median citizen added their voices and shifted the locus of effective power.

The puzzle in the United States is why commutation was abolished and substitution was not. In fact, the abolition of commutation increased rather than reduced inequities. In private correspondence, Lincoln noted:

Without the money provision, competition among the more wealthy might, and probably would, raise the price of substitutes above three hundred dollars, thus leaving the man who could raise only three hundred dollars no escape from personal service. . . . The money provision enlarges the class of exempts from actual service simply by admitting poorer men into it. How then can the money provision be wrong to the poor man? The inequality complained of pertains in greater degree to the substitution of men and is really modified and lessened by the money provision. The inequality could be perfectly cured by sweeping both provisions away. (Cited in Murdock 1971: 202–3)

Indeed, with the abolition of commutation, the price of substitution soared to $1,000 in some locales (Murdock 1971: 190, 266). Moreover, the public debt of many state and local governments increased as they furnished stipends to help purchase substitutes in order to avoid a backlash from an electorate to which all draftees and their adult male relatives belonged (Chambers 1987: 61).

The answer to the puzzle is largely one of class and politics. Commutation was visible and offensive to urban, industrial populations while substitution was more of a rural and small-town phenomenon, highly integrated with local militia traditions. The urban opponents mobilized and rioted against commutation, making the practice sufficiently costly that government acceded to their demands even though many of the rioters, immigrants and nonpropertied, lacked the vote. They were indifferent to substitution, which did not affect them.

Substitution, on the other hand, was implicated in the history and local prerogatives of rural America, but it was also a means for a rural community to protect its own men and economy against the demands of centralized government. In fact, the rural and small-town proponents of substitution rallied in its behalf. Substitution, particularly if subsidized by local and state governments (as it often was), was a means to legally avoid conscription. As long as they relied on their own forms of draft to provide their quota to the army, substitution provided a safety valve for those who wished to avoid service and, at the same time, ensured that there would be someone else to do the job. Commutation was only a means of buying one's way out of service; it did not require finding another body in one's place.

Thus, substitution more than commutation served the interests of the middle and upper classes, whose representatives dominated Congress. The *New York Times* (June 22, 1864, cited by Chambers 1987: 61) defense of substitution exemplifies the rationale for its maintenance as

... the only means of sparing the class of the community whose labors are of most value to the nation, and who, once lost, cannot readily be replaced; namely those who work with their brains – who do the planning and directing of the national industry.

This sounds remarkably like the early-nineteenth-century French defense of replacement and substitutes. Indeed, the United States case presents little evidence of ideological change during this period. Rather, the story is one of political clout. Those who had the vote captured the median legislative position. Those who did not have the franchise produced other sorts of political pressure to influence the median legislator.

Over the next decades, an ideological shift did take place, however.

Despite its maintenance during the Civil War, substitution was in its death throes. Following the war, the discussion of what constituted an equitable and democratic draft began to take shape. The arguments for increased democracy and universalism that led to extensions of the franchise and political reform arguably created a new norm of fairness in which equality of treatment, irrespective of class (and, eventually, of race) became the standard. The discussions of military service, at both the state and the national levels, increasingly rejected substitution. By World War I it had not been in use for years, was not raised in the discussions of the selective service system, and appears not even to have been "thinkable." The administrative costs of achieving compliance to a military system that so blatantly exempted the rich was no longer feasible. The prevailing ideology of fairness made such a transaction unacceptable.

CONCLUSION

The French were the first to link mass conscription and citizen obligations with the extensive use of replacement as a means to assuage discontent that accompanied the transformation of military service. Replacement eventually became a common solution to similar needs in Sweden, Holland, Spain, Belgium, and other countries in Europe. The excesses of intermediaries were a problem everywhere, and over time most European countries abolished private brokerage (Sales de Bohigas 1968: *passim*). After 1848 the idea of commuting service with a fee, previously identified with feudalism, was once again on the political agenda. Proponents seemed to view it less as a noble privilege than as an effective market mechanism for funding the administration of the draft and determining who should be in the military. Widely adopted, commutation was not abolished until 1904 in Sweden[3] and 1920 in Spain. In Britain, recruits who had accepted the king's shilling could pay "smart money" to avoid the service for which they presumably contracted. By 1882 this practice no longer existed.[4]

Commutation, a fee paid to the government in lieu of military service, can be, *ceteris paribus,* a gain in trade for both those who pay the

---

[3] Bo Rothstein informs me that, commencing in the late nineteenth century, there was a campaign around the slogan, "One man, one gun, one vote." Its participants demanded both the vote and an equitable, universal conscription system. Once again, the abolition of commutation preceded the extension of the franchise but followed a democratizing campaign. Voting rights were extended to all males in 1907, but the vote was proportional to property ownership. In 1917 property qualifications were removed, and in 1921 Sweden granted suffrage to women.

[4] The most thorough account of the development of the British army is in Spiers (1980).

supplementary tax and for the government that receives a supplementary tax in its coffers. Substitution and replacement are mechanisms by which someone else serves instead of a young man who is drafted. In the absence of coercion these substitution and replacement are Pareto optimal for those who purchase and those who sell. Today, a market in purchase, commutation, substitution, and replacement is unacceptable. The trade of money for position or in lieu of service is what Tetlock et al. (in press) label a nonfungible value and Walzer (1983: 98–103) a blocked exchange. Payment for soldiering is, of course, thinkable; mercenaries still exist, and paid voluntary armies are common in twentieth-century democracies. Exemptions are also thinkable and quite common, despite the inequities they generally produce. What is now unthinkable, at least in democracies, is for a young man to contract with someone else to take his place in the military or to pay the state directly for an exemption.

What accounts for this change? There are several kinds of explanations offered in the literature. The first is the lack of fit between the practice of buying one's way out and increasing democratization. Sales de Bohigas (1968: 262) makes the strong claim that: "Commutation and censitary systems,[5] i.e., electoral systems in which voting is restricted to the propertied classes, are commonly twin institutions." Thus, the extension of the franchise and the growth of political parties representing the interests of workers and peasants increased the pressure to change a military system that was the product of unrestricted bourgeois and landed power.[6] When the bourgeoisie constituted the bulk of the electorate, their consent was bought by the state; when the franchise was extended, policies changed.

At first glance, the abolition of buying out does appear to have been an effect of the extension of the franchise. As more people gained the vote, policies that so clearly advantaged the wealthy and privileged became less acceptable. A second glance suggests a major problem with this argument: In France universal male suffrage did not become a reality until 1875; in the United States, both blacks and illiterate whites, generally Irish, were denied the vote until after the Civil War (Therborn 1977: 13–16), yet they managed to force the elimination of commutation, if not substitution.

Another line of argument is military efficiency. Challener (1955), for example, argues that France and other countries sought to emulate the extraordinary success of the Prussian military in the late 1860s and early 1870s by reorganizing their militaries along Prussian lines. Since 1813 Prussia had relied on universal military service that permitted no replace-

---

[5] I have been unable to find censitary in the dictionary; I believe this very nice term may be Sales de Bohigas's creation. It refers to property qualifications.

[6] Challener makes a similar argument, as does Schnapper (1968).

ments, substitutes, commutation, or free exemptions. Large-scale warfare and changing military theory that required mass mobilization, rather than a small professional army run by an elite corps of officers, reinforced acceptance of reform. However, a universal obligation to serve is not necessarily inconsistent with exemptions for those unfit to serve or who could better serve their country as civilians. Throughout most of the nineteenth century, even during the extraordinary mass mobilization of the Revolutionary and Napoleonic periods, the supporters of replacements and commutations claimed that those who chose to pay their way out were precisely those whose value to the state lay in running the economy or continuing their training in the liberal professions. Moreover, by setting the price high enough, government could ensure the loss of only the marginal soldier. Military efficiency seems more likely to account for the maintenance of the system than for its change.

Perhaps the explanation is the opposition of the military hierarchy to these practices. Without exception, the high commands opposed substitution, replacement, and commutation. In large part, this was because they opposed universal military service and preferred a professional army. Even when they recognized the usefulness of conscription, they tended to consider buying out as creating problems of adverse selection and exemplary of civilian intervention into military administration of recruitment. Abolition was consistent with military preferences but demonstrably not the cause of policy shift in any of the countries examined above.

High transaction costs of finding suitable replacements, regulating intermediaries, and achieving compliance is an explanation that may fit France, but it describes neither Prussia, which experienced no significant inefficiencies nor the Union, which retained substitution.

The first and foremost source of change was the exigencies of war, which combined with experience of past policies to shape the nature of the military format sought by government actors. To the extent that there were wars, there was a need to mobilize men. To the extent that a country was successful in warfare, it had little impetus for organizational change. There was, however, a second impetus to reform, namely the changing political clout and political views of those expected to serve. Increasingly, the contingent consent of the potential rank and file was necessary before a military policy could be enacted, successfully implemented, or sustained.[7]

What explains the change in all these countries, however, is a change in the preferences of the pivotal legislator toward an ideology of univer-

---

[7] Finer (1975) makes a somewhat similar point in a very wide-ranging essay.

salism. In Prussia, the ideology was imposed from above by a reform-minded set of ministers well before the onset of democracy. Initially, the governments of France and the United States perceived buying one's way out of the military as a way for governments to secure the cooperation and consent of those with political clout. Later, as democratization movements gained strength, the median legislative position became more universalistic.

Indeed, at least in France and the United States, there was always some appeal to norms of fairness. Given that the government actors and the members of powerful constituencies often had common economic and class interests, it is not surprising that they all rationalized practices of buying out on similar grounds. They argued and believed that the bourgeoisie usually provided more valuable services to the nation than did the average peasant or worker and that the bourgeoisie would suffer far more in uniform than someone whose services he could contract. What is interesting is that they appealed to equity at all, rather than to natural right or, more simply, superior power and influence. This suggests that even in a censitary democracy, there is a need to demonstrate the relative procedural fairness of governmental policy to those not in the electorate but whose cooperation is essential to effective military organization.

Buying out may have emerged as an accompaniment to bourgeois democracy, but it was less compatible with the increasingly universalistic norms of a broader electorate. Over the course of the nineteenth century, opposition arose to commutation, replacement, and substitution even among many who would seem to have a class or personal material interest in their maintenance. Two circumstances correlate with this shift. First, the experience of conscription made individuals aware of the differences in the available arrangements and bargains. This certainly was part of the complaint of the draft rioters in the United States. The introduction of *exonération* in France not only had these effects, but it also increased the chances of someone with a lower number having to serve as those above paid the commutation fee. For the first time, even many peasant proprietors experienced this particular invidious comparison. Although considerations of military and political efficiency were probably a major cause of shift in the median legislative position toward the abolition of commutation, the debates suggest that fairness concerns were also at issue.

Second, the ideology of democracy changed over the course of the nineteenth century. Democratic rights were no longer the exclusive privilege of the propertied; they were to be the privilege of all adult males. This notion of a more universalistic polity extended to the institutions of government. Equality before the law and equality of sacrifice increasingly became the standard by which citizens evaluated government. This ideology took hold even in those whose sons might benefit from some form of commutation, as evidenced by the relative class similarities of proponents and opponents in the French Second and Third Republics.

The combination of experiences that provoked invidious comparisons and of a rising democratic ideology seem to have influenced the legislators as well as the population. Although substitution was practiced throughout the Civil War and replacement was not finally abolished in France until 1872, the new equilibrium policy bargain on democratic conscription was beginning to emerge. Once a universalistic conscription policy was in place, it became the equilibrium policy, at least as long as there was democratic government. Prussia, a nondemocratic state and the first to eliminate substitution and commutation, appears to falsify this assertion.[8] However, later in the nineteenth century, Prussia reverted from the commitment to universalistic principles of service and back toward privileging the aristocracy and wealthy. Although in France, too, there was some seesawing over the century between an ideology of equity and one of class bias, the trendlines in the two countries are quite divergent. The commitment to universalism and the recognition of the importance of contingent consent that motivated the Prussian reformers could not be sustained without democratic institutions.[9]

Despite pressures in France, the United States, and other democracies to return to practices that benefited the economically advantaged and although governments gave in to these pressures to some degree by creating exemptions and loopholes, there was nowhere a return to commutation, substitution, or replacement. A democratic and universalistic ideology took hold that made unthinkable the direct exchange of money as a means to escape military obligations.

At the commencement of World War I, even before governments recognized the need for total mobilization, the possibility of commutation, purchase, and the like did not arise. The standard of fairness by which subsequent conscription practices have been judged in democracies has been equality of service and sacrifice. The fact that the well-off are still better equipped to obtain medical, psychiatric, and occupational exemptions remains an issue whenever and wherever there is a draft. Exemptions based only on purchasing power are not. Commutation, substitution, and replacement, once acceptable, are now unthinkable.

---

[8] For a fuller discussion of the Prussian case, see Levi (forthcoming).
[9] I thank Daniel Verdier for helping me to see this point.

5

The institution of conscription

Johnnie get your gun, get your gun, get your gun,
Take it on the run, on the run, on the run,
Hear them calling you and me,
Ev'ry son of liberty.
    George M. Cohan, "Over There"

Hurry right away, no delay, go today,
Make your daddy glad to have had such a lad,
Tell your sweetheart not to pine,
To be proud her boy's in line.

Why is your face so white, Mother?
Why do you choke for breath?
"Oh I have dreamt in the night, my son,
That I doomed a man to death.

"They gave me the ballot paper,
The grim death warrant of doom
And I smugly sentenced the man to death
In that dreadful little room."

    "The Blood Vote," anticonscription propaganda, Australia, 1916

The chronicle of mass conscription in modern democracies is the story of the changing relationship between the state and its citizens, and the Great War is one of the major turning points, especially in the Anglo-Saxon democracies. The institution of conscription significantly extends the obligations of male citizens and the reach of the state. Its history offers insight into both the institutional arrangements that promote or undermine the consent of the governed and the changing bases for that consent.

The high degree of citizen support necessary for conscription hinges on the perception of an acceptable policy bargain whose terms government actors are likely to uphold. The minimal terms of the democratic conscription bargain are that government will conscript according to some legislated and relatively equitable formula. The history of conscription in France throughout the nineteenth and early twentieth century is one of ongoing negotiations between citizens and state officials

107

over what makes for equitable rules governing conscription. In the Anglo-Saxon democracies of Britain, the United States, Canada, Australia, and New Zealand, where conscription followed the extension of democratic participation, there was a further requirement, at least for its initial imposition: Conscription could be imposed only during war and, moreover, only during a war of defense although the definition of "war of defense" varied among countries and among groups within countries. Seldom, however, were even these terms adequate to garner universal support. There are numerous cases in which citizens agree to conscription only when they believe government has kept other policy bargains as well. Citizens who lack confidence in the ability of state officials to make credible commitments are unlikely to consent to greater government control over their lives.

The empirical focus of this chapter is how the obligations of citizens are determined and shaped and how the institutions of government are transformed during World War I in the United States, United Kingdom, Canada, New Zealand, and Australia. It was not until World War I that a full-scale modern, national draft came into being in these Anglo-Saxon democracies. Conscription for local militia was not uncommon, and several of the countries experimented with some form of the draft prior to 1914. Both the Confederate and the Union armies relied on conscription during the Civil War, and Australia and New Zealand required national training for home defense early in the twentieth century. All, but especially the countries in the British Commonwealth, share some rules and traditions. The comparison of these five countries highlights some interesting variation in policy results. New Zealand and the United States established conscription relatively easily. The Australian government was unable, despite major efforts, to impose overseas conscription in World War I. Britain effectively exempted the Irish from conscription. Canada, faced with vociferous opposition from the francophones, nonetheless succeeded in establishing a universal male draft. What accounts for the variation in these policies?

Government demand for troops was high in all of these countries although clearly highest in Britain, one of the major protagonists of the war and under serious military threat. Demand in the other four countries was somewhat lower but sufficient to require large-scale mobilization. Thus, in all five countries, government actors attempted to eliminate the choice of a volunteer army and to promote selective service. Relative bargaining power of relevant groups is clearly critical to the account of the position of the median legislator and, thus, which policy outcome emerges from debate. To the extent that a group of citizens can make reelection or implementation impossible or highly unlikely, then a policy will fail to emerge or will have important concessions attached to it.

Government actors make policy strategically; they consider the likely reactions of citizens to the policy. In democracies, government actors generally insist only on those policies the median voter is likely to approve. To the extent that a set of citizens perceives its interests as insufficiently represented and government actors as untrustworthy and incapable of credible commitments, that set of citizens, or more likely their representatives, will vote against a policy. According to the model of contingent consent, however, the compliance of the citizens is as important a determinant as their direct political influence through votes, lobbying, or the like.

A conscription policy bargain delineates the conditions under which compliance can be demanded by government; the services, money, or obedience citizens must provide; what government actors must do in return; and the penalties for failure to uphold these terms of trade. Legislative approval of the policy bargain is a necessary but not sufficient condition for contingent consent. For those who believe their concerns were ignored, it is as if no policy bargain exists. Even for those who feel the negotiation process was fair, even if they are not in total agreement with the outcome, contingent consent has at least one further condition: the existence of institutional arrangements that enforce government's commitments. Without a policy bargain, the policy lacks legitimacy. Without appropriate institutional arrangements, the policy bargain lacks credibility. Contingent consent will expand with increased citizen confidence that government is trustworthy, meaning key government actors will keep their policy promises and government will nondiscriminatorily enforce the compliance of those who attempt to free-ride.

The previous chapter documented the shift from a policy of elite exemptions to one of relatively impartial selective service in France; the narrative of this chapter will reveal the extent to which the commitment to such a policy evolved in the Anglo-Saxon democracies. Of particular interest is an argument that claims a relationship between the extension of the franchise and universal conscription (e.g., Sales de Bohigas 1968). This chapter, therefore, considers the following hypotheses:

(4) *The more troops government needs, the greater the likelihood government policymakers will try to institute conscription.*

(5) *The more democratic the regime and the more universalistic its laws, the more likely it is that citizens will comply with a policy of universal conscription.*

(5a) *As the norms of citizens change toward more democratic norms, the more likely it is that citizens will comply with universal conscription.*

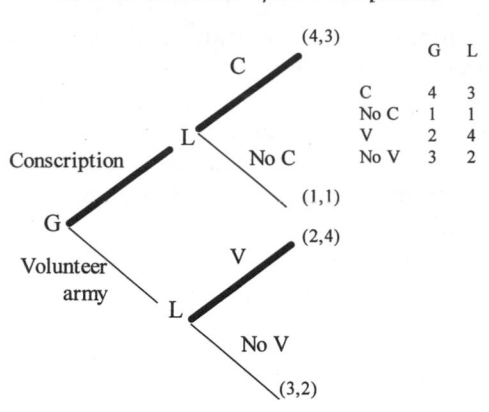

Figure 5.1. Large demand game I.

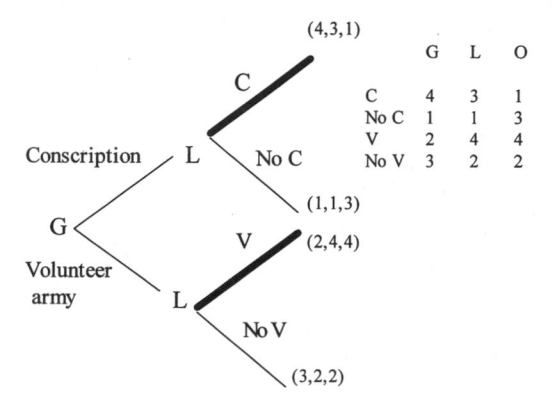

Figure 5.2. Large demand game II.

(5b) *As the franchise includes more of the population, the more likely it is that citizens will comply with universal conscription.*

There are also possible explanations based in geopolitics, national cultural attitudes about conscription, and the nature of the social structure, most particularly class and social cleavages, and all of these will receive exploration.

The government policy decision tree (see Figure 2.3) and two versions of the large demand game (Figures 5.1 and 5.2) guide us through the narrative. Given the high demand for troops, government officials will try to eliminate a volunteer army from the legislative choice set. They may bargain over the kinds and numbers of exemptions, but they will try to make some form of conscription a given. Assuming that the median legislator represents a majority of the citizens, the pivot will prefer selective service to various forms of conscription with numerous exemptions and exceptions.

However, the existence of significant opposition leaves the outcome indeterminate. If the opposition is strong enough, it will change the locus of the pivotal legislator and make volunteering the outcome. If the opposition is strong but insufficiently strong to secure its preference for a volunteer army, it may win concessions in exchange for its support. If it is weak, government can simply ignore it. The game tells us the preferences but not the clout behind those preferences (Figure 5.2).

The two possibilities for the simple conscription game pose questions the narrative must answer: First, were the pivot's preferences different in different polities? Second, if they were different, why were they different? Third, if the preferences of the pivot were relatively constant across the cases, what accounts for the variety of outcomes?

A SHORT HISTORY OF WORLD WAR I CONSCRIPTION

United Kingdom

Britain was the first of the Anglo-Saxon democracies to institute a full-scale draft that included overseas duty. The two Military Service Bills of 1916 made provision for the wartime conscription of males between 18 and 24 years of age; they were reinforced and extended by the Military Amendment Bill of 1918.

The British commenced World War I with voluntary recruiting (see esp. Simkins 1988). Initially, it seemed likely to succeed but quickly proved unsatisfactory. Voluntary recruiting depends on peer and community pressure, and this was considerable during the first months. There was a noteworthy white feather campaign in which women would stigmatize nonenlistees by sending them or presenting them publicly with a white feather as a sign of cowardice.[1] Many cities, particularly northern industrial cities such as Manchester, Birmingham, and Liverpool, competed to field Pals battalions, composed of local young men who could sign up and serve together. These were successful at their start, but the energy soon burned low. In fact, the recruiting boom was relatively short-lived. There may have been enough potential recruits, but there were not enough volunteers, particularly as the war dragged

---

[1] The origins of this campaign remain cloudy although there is reason to believe the campaign commenced in Folkstone in the early days of World War I at the initiative of an admiral (conversation with Peter Simkins).

111

on. Moreover, voluntary recruiting led to geographical and occupational inequities. Not all communities were active in raising Pals battalions; southwest England and rural counties, such as East Anglia, never even tried. Perhaps even more importantly, because voluntary recruitment was unrestricted, the effects on industry were uneven, sometimes adversely affecting essential wartime industrial production (Simkins 1988: 111–2; Parker 1957; Perry 1988: 16; Adams and Poirier 1987: 90–1). Winter (1985: 35) notes that "one of the striking features of the early phase of enlistment was the high rates of recruitment, not from among workers in precarious trades who had little or nothing to lose by joining up, but rather from among skilled workers in trades that were not threatened by unemployment."[2] As the war progressed, civilian wages and employment opportunities improved. According to Simkins (1988: 108), the recruiting boom transformed a prewar "labour surplus into a labour shortage in many trades."

In May 1915 Liberal Prime Minister Herbert Henry Asquith announced the formation of a Coalition Government (see esp. Hazlehurst 1971). The Cabinet was composed of twelve members from the Liberal Party, eight from the Conservatives, one independent, and one from Labour (Adams and Poirier 1987: 82). One month later, David Lloyd George, Minister for the new Department of Munitions, introduced the Munitions of War Act, which was "one of the initial steps in the creation of what turned out to be the greatest network of state-owned or regulated manufacturing facilities since the coming of the Industrial Revolution" (Adams and Poirier 1987: 93). A crucial part of the new legislation was an industrial census. This was soon followed by a National Registration Act, introduced by Walter Long, the President of the Local Government Board. The evidence from these two censuses suggested that the industrial capacity of Britain was being threatened by the loss of critical workers to the military. It further revealed that there were large numbers of men in unreserved occupations who had yet to enroll (Simkins 1988: 148).

Asquith was faced with a campaign within the Cabinet and without to introduce compulsory enlistment, but he also had to contend with considerable opposition. His leadership was in jeopardy. His solution was to push voluntary recruitment to its limits. The resulting Derby Scheme, as it came to be called, involved social pressure on potential

---

[2] The highest percentages, both under voluntary recruitment and during conscription, were among those in commerce, entertainment, and the professions. This in part reflected patriotism, in part their flexible employment situations, in part their ability to attain commissions, and in part a government manpower strategy that made it increasingly difficult for men to leave industry for the army (Simkins 1988: 110; Winter 1985: 36–7; 41).

enlistees through the publication of all the names in the National Register in a new set of forty-six age classifications, which were then circulated to all men between 19 and 41 (Adams and Poirier 1987: 120–1; Simkins 1988: 152–6). The men were encouraged to either join up directly or "attest" to a willingness to serve if called – with an emphasis on single men. Those who attested were given 2s 6d and an identifying armband. Workers with skills or in trades considered to be of national importance wore special armbands. The government established local tribunals to consider exemptions and other disputes. The Scheme did not apply to Ireland.

The Scheme failed, as many suspected it would. Asquith's government, however, had so far survived. In January 1916 he introduced what was to become the first Military Service Act of 1916. It involved the immediate compulsory military enlistment of unmarried males between the ages of 18 and 41 who did not fit one of the listed exempt categories. Conscription was soon extended with the second Military Service Act of 1916. Consequently, married men were drafted, the duration of service was extended to the duration of the war, and the standards for rejection from service were changed and men reexamined. Ireland, which had recently experienced the Easter uprising, was not, however, subject to conscription. Labor was appeased by the commitment to refrain from industrial conscription, to which they were inalterably antagonistic (Simkins 1988: 157; Adams and Poirier 1987: 191–2).

By 1918 the manpower crisis was severe. The length of the war and the tremendous losses already sustained were compelling the Coalition Government, headed since 1917 by Liberal Prime Minister Lloyd George, to consider revoking exemptions and redefining indispensable civilian work. The Prime Minister was especially concerned about the reactions of the organized working class and of the Irish. Lobbying by trade union leaders against any form of civilian national service was augmented by widespread and vehement strikes in May 1917 (Adams and Poirier 1987: 202–3). To appease labor, Lloyd George engaged in a series of negotiations and concessions, the most important of which was to reinforce Asquith's earlier commitment to refrain from industrial conscription (Winter 1985: 41; Adams and Poirier 1987: 201–5; 209–10).

The Irish presented greater difficulties. Field-Marshall Lord Kitchener, Secretary of State for War, overcame his reluctance to grant war office authority for the Ulster Volunteers, a unionist group. The Ulstermen were enthusiastic supporters of the war effort, and initially so, too, were many of the nationalist Irish (Callan 1987). John Redmond, the leader of the Irish nationalist parliamentary party, encouraged enlistment in the Irish Volunteers (Simkins 1988: 94; Denman 1992: 20–7, 133). Sinn Fein adamantly opposed Irish enlistment. Redmond believed, however, that active endorsement of voluntary recruiting by the Irish party would help in the party's campaign for home rule, that serving together in the trenches might help reunite the Irish, and, if all else failed, that the training provided to the recruits would serve them well in the subsequent battle for independence. The link between home rule and Irish party support of enlistment was relatively explicit; speech after speech by Redmond and others in the Commons emphasized Irish cooperation as long as England treated Ireland fairly (Denman 1992: 29–30). This implied not only home rule but also authorization of the Irish Volunteers, which Kitchener continued to stall.

As recruitment figures became available, the question of Irish participation became an issue of public debate. Callan (1987: 50–2) reports heated exchanges concerning the 1916 *Report on Recruiting in Ireland,* which seems to have confirmed everyone's prejudices. Protestant Ireland claimed it was contributing disproportionately, many in the government and army continued to believe that Ireland was not doing its share, and the nationalist press argued that the report was misleading about the extent of their contribution. A 1917 parliamentary report seems to have fueled the flames even more. In fact, there is some question about whether Irish Catholic and nationalist participation was particularly low or only appeared so in contrast with the extraordinary level of Protestant, particularly Ulster Protestant, enlistment (see esp. Fitzpatrick 1992b, but also Callan 1987: 53). Even so, there can be little doubt that the nationalist opponents of military service were effective in raising the costs to the British government of conscription in Ireland.

The Easter Rising of 1916 transformed the relationship between England and nationalist Ireland forever. The British army experienced particular difficulties in maintaining the strength of Irish units after the initial rounds of recruitment in 1914–15, and this situation worsened considerably after the Rising (Denman 1992: 132–6; Perry 1988: 20). Conscription was unthinkable in nationalist Ireland, where the costs of enforcement would be insupportably high. Lloyd George and his government perceived that a policy bargain on conscription acceptable to the majority of Irish Catholics depended on the granting of home rule – and even that might not suffice. On the other hand, a policy bargain on home rule acceptable to the rest of Britain, especially the Unionists, depended on the conscription of the Irish.

Given that all other eligible men were being drafted and that eligibility itself was being extended, the anomaly of exempting the Irish began to have serious political repercussions for the government. In the view of many, the Irish were not doing their share, and the government should be compelling them to. The fairness of the draft was in question. Dangerfield (1979: 272) believes "judging by his maneuvers from this time on, that Lloyd George intended to solve this dilemma by offering home rule as a quid pro quo for conscription, and then seeing to it that both were indefinitely postponed."

Although Lloyd George recognized that it would be very costly and difficult to enforce the draft in Ireland (Dangerfield 1979: 272–3), he introduced the Military Service Amendment Bill of 1918, including Ireland but without simultaneously introducing home rule. His speech made clear, however, that home rule was on its way. His actions made clear that he would not expend a great deal of resources enforcing conscription in Ireland.

Various and quite diverse Irish groups strongly expressed their continued opposition to Irish conscription. While the bill was being debated in Parliament, the Irish Republican Army (IRA), through a group called the Volunteers, began organizing against conscription as well as for land redistribution (Dangerfield 1979: 258–9). The Irish Parliamentary Party left the Commons upon passage of the 1918 bill (Townshend 1983: 280) and formed an alliance with the Sinn Fein aimed at building united opposition to compulsory military enlistment (Dangerfield 1979, 279). They developed a pledge to be taken by all Irishmen:

Defying the right of the Government to enforce compulsory service in this country, we pledge ourselves solemnly to one another to resist conscription by the most effective means at our disposal. (Dangerfield 1979: 279)

The Catholic Church supported Irish resistance, and clergy read the pledge at masses (Dangerfield 1979: 280: Townshend 1983: 281).

Given such concerted Irish opposition to his policy, why did Lloyd George continue to pursue it? There are several possible answers (Adams and Poirier 1987: 240–1): It enabled Lloyd George to take repressive measures against the Sinn Fein leadership while appearing moderate through his support of some version of home rule; the policy appeased the French, who wanted commitments of men, and the Americans, who wanted concessions to the Irish; Lloyd George was a brilliant strategist whose mix of promises and concessions enabled him to stay in power and eventually realize home rule. Another explanation is that the most important policy bargain was with those already subject to conscription. This required the government to enforce its conscription policy universally and fairly. Continued legal exemption of the Irish represented a broken contract with the mass of the British citizenry.

New Zealand

New Zealand introduced conscription in August 1916, just months after Britain. Among the countries being compared here, New Zealand experienced the least turmoil over compulsory enlistment. Indeed, Baker (1988) argues that conscription might have been introduced even sooner if the National Government, a coalition government formed in 1915, had not been mistakenly fearful of opposition, especially from organized labor.

Entry into the Great War had nearly universal support, and there was an initial rush by young men to volunteer. The illusion of the war as a short and relatively low-risk adventure was shattered in May and June of 1915 with the word of the losses at Gallipoli and the sinking of the *Lusitania*. The effect of these events seems to have created a new surge of volunteers, but it also increased the numbers of enlistees considered necessary for a full fighting force. Although government began to have a sense of both a shortage of soldiers and a misallocation of manpower generally, conscription was not yet a popular option. According to Baker, a resort to conscription "would be an admission that New Zealanders had to be forced to fight" and that, therefore, they "were less manly or patriotic than the men of other British nations" (1988: 31).

August 1915 witnessed the formation of a National Government, in which Massey was Prime Minister, Ward his Deputy, and Allen the Minister of Defence. Reform and Liberals shared the remaining twelve Cabinet seats. Labour refused a seat. Allen preferred conscription as the best way to efficiently and equitably mobilize manpower, but he and the Cabinet chose to push voluntarism to its limits before introducing compulsory enlistment (Baker 1988: 42–3). Baker argues that fear of strikes, resistance, and other disruptive behavior by organized labor was the primary reason for delay (1988: 43ff. and *passim*).

The alternative to conscription was intense moral suasion, exercised both through private pressure on those presumed to be eligible and through bureaucratic tactics. There was considerable antipathy expressed toward anyone perceived, justly or not, as a shirker. Employers denied jobs or fired "shirkers"; neighbors ostracized them; churches and newspapers denounced them; and there was a noteworthy white feather campaign. Even wounded and returned veterans found themselves recipients of white feathers if they appeared to be fit. One such young man complained "he could make a feather duster with the white feathers he'd been sent" (quoted in Baker 1988: 51). The government ultimately found it necessary to issue badges to identify the "worthy eligibles."

The government itself also tried to persuade eligible young men to join with its own modified version of the National Register and the Derby Scheme. The War Regulations permitted government censorship and other abridgments of civil liberties, and the government was not loath to repress those who spoke against the war or were disruptive of the recruitment effort.

By 1916 it was increasingly clear that a majority of the population supported conscription. There was some evidence that voluntarism was not producing sufficient enlistees. Perhaps as important was the recognition that only conscription could ensure equality of sacrifice. In addition, it would permit the government to mobilize and allocate the labor of the male population in an orderly, efficient, and sensible way. The introduction of conscription in Britain removed the last major obstacle. New Zealanders need not be ashamed of requiring their men to fight.

The Military Service Act was introduced in May 1916, passed in August and implemented in November. It differed from the British bill in its categorization and ordering of potential enlistees. It had fewer exemptions but a clear hierarchy of recruitment. The New Zealand legislation continued to encourage volunteering by dividing the country into military districts and the population into types. Each had quotas, but in New Zealand compulsory enlistment was by a monthly ballot that took place only when the quota was unfilled. In addition, Military Service Boards, composed primarily of civilians, would hear appeals for exemptions (Baker 1988: 86–7).

Prior to the passage of the Military Service Act, members of the labor movement called for a referendum, but the government refused to hold one (Baker 1988: 71). Defence Minister Allen, when he heard of the defeat of conscription by referendum in Australia, told Prime Minister Massey, "Thank goodness we have avoided that blunder" (quoted in Baker 1988: 155). With the introduction of conscription, several unions threatened strikes. However, the government's fear of massive labor disruption proved ungrounded.

United States

The United States was the last of the Anglo-Saxon democracies to enter the war and the third to introduce national overseas conscription. The United States experienced less overt conflict over the issue than any of the other countries being compared. Several factors distinguish it: previous experience with conscription by the central state during the Civil War; the relative weakness of organized labor; and the absence of a territorially defined cultural group. In addition, both its leaders and citizens had the opportunity to observe the experience of Britain in its efforts to achieve efficient and equitable manpower allocation. Equally important were institutional arrangements that permitted a strong president to achieve his policy preferences during wartime.

The institution of conscription

With the advent of the war in Europe in 1914 there was significant mobilization by pro-conscriptionists. There was also considerable opposition to the draft by members of the Democratic party, particularly the agrarian wing, peace groups, left-wing political organizations, and various sectors of both the immigrant and rural populations. Some of the opposition fell away with the passage of the Selective Draft Act in April 1917, and the voices of many who maintained their opposition were repressed, most notably members of the Socialist Party and of the International Workers of the World (IWW).

As the war proceeded, the industrial and social elite came to favor a selective service system during wartime. President Woodrow Wilson initially, probably for reasons of political expediency, preferred to institute the draft only after first trying a volunteer system. He was always committed to the eventual use of conscription, however. He believed a selective draft would be the most efficient means of mobilizing manpower with the fewest disruptions to the economy. During the debate in Congress over the draft in May 1917, he wrote,

The idea of the draft is not only the drawing of men into the military service of the Government but the virtual assigning of men to the necessary labor of the country. Its central idea was to disturb the industrial and social structure of the country as little as possible. (Quoted in Chambers 1987: 126)

Nor, it should be added, was Wilson averse to extension of state intervention in the economy. A wartime draft was consistent with this perspective, particularly given the proven inadequacy of the volunteer system.

On April 2, 1917, Wilson asked Congress for a declaration of war. On April 6, the day after war was officially declared, the Secretary of War submitted an army bill that included a request for immediate authorization of the draft. On April 28, after considerable debate, the bill was passed; resolution of differences between the houses was achieved by May 8.

According to Chambers (1987: 177), "The wartime replacement of the U.S. Volunteers by a National Army of draftees in 1917 is best understood as a victory for the values of a cosmopolitan urban-industrial elite over rural-agrarian traditions." This was not a conservative-progressive split but a division between "modernizers" and their opponents.

The introduction of conscription was not wholly consensual in the United States. Government acted to prevent dissent from having major political consequences by breaking up protests, jailing Socialists and others who were considered problems, engaging in "slacker raids," and prosecuting draft evaders. Even so, a large number of young men managed to escape the system. By one estimate, three million may have failed to register (Chambers 1987: 211). There is little evidence, however, of the serious ethnic cleavages that divided Britain or Canada both before and after the introduction of conscription, nor of the politically significant opposition of organized labor that characterized New Zealand, Australia, and Britain.

The absence of politically effective popular opposition made it easier for Wilson to negotiate a policy bargain with Congress. By making it a *selective* service system, Wilson was able to win support through concessions to legislators and special interest groups who had the capacity to block the legislation or make its implementation problematic. The strong powers of the executive, particularly during war, facilitated the negotiations even with many of those in the House and Senate who had been opponents of conscription.

Canada

Canada[3] introduced universal male conscription in World War I despite immense controversy and bitter opposition by the francophone population.

When Britain declared war on Germany in August 1914, the Canadian government, headed by Conservative Prime Minister Robert Borden, announced it would rely on volunteers to fill the ranks of its armies. The strength of the response seemed to indicate the voluntary system would serve all of Canada's military needs for what nearly everyone thought would be a short war (Armstrong 1974 [1937]:60). Within months the initial enthusiasm for military service waned. Recruiting levels dropped everywhere, but the level of recruiting in Quebec was especially low. By late 1916 the Borden government, faced with what appeared to be a military manpower shortage and by a failure of all other efforts to encourage sufficient volunteers, began to consider conscription. Borden's last attempt to mobilize recruits involved a national, but noncompulsory, registration. Much of the public perceived registration as a precursor to conscription, despite Borden's disclaimers (Granatstein and Hitsman 1977: 42–7), and they were proved right.

On May 18, 1917, Borden introduced compulsory conscription with the Military Service Act of 1917. Explicit opposition to conscription was strengthened where it had already been expressed and surfaced where it had not been before. The antagonism of the francophone *nationalistes* and the Nationalist Party under Henri Bourassa was no surprise, but

---

[3] The section on Canada has largely been co-authored with Shane Fricks (see Levi and Fricks 1992). The Canadian conscription crises will receive more extensive treatment in Chapter 6.

they were joined by important figures in the French Catholic Church and by nearly the entire Quebecois press. Sir Wilfrid Laurier, leader of the Liberal Party and former prime minister, came out strongly against conscription and demanded a referendum, which was denied. Parliament passed the bill on August 29 by a vote of 119 to 55. All thirty-seven Quebec Liberal MPs voted against it. The Quebec Nationalists also were opposed (Granatstein and Hitsman 1977: 69; Wade 1967, v. II: 762–3). Following its passage, there were riots throughout Quebec; particularly noteworthy were the ones in Montreal and Quebec City.

The clear split along "racial"[4] lines in the support for conscription tends to obfuscate the existence of opposition in English-speaking Canada as well. Organized farmers and organized labor throughout Canada lobbied against conscription (Granatstein and Hitsman 1977: 73–6). There were sixteen Labor Party candidates in the 1917 election, nearly all of whom allied with the Opposition (Scarrow 1962: 28–9). Nor was there much support for the government evident among non-British naturalized citizens (Granatstein and Hitsman 1977: 71).

In the immediate aftermath of the passage of the Military Service Act, Borden formed a new coalition Union government, composed of pro-conscription Liberals as well as Conservatives. Faced with the prospect of a general election, this government achieved the passage of the wartime Elections Bill, which enfranchised close female relatives of military personnel and servicewomen (giving some women the vote for the first time in a federal election), disenfranchised conscientious objectors and naturalized citizens from enemy countries, and permitted the government considerable leeway in assigning the votes of service personnel to any riding it chose.

Victory in the 1917 general election, characterized as a vote on conscription, went to the newly formed coalition Union government under Borden's leadership. The Liberals under Laurier won only 82 seats to Union's 153. The anglophone vote was not uniformly Union, however. The civilian vote was relatively close, 841,944 to 744,899. If one eliminates the francophone ridings and the 14 seats procured through the manipulation of the military vote (Beck 1968: 146), there still remain a number of ridings that voted against Borden's government.

The linguistic split was, nonetheless, pronounced. Indeed, this election forevermore transformed Quebec politics. Quebec voted overwhelmingly Liberal (Opposition), as did French-Canadian ridings in other provinces. For the first time since Confederation, the francophones of

---

[4] The literature of the time discussed the francophones and anglophones as separate races.

Quebec elected no Conservative party member to a seat in parliament (Beck 1968: 143).

Australia

The Australian government sought to introduce overseas conscription during World War I but was thwarted in its endeavors. Limited overseas conscription was introduced toward the end of World War II. Indeed, Australia was the only one of the Anglo-Saxon democracies that did not institute conscription during the Great War. It was also the only country that held direct, popular referenda on the question.

As the war in Europe became imminent, Australia had an increasing number of young men who had been trained for military service and who were subject to conscription for defense of Australian territory but not for overseas duty. The Australian government followed the lead of the New Zealand and Canadian governments in offering a contingent of troops for the Imperial Forces. By the provisions of the Defence Act, these had to be volunteers.

By October 1915 the experience of Gallipoli and the sinking of the *Lusitania* confirmed the intensity and likely long duration of the war. At this point, Hughes took over the leadership of the Australian Labor Party (ALP) and became Prime Minister. As Attorney-General, Hughes had implemented the War Census Act of July 1915, which was Australia's registry of the fit and eligible. This was followed by a questionnaire sent to 60,000 eligibles to determine who was ready to enlist, when, and if not, why not. As in all the other countries in this study, potential volunteers were subjected to moral suasion, including a white feather campaign, and bureaucratic pressure. As in the other cases, the government deemed that volunteering was an inefficient and inadequate means of mobilizing manpower and led to inequality of sacrifice. Hughes sought conscription as the solution.

The War Precautions Act enabled the Prime Minister to institute conscription if he could get a majority in both the Senate and House. He could not. Although the head of a Labor Government, his party was split over the issue of conscription, and anticonscription Labor Senators had enough votes to block a majority. Hughes decided to go to the people with a referendum. On October 28, 1916, the electorate was asked,

Are you in favour of the Government having, in this grave emergency, the same compulsory powers over citizens in regard to requiring their military service, for the time of the term of this war, outside the Commonwealth, as it now has in regard to military service within the Commonwealth?

The only other such referendum on policy in Australian history was the second vote on December 20, 1917. This one asked:

Are you in favour of the proposal of the Commonwealth Government for reinforcing the Australian Imperial Forces overseas?

Neither referenda carried. The "no" votes on the second were greater than on the first. In both cases, Hughes campaigned hard. He even had sufficient confidence before the first referendum to call up the home forces and to attempt to disenfranchise the men who did not respond to the call. In 1916 the vote was 1,087,557 votes for and 1,160,033 against, and in 1917 the results were 1,015,159 versus 1,181,747. Among the states, it lost in New South Wales, Queensland, and South Australia, and in 1917 in Victoria as well. The defeat of the plebiscites were hardly overwhelming. Nearly half of the electorate signaled their support of both the war effort and conscription by voting "yes." [5]

There are other indicators of strong support for the war effort among much of the population. The reelection of Hughes is one. In the interim between the two plebiscites, Hughes was expelled from the Labor Party and formed the Nationalist Party, but he still won the general election for his new government in 1917. Thus, one of the most interesting facts about the conscription referenda is that while they were defeated, Hughes was not. This suggests that a general election is not always a proxy vote for citizen attitudes on important policy questions. Propaganda in the period leading up to the referenda, even by some of those opposed to conscription, was disproportionately pro-war. There were numerous and large rallies on behalf of the recruits. Most importantly, approximately 40 percent of eligible white males joined the AIF. Why, then, did so many Australians vote against conscription?

There are a multitude of analyses of the defeat of the referenda (see e.g., Jauncey 1935; Scott 1938; Robertson 1959; Gibson 1963; Smith 1981 [1966]; Inglis 1968: 39; Gilbert 1969, 1971; Pearson 1974; Lake 1975; McKernan 1977; Withers 1982). Among the most popular explanations are labor opposition and nationalist sentiment among Irish Catholics who opposed compulsion to fight in a war on behalf of Britain while it was repressing the Catholic Irish and denying them home rule. Wither's (1982) cliometric analysis finds that organized labor and Catholics did tend to vote "no," but there is no statistical significance to the Catholic vote. Moreover, Irish Catholics and workers made up a signifi-

---

[5] Both referenda won among the soldiers overseas, but the vote was extraordinarily close. These soldiers were, after all, volunteers. Perhaps the opponents wished to glorify their own patriotism, perhaps they had an ideology against the compulsion of conscription, or perhaps they did not want to require anyone else to experience what they had experienced.

cant proportion of the AIF. Forty-one percent of the AIF had been industrial employees and 22 percent laborers. Twenty percent were Catholics, which was approximately the same percentage of the population (Grey 1990: 91–2). On the other hand, primary producers, who were losing valuable manpower to the war effort, tended to vote in favor (Withers 1982: 43–5; Stock 1985) and to enlist earlier (McKernan 1980b: 190; McQuilton 1987: 4–5). Thus, a narrowly rational calculation of costs and benefits or a social structural explanation derived from material interests cannot adequately explain the composition of either the opposition or the volunteers.

A more compelling explanation is that the negative vote reflected a combination of anti-statism, pro-labor sympathies, and distrust of the Hughes government to implement conscription fairly. These values coincided with and were reinforced by the war weariness that began to set in around 1916 and was quite evident by 1917. Hughes's recruitment efforts in the form of the War Census of 1915, the "Call to Arms" that same year, the centralization of the recruiting effort, war censorship, and the conscription plebiscites had the effect of undermining the volunteer system (Robson 1970: ch. 4). At the beginning, the success of recruiting lay in state efforts to appeal to its citizens and to "snowball" recruiting, relatively spontaneous marches begun by a few men but intended to pick up additional recruits on the road to distant recruiting offices (Robson 1970: 57–8; McKernan 1984: 31–3). Increasing reliance on Commonwealth agencies muffled locally generated recruitment and raised fears of an increasingly powerful central state. The Hughes government's anti-union reaction to the great strike of 1917 (McKernan 1984: 46–7) and the revelations in 1916 and 1917 of the true costs of the war (Robson 1970: 71–4) fueled distrust of Hughes and his government. The general election indicated the population's confidence in the ability of the Prime Minister to wage the war with enthusiasm; the referenda indicated their lack of confidence in him to protect the rights of the citizenry. A significant proportion of the Australian citizenry voted against conscription as a means of taking a stand against government's increasingly heavy hand.

ANALYSIS

What accounts for the differences among these countries? It is certainly not variation in government demand for troops. Britain's demand was arguably the greatest, but it exempted the Irish. The governments of the other countries also argued for widespread military mobilization. The differences in demand were slight relative to the differences in policy outcomes, as the median legislature diagram illustrates (Figure 5.3).

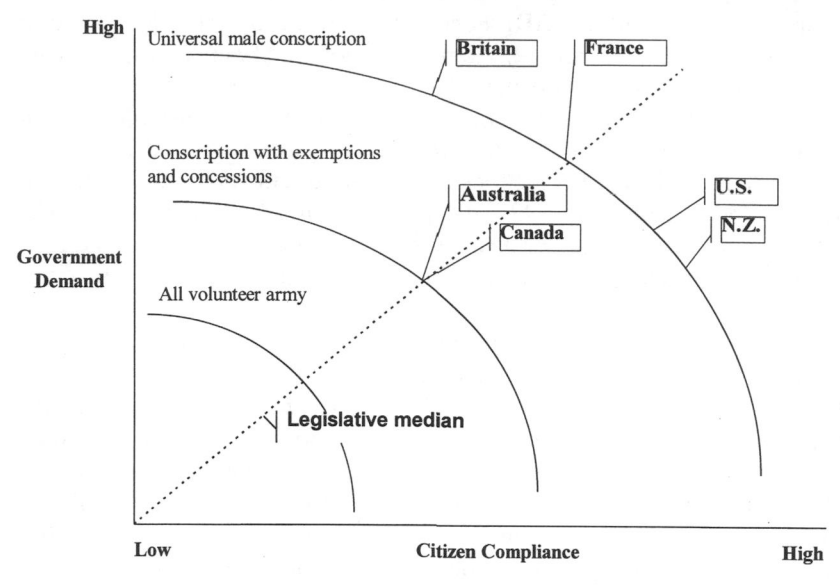

Figure 5.3. Legislative median for World War I.

One possible explanation is geopolitical. Perhaps the countries far-thest away from the battlefield were least likely to be able to mobilize their population to support conscription. Another possible explanation is cultural. Perhaps the Australians are more independent than the Americans, the francophones and Irish more contentious than most other ethnic, linguistic, and social groups, and the New Zealanders more jingoistic than anyone else. Not only are such explanations ad hoc, they simply do not fit the evidence and they certainly contradict each other. New Zealand and Australia were equally distant from the con-flict in Europe, but one implemented conscription while the other did not. The frontier culture of the United States and the isolationist procliv-ities of the citizenry would certainly make its population at least as likely as Australia's to oppose conscription. If anything, the Dominion status of Australia and the strong identification with "King and Country" should have made its cultural and ideological heritage a prop of con-scription, as it seems to have been in New Zealand and in anglophone Canada.

A more compelling explanation is that class, social, and religious cleavages account for the strength of and variation in opposition. In the Anglo-Saxon democracies the major types of opponents fell into at least three categories:

(1) ideological groups, such as some of the left-wing political parties, anarchists, and pacifists, who felt the war was morally and politically wrong;
(2) economic groups, such as some unions, working-class organizations, and certain farmers' lobbies, who believed that they would be the primary losers from universal conscription;
(3) religious, ethnic, and other cultural groups, such as the Irish in Britain or the francophones in Canada, who had lost confidence in government promises.

For some members of the first group, contingent consent was impossible; for others it was possible only with a policy that permitted alternative service. For the second and third groups contingent consent was possible only if government actors provided sufficient assurances that citizens would receive benefits selectively promised to them.

There is considerable evidence of opposition by ideological groups in all of the Anglo-Saxon democracies. It is difficult to make estimates of their relative strength, but they were everywhere too small and politically weak to make much difference in the policy outcome.

There was more variation in the political clout of the organized working class.[6] In 1913–14 the percentage of the labor force in unions was 25 percent in Australia, 22 percent in the United Kingdom, 15 percent in New Zealand, 7 percent in the United States, and 6 percent in Canada (Stephens 1979: 115). Not only did Australia lead in unionization, it also was the first to have a Labor Party that formed governments, including the one running the country soon after the outset of the war. The British and especially New Zealand governments also experienced considerable working-class political activity. The United States and Canada were the laggards. The political organization of the working class was insignificant in those countries.

The other major variation was in ethnic cleavages. Both Britain and Canada had territorial regions of the country that were distinctive from the rest of the population in religion, culture, and language. All five of the countries had large numbers of cultural minorities who could not make a territorially based claim but nonetheless were capable of some degree of solidary action.

Pronounced cleavages do not necessarily translate into the ability to transform grievances into political clout. Cleavages are explanatory only where there is not only a reason for opposition but also a capacity to act. The relative clout of oppositional economic and social groups goes

[6] I am drawing here largely from a conversation with Francis G. Castles, as well as from information in his 1985 book.

a long way to explaining the intensity of the conflict over the introduction of conscription. The Irish in Britain, the francophones in Canada, and both the Irish and the working class in Australia all waged strong anticonscription campaigns.

The existence of opponents and their organizational capacity provides only part of the explanation of the genesis and relative effectiveness of the campaigns. The model of contingent consent helps fill out the account by explicating the reasons for opposition to conscription and by suggesting the factors necessary for success in either vetoing the proposed policies or winning concessions sufficient to effect consent.

To understand who was likely to oppose conscription we must turn to the historical relationship between the relevant groups of citizens and the states. In all the countries under study certain groups gave their consent with their voices and their actions. Everywhere there was war fever in the elite universities and among workers and professionals well up in the occupational status ladder. This is best documented for Britain (see esp. Winter 1985), but it seems to have been a general phenomenon. One possible interpretation is that those who benefited most from the state and found it most trustworthy were those most likely to volunteer.

Opposition came from a variety of sources. Segments of the organized working class expressed questions about whether this was a war on their behalf. For some the first precondition of conscription had not been met; they remained unconvinced that the war was in defense of the nation. This perception also marked some of the cultural groups, most notably the Canadian francophones. In addition, all five countries had experienced waves of recent immigration, and some of these immigrants clearly did not define the war as their own. The Irish immigrants tended to place their allegiance to Ireland ahead of their allegiance to Britain. German immigrants were perceived as having split, unclear, or pro-Hun loyalties.

Distrust of government was another major source of oppositional feeling. Both the British Irish and the Canadian francophones had long-standing grievances against the state that gave them little basis for confidence in promises of equitable treatment under conscription. In addition, there were the native populations of the United States, Canada, Australia, and New Zealand, as well as American blacks, who had cause for doubting their government's credibility. To the extent that peoples from such groups were interested in joining the military, it was generally as a way to prove their loyalty and hopefully to gain fuller rights of citizenship.[7] Some among them joined the opposition to conscription.

[7] See esp. Petersen (1989) for a discussion of this phenomenon. Among other groups, he cites the Nisei Japanese in the United States in World War II, the blacks in Rhodesia in the 1970s and in South Africa today, and the Druse in Israel. There are

This was particularly true of the significant numbers of Irish immigrants to both the United States and Australia.

Distrust of government was not confined to opponents of conscription, however. Most of those who supported the war effort and some form of draft also wanted assurances. Soldiers and their families needed asssurances that government would produce the benefits it promised to soldiers and their families, industry assurances that it could retain workers and keep wages from spiraling up too high, and the contingently consenting citizen assurances that the draft would be equitably implemented.

The credibility of government commitments to minorities and special interests required a mechanism that enabled representatives of these groups to either veto a proposed policy or punish government actors who broke the terms of the consequent policy bargain. In some cases, for example, the Irish in Britain or business interests in the United States, the veto was partially an effect of institutions but even more so of sufficient capacity to impose costs on a government that did not make adequate concessions in return for agreement to conscription. In others, for example, the Australian working class, their active incorporation into a major party gave them access to insitutions such as the referenda through which they could express their veto. In other cases, for example, the francophones in Canada, the rules of the game made them always the minority on any issue that divided their preferences from those of the anglophones.

There is one additional feature to this story that also affected the outcomes. In all of the countries in this sample, the narrative reveals that the pivotal voter was perceived by government decisionmakers as feeling strongly that conscription, *if* introduced, must be universal in order to ensure equality of sacrifice. To the extent that there were to be exemptions, they should be based on such categories as physical disability or a civilian's value to the war effort. Ethnic distinctiveness should certainly not be the basis of exemption,[8] nor should wealth and class status.

Thus, government advocates of conscription had to alleviate two different kinds of distrust of government: distrust by minorities based on a past history of broken promises; and distrust by majorities that certain groups would get special treatment. To gain the trust of minorities

several interesting accounts of Australian aboriginal involvement in the military (Hall 1989; Jordens 1989a; Ball ed. 1991). Enloe (1980: 190) discusses the Maori involvement in the New Zealand army.

[8] There is, of course, one caveat here. In Canada, the United States, and Australia, aboriginal peoples and blacks were still considered subcitizens and were not expected to be subject to the same conscription rules.

might, however, require just the sorts of concessions and exemptions that would confirm the distrust of majorities.

The explanation for the exemption of the Irish from general British conscription is a relatively straightforward story of costs and benefits to the British government as a consequence of the demonstrated organizational effectiveness of the Irish opposition. The Irish were at the point of rebellion. This gave them the clout to negotiate a distinct policy bargain. However, the government's fear of alienating its supporters with a non-universal policy meant that conscription was instituted without the promised Home Rule. The lack of an institutionalized veto meant the Irish could not enforce the verbal commitments of government officials to Home Rule. In the end, the de facto exemption of the Irish from universal conscription did not suffice to prevent their continued struggle for independence.

Canada, too, had a territorially based and politically numerous minority, the francophones. Moreover, as in the case of the Irish, the francophones, and especially the francophone Quebecois, had a significant parliamentary presence. Indeed, the leader of the Liberal Party was both francophone and an opponent of conscription. Several scholars have recently noted that the recurring appearance of a francophone as prime minister is a means to offer the francophones a credible commitment that their interests will be taken into account by the government (see, e.g., Hardin 1995). However, during the conscription crisis of World War I, the francophones lacked the credible threat of rebellion that the Irish possessed. The francophone representatives in the Canadian parliament had insufficient bargaining power to block conscription or win de facto exemption. They even lacked the capacity to compel Borden to hold a referendum that might have enabled them to reveal a more general opposition among the population to conscription. The pivotal Canadian voter may have preferred conscription, but there is at least a possibility that, as in Australia, sufficient distrust of government would have provoked a negative overall vote. On the other hand, the francophone threat of noncompliance seems to have hardened the pro-conscription position of at least some proportion of the anglophones who wished to ensure that the francophones would contribute their "share" to the war effort.

The hardest case seems to be Australia, in which both volunteering for military service and opposition to conscription were high. What fundamentally distinguished Australia – indeed what makes Australia unique among all five of the Anglo-Saxon democracies – was that the opposition had institutional power. The Australian Labor Party could affect the process by which the conscription decision was made and not just rely on protest and threats of noncompliance. The ALP provided the opposition to conscription with a means to veto policies they strongly disliked or to enforce promises made in exchange for their acquiescence.

Although the most vociferous opponents of conscription, the working class and the Irish organizations, could not always constitute a plurality in Australia, they were sufficiently numerous and dispersed throughout the country that they could use existing institutional arrangements effectively. Moreover, the ALP was a sufficiently broad-based and multi-issue party that it could forge an agreement on an anticonscription position. It was an alliance of many groups within the population, not the representative of only one. It could coordinate anticonscription feeling across various populations.

Hughes found himself in a bind that the other chief executives could avoid. Hughes was the leader of the Labor Party, but his party opposed conscription for overseas duty. The only way Hughes could introduce conscription was by end-running the legislators and winning the approval of the electorate through a plebiscite. The plebiscite was available as a political tool throughout the Anglo-Saxon democracies, but only Hughes felt compelled to initiate two direct referenda on conscription, on which every citizen, including women, could vote. Borden felt some of the same pressures as Hughes to obtain a popular mandate, but he avoided a referendum. Instead, he defined a general election as a vote of confidence. The Hughes government was also reelected during the course of the war, suggesting that if Hughes could have used a general election as a proxy vote on conscription the way Borden had, he might have been able to institute conscription.

The other remaining question is why the United States and New Zealand were able to institute conscription with such relative ease. There was opposition in both countries and a significant working-class movement in New Zealand. In the United States, the opposition was heterogeneous and diffused and without significant organizational capacity or institutional clout to influence the definition of the policy bargain. The presidential system further reduced the capacity of opponents to affect the outcome, particularly given presidential wartime powers and popularity. In New Zealand, as in Britain, the parliamentary system encouraged negotiations in which organized labor could veto particularly hateful aspects of the policy and win relatively enforceable concessions that sealed its acceptance of the resulting conscription policy bargain.

The narrative suggests that the populations of all the Anglo-Saxon democracies had a long-standing resistance to conscription in the hands of the national government. It is at least plausible that if the other governments had held referenda, conscription would have been defeated.

In other words, the preferences of the pivotal legislator and pivotal voter were not identical.

If the preferences of the pivotal voter were in fact the same in all of these countries, why then were the outcomes so different? These cases illustrate the importance of institutional arrangements that enabled government to impose conscription without a general vote but that were, nonetheless, perceived as adequately representative to reassure most of the population of the fairness of the decision-making process. Institutions were also essential for promoting contingent consent among those groups and actors whose initial position was one of skepticism or outright opposition as well as among those willing to support conscription in exchange for concessions. Contingent consent required institutions that ensured both the opposition and special interests a voice and a veto in the negotiations and a means to punish government actors who broke their promises.

The cases also point out the importance to government actors of winning the contingent consent of the general population. Not only did the majority need to find government trustworthy, it also had to receive assurances of ethical reciprocity among the bulk of citizens. This created the central contradiction for government actors: To appease oppositional groups required concessions, even to the point of exemptions. However, such concessions might undermine the contingent consent of the majority if they believed that other citizens were neither voluntarily doing their share nor being compelled to contribute.

The paradoxical finding of this comparison is that the intensity of ethnic-based opposition may have altered the preferences of the pivotal voter from a slight antagonism to conscription to support. A simple schematic that contrasts Australia, Britain, and Canada is illustrative (Figure 5.4). In Australia, where there was evidence of widespread participation in the war effort, the ALP opposition position was closer to the pivot than was Hughes's. In Britain and Canada, on the other hand, the opposition of the Irish and the francophones roused fears that there would be inadequate ethical reciprocity. The only way to ensure the contributions of these groups was, thus, through coercion, and so the pivot shifted to support of conscription.

CONCLUSION

The institution of conscription in the Anglo-Saxon democracies during World War I represented a redesign of the democratic state and a redefinition of the obligations of citizenship. Voluntary citizen soldiers had been the mark of the military format of the Anglo-Saxon democracies. The Great War demonstrated the problems with voluntarism. It failed to

Conclusion

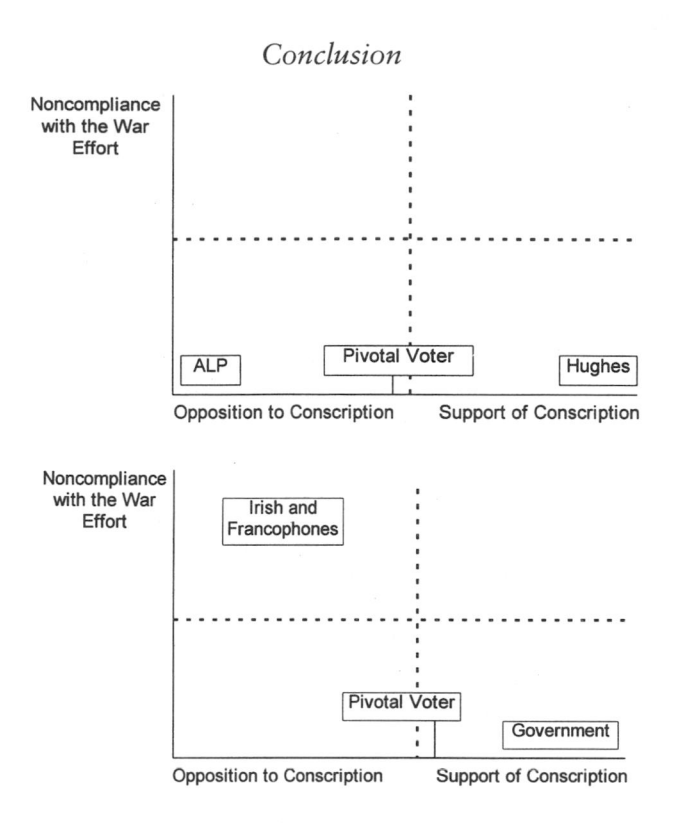

Figure 5.4. Support for conscription contrasted: (a) Australia with (b) Britain and Canada.

produce enough enlistees or permit efficient mobilization of their labor. It led to unattractive and often inappropriate forms of moral suasion. It created bureaucratic mechanisms, such as the national registers, that may have discouraged as many volunteers as they encouraged. By publicizing the shortages in manpower, these censuses made evident the numbers who might be considered "shirkers." Such knowledge could make those who had enlisted as well as those who had not think twice about volunteering. If there were not to be enough men anyway, why make the sacrifice?

The voluntarism that characterized all the Anglo-Saxon democracies, except the United States, at the commencement of World War I, relied on a large number of contingent consenters. Not all citizens chose to contingently consent, however. Many preferred to free-ride, and only a selective incentive such as coercion altered their calculations. At the same time, at least some of those who had not yet volunteered might have preferred to volunteer but only with assurances that others were also going to participate. Finally, those who did volunteer increasingly

131

had an interest in manpower reinforcements, on the one hand, and, possibly, legitimizing their own choice, on the other. Thus, many among them supported conscription, as the elections in Canada and the referenda in Australia demonstrate.

Conscription solved manpower allocation problems during the war and, in most cases, extended the reach of the national state forevermore. The institution of conscription creates as well as solves problems for democratic governments, however. A major argument for conscription was – and is – its equity. Within democracies there develops a new standard by which to evaluate the implementation of conscription: equality of sacrifice. To the extent that governments permit exemptions on non-universalistic grounds, they will experience an increase in refusal to consent. The pressure to do just that remains, especially during wars, such as Vietnam, that do not require total mobilization (see Chapter 7).

A related problem for democracies is the imposition of conscription without the approval of some of those it affects or despite the opposition of certain groups. This, in the long run, is a problematic strategy for democracies, as the cases of the Irish in Britain, the francophones in Canada, the aboriginals in Australia, the blacks in the United States, among others, have demonstrated. Individuals excluded from the policy bargain, whose concerns have not been incorporated, or who have lost confidence in the levelness of the playing field will not give their contingent consent. They may be momentarily compliant due to the existence of coercion, but they are not contingently consenting.

Although conscription seems to be one of those kinds of governmental institutions that, once imposed, becomes a right of government and can be reimposed, the initial institution of conscription does not necessarily establish the policy bargain once and for all. All of the Anglo-Saxon democracies have reconsidered their military recruitment and training policies many times since World War I. Further overt conflict over conscription erupted in Canada during World War II (see Chapter 6) and in Australia and the United States during the Vietnam War (see Chapter 7).

In the heterogeneous polities of most democratic states, the achievement of an acceptable policy bargain requires the creation of a shared community that overrides the particularistic social groupings with which many people identify. What this means in practice is the reduction of the availability and salience of information discrediting government's trustworthiness or the benefits of the proposed policy bargain. To some extent this occurs as a natural by-product of mass society. Cultural, economic, and ideological organizations begin to lose members or to be transformed into groupings that are more social than political in purpose. Yet even in Britain, the oldest of the modern democracies, such ties tend to periodically redevelop political meaning. Among some groups, such as American blacks or francophone Canadians, it is not clear that they have ever receded.

Perhaps a more realistic and common goal of democratic government is the achievement of a policy bargain that recognizes the variety of interests and perspectives reflected in the polity. This implies, however, effectively different bargains for different groups. There are bound to be inequities in such bargains, inequities that will probably take on political salience over time. Pressure for renegotiation of the terms of these bargains is one likely consequence. Another is considerable antagonism against government and among groups as each cites the others for a failure to contribute its fair share.

6

Giving and refusing consent: Citizen response in the Canadian conscription crises

Je me souviens
> Motto on Quebec license plate

A major effect of the Canadian conscription crisis of 1917 was the deepening of the rift between francophones and anglophones. The government's imposition of conscription, in spite of francophone opposition, infuriated much of the French Canadian community. The francophone campaign against conscription and evidence of francophone draft evasion and desertion infuriated anglophones, who felt the francophones were not doing their share in the war effort.

One of the givens of military sociology is that unemployed and relatively poor young men are more likely to volunteer for the army than are other individuals from more opulent segments of the population. This is the popular explanation of why blacks were overrepresented among the U.S. volunteers for Vietnam and the Irish among the volunteers for the nineteenth-century British military. In the cases of both U.S. blacks and the British Irish, and in others, the populations were relatively low in income but also victims of discrimination. There were reasons that they might not feel well served by the state for which they were willing to die. Yet they volunteered. The francophone Canadians, on the other hand, were not so willing to give their compliance, at least not in the form of their participation in the national military.

Analyzing the variation in responses to Canadian government proposals for introducing conscription during the First and Second World Wars helps illuminate the conditions under which citizens give or refuse their contingent consent to military service. Linguistic and cultural division between anglophone and francophone Canadians highlight these conditions. Investigating the causes of variance in compliance and consent

This chapter draws on a paper, jointly written with Shane Fricks (Levi and Fricks 1992). I have revised it significantly for this book.

134

between two groups ruled by the same government offers a way to sort out the effects of different cultural contexts and different institutional resources. It also offers a means to better understand the interplay between tangible interests and ethical concerns.

This chapter explores the argument that variation in support of conscription in Canada is a reflection of variation within its population, and population subgroups, in evaluations of the trustworthiness of government and the extent of ethical reciprocity to either comply or refuse to comply. During World War I, the government failed to convince French Canadians that conscription was within the realm of the previous, encompassing policy bargain. They failed to provide adequate institutional assurances, side payments, or concessions to overcome opposition. Moreover, the federal government fueled, rather than doused, the distrust francophones already felt. The nationalist organizations and even the Church, on the other hand, created an ethical environment in which noncompliance was the "right thing to do." There was, therefore, a higher probability that French Canadians would reject the policy and refuse consent. Anglo-Canadians, who had a different interpretation of both the policy bargain and government's trustworthiness and whose ethical reciprocity was based on an obligation to comply, were more likely to accept government policy and engage in contingent consent.

In World War II, francophone nationalist organizations once again activated opposition to conscription. However, the prime minister and his government were more willing to make concessions to anticonscription forces and demonstrated a greater trustworthiness. The federal government was able to convince a greater number of citizens that conscription was appropriate and government commitments credible. Even though francophones were still less likely than anglophones to volunteer or support conscription, contingent consent was more widespread even among the francophone population.

HYPOTHESES

Why did so many francophones refuse to consent during the world wars, and why was there more consent among francophones in World War II than in World War I? This chapter permits exploration of two contrasting explanations, one based on the model of contingent consent and the other on the model of opportunistic obedience. In particular, the narrative explores the following hypotheses:

(1) *The more trustworthy citizens perceive government to be, the more likely they are to contingently consent to its policies and, therefore, comply.*

135

(2) *The larger the proportion of citizens contributing from a given population, the more likely others from that population will also contribute.*

(3) *Government policymakers, their supporters, and their opposition will devote resources to disseminating information about the trustworthiness of government and the probability of ethical reciprocity among the relevant population.*

Alternatively:

(alt. 3) *The greater the marginal benefit to each individual from compliance, the more compliance.*

It is possible to make these hypotheses even more precise. In particular:

(I) *Volunteering and support of conscription will be highest among those groups of citizens:*
   (A) *with whom the federal government has a demonstrated history of trustworthiness; and*
   (B) *who believe others in their relevant subgroup will also volunteer and/or support conscription.*

Hypothesis IA captures the condition of trustworthy government and IB the condition of ethical reciprocity.

The major competing hypothesis has the factors producing opportunistic obedience doing all the work. In other words, tangible costs and benefits, economic and social, would be the determinative influences on volunteering, voting, and protest. If this hypothesis is correct, those who are unemployed are most likely to enlist and to accept conscription, while those who are employed, whose livelihood would be harmed, or for whom military service offers a relatively poorer economic payoff than their current occupation are less likely to enlist and more likely to resist the introduction of conscription. According to this logic, the probability of exemptions or deferrals should also affect the behavioral choices of healthy, military-age men. Among the employed, we would expect that those who do not anticipate exemptions would be more likely to oppose the introduction of conscription. Although the unemployed would also anticipate no exemptions, we expect relatively little opposition from this group given that they stand to gain economically from being drafted. Thus, we hypothesize that:

(II) *Volunteering and support of conscription will be highest among those who stand to gain economically from being in the military and lowest among those who stand to lose economically.*

Hypotheses

Local and cultural organizations may impose additional costs on those considering compliance. To the extent that such organizations offer interpretations of the policy bargain, provide information about government's promise-keeping capacity, and provide information about the extent of the refusal to consent among an individual's reference group, their activity contributes to ethical reciprocity and is consistent with the model of contingent consent. This argument is captured in Hypothesis IB. To the extent that such organizations significantly raise the costs of compliance or provide sufficient incentives for behavioral dissent, they contribute to opportunistic obedience (or disobedience). Perhaps the most important sanction available to cultural groups is ostracism (Petersen 1989: 572–4), but there can also be violent reprisals, side payments, or other combinations of threats and offers. Thus, we have an alternative hypothesis about the effects of the activities of organizations active in the war effort:

> *(IIA) Volunteering will vary with the willingness and ability of cultural organizations to sanction individuals who do not act in accordance with the behavioral requirements of the organization.*

Volunteering and support for conscription are not, of course, the same kind of behaviors. Volunteering commits the person who volunteers; support of conscription commits others and not always one's self. The analysis in the previous chapter suggested that support of conscription should rise in the dominant group with evidence that a significant segment of the population was not volunteering and particularly if that segment had a clear aggregate identity. Thus:

> *(IC) Support for conscription will rise among those who perceive considerable nonvolunteering, particularly if the nonvolunteers tend to share a common identity.*

What this means is that evidence of volunteering within one's own subgroup will increase one's willingness to volunteer, but evidence of nonvolunteering by another subgroup will, at the same time, increase one's willingness to support conscription as a way to ensure generalized ethical reciprocity.

The opportunistic model implies that what others do should not affect one's own choice, and this may certainly be the case with volunteering. However, conscription is a collective good. Even those who value the form of national defense provided by conscription may not want to be the ones to bear the cost. A number of motivations can exist. For example, large industrial interests may value the draft as a spur to the economy and as the best defense of their plants and trade. They may, nonetheless, want their workers exempted from such a draft. Ordinary citizens who are profiting from the war effort, who do not wish to endanger themselves, or who simply do not want to leave home may also support conscription but only if they are in an exempt category. If getting others to provide a collective good on which to free-ride is the explanation of support for conscription,[1] then:

(IIB) *Support for conscription will be highest among those who endorse the war effort and can avoid military service.*

The indicators of compliance are acts of volunteering for military service and of votes and campaigns in favor of the draft. Evidence of noncompliance is failure to enlist and votes, campaigns, and protests against the introduction of conscription. Newspaper accounts, propaganda, and statements by important representatives of the relevant groups are the sources of information on popular perceptions of government trustworthiness. Also indicative are the contests that have emerged over the implementation of past policy bargains. Another indicator of government trustworthiness is the existence of institutional arrangements that make their commitments credible. Economic and social costs and benefits are fairly straightforward. The most difficult factor to measure is ethical reciprocity, which is invisible except through an assessment of the numbers volunteering or supporting conscription, the dependent variables. However, ethical reciprocity is at least partially an effect of how many complied with an earlier set of government demands. Where there are active organizational efforts but little evidence of direct sanctions, ethical reciprocity is presumed to be at work.[2]

Three clarifications are necessary before detailing the Canadian experience in the First and Second World Wars. First, it is reasonable to assume that fear of death played a very small role in most individuals' calculations during the initial period of recruitment. It was a common belief, at least at the beginning of the war, that the war would end quickly and with little loss of life. Moreover, for both wars the information on the rise in the death rolls appears to have been equally available to those who signed up and those who did not. Given the high value individuals generally place on their lives, it is reasonable to assume no variation in behavior due to this factor by language, "race,"[3] or place of birth. Second, the emphasis here is on volunteering and on behavior

---

[1] This is one possible, but very cynical explanation, of the high proportion of women who voted for conscription in Australia in World War I (see Chapter 5).

[2] In future research with Kjell Hausken, I shall explore a means to measure this variable more directly.

[3] Both the francophones and the anglophones referred to themselves as distinct races, particularly during the earlier part of this story.

relevant to the introduction of conscription, not reactions to actually being conscripted. Once conscription is introduced, the calculation changes. It is in the self-interest of most to comply since they are effectively punished if they do not. This is true even of those who previously opposed conscription either out of self-interest or due to their perceptions of the contingencies of consent.[4] Third, individual-level data of the measures being using for compliance are not available. What is available are correlations between the relative prevalence of these factors and the relative prevalence of certain behaviors that make it possible to offer a strong plausible case based on the combination of the narrative, the data, and the analytics of contingent consent.

1914–1918

In 1911 the Conservative Party, under Sir Robert Borden, defeated the Liberal Party, headed by Sir Wilfrid Laurier, who had served as prime minister since 1896. The two major issues were Laurier's proposals for a Canada–U.S. trade reciprocity agreement and for building a navy. The Nationalists, led by Henri Bourassa, were opposed to both the reciprocity agreement and the navy, which they claimed would be subject to the whims of Britain and forced to fight in Imperial wars (Wade 1968: 621–3). The Nationalists argued that Laurier had sold out to the anglophones (Granatstein 1969: 4), and, as a reward, they were invited to join the government (Granatstein 1969: 4). Consequently, Laurier suffered a national defeat, and his party lost twenty-one French seats, including some in rural districts he had predicted he would retain (Beck 1968: 132–3). According to one observer, the Nationalists had "helped to establish the more imperialistic of the two national parties" (as cited in Beck 1968: 133), which may account for their relatively belated declaration of opposition to the war.

When Britain declared war on Germany in August 1914, the Canadian government, still headed by Conservative Prime Minister Borden, announced it would rely on volunteers to fill the ranks of its armies. The strength of the response seemed to indicate that the voluntary system would serve all of Canada's military needs for what nearly everyone thought would be a short war. Within months the initial enthusiasm for military service waned throughout Canada. Recruiting levels had dropped everywhere by March 1916 (Brown and Loveridge 1982: 59–61) when Borden announced a recruiting target of 500,000 men. Yet Borden continued to call for voluntary recruits; between 1914 and 1917

---

[4] Even so, there should be more who choose to evade, desert, or exit among those who refused to volunteer or fought conscription on political grounds. This possibility will also be explored in the case.

he followed the initial drive (which produced the first contingent) with what were labeled Militia Recruiting and Patriotic Recruiting.

By late 1916 the Borden government, faced by what it considered a military manpower shortage and by a failure of all other efforts to encourage sufficient volunteers, began to consider conscription.[5] Borden's last attempt to mobilize recruits involved a national, but noncompulsory, registration. Much of the public, however, perceived registration as a precursor to conscription, despite Borden's disclaimers (Granatstein and Hitsman 1977: 42–7). Their perceptions proved correct. On May 18, 1917, the Borden government introduced compulsory conscription with the Military Service Act of 1917. The Quebec Liberals and Nationalists were unanimous in their votes against the bill, but it passed handily by a vote of 119 to 55. Quebec Nationalists, nearly the entire Quebecois press, and even several important figures in the French Catholic Church expressed verbal opposition (Granatstein and Hitsman 1977: 69; Wade 1968: 708–80). Following passage of the Act, there were riots throughout Quebec.

There was significant variation in volunteering among cultural groups. Initially, only the British-born Canadians responded in significant numbers. By March of 1916 anglophone Canadians were also providing significant numbers of volunteers – although still well below the British-born. The level of voluntary enlistment among French Canadians began and remained low. In fact, neither French nor English Canadians were recruiting sufficient numbers of volunteers, given the target figures.

The exact number of francophone enlistees is nearly impossible to ascertain; the army has no statistics on its recruits by race or language (Pariseau and Bernier 1987: 82–84). However, there does exist at least one breakdown of francophone and anglophone recruits. It appears that the responses of the anglophone and francophone Canadians to the call for volunteers were distinctly different. Table 6.1 shows that all relevant population groups, except the British-born, were enlisting far below the rate needed to meet government goals. In fact, the British-born population group was providing nearly 60 percent of the volunteers, despite comprising less than 12 percent of the total population. English Canada was providing 30.1 percent of total recruits while comprising 43.9 percent of the population. French Canada was providing 4.3 percent of the recruits while comprising nearly 29 percent of the population. A graphic presentation of the difference is presented in Figure 6.1. Furthermore,

[5] There is some contention in the literature that the war needs of Canada's military was not the primary motivation for conscription. Several scholars (see esp. Willms 1970 [1956]) have suggested that Borden used the conscription issue to split the Liberal party in order to retain Conservative control.

Table 6.1. *Enlistment in the Canadian Military, as of March 1916*

Group[a]	Population[b]	Population (%)	Number of volunteers	Volunteers (%)	Target[c]	Numerical (percent) deficit
All Canadians	7,206,000		282,000		500,000	-212,000 (-42.4)
French Canadians[d]	2,062,000	28.6	12,000	4.3	143,000	-132,000 (-92.3)
British Canadians[e]	3,165,000	43.9	85,000	30.1	220,000	-135,000 (-61.4)
British born[f]	835,000	11.6	166,000	58.9	58,000	+108,000 (+186.2)
Other[g]	1,145,000	15.9	19,000	6.7	80,000	-61,000 (-76.3)

Note: All figures are rounded to nearest one-tenth of 1 percent.
[a] These figures come from estimates provided by a Conservative Senator General Mason in 1916.
[b] Urquhart (1965: 18). Population figures are drawn from the 1911 Census.
[c] The target for all of Canada was set by Prime Minister Borden in 1916. The determination of the appropriate target for each group was made by us based on the percentage of the population represented by that group.
[d] Mason based his estimates of French Canadian volunteers on information supplied by the Ministry of Militia regarding the number of enlistees assigned to French Canadian military units and the number of enlistees with French names in English-speaking units (Hansard 1916: 406; cited in Armstrong, 1937: 121–122).
[e] Born in Canada with British ancestry.
[f] Born in England, Wales, Scotland, Ireland, Newfoundland, and other British Commonwealth countries.
[g] Born in Canada but not of British or French ancestry or born in a country that was not in the British Commonwealth

according to the *Official History of the Canadian Forces in the Great War* (cited in Granatstein and Hitsman 1977: 23), of the 36,267 soldiers who comprised the first Canadian contingent 10,880 were Canadian born; of those 1,245 were French Canadian.

The low rate of volunteering in French Canada surprised the government. Colonel Sam Hughes, the Minister of Militia and Defense, and other high-ranking government and military personnel believed that an obligation inherent in "saving the homeland" would produce ample volunteers from among both French and English Canadians (Berger 1970: iv).[6] However, the plea to fight on behalf of France did not succeed among a population who felt France had deserted them at the end of the eighteenth century and then, to add insult to injury, tolerated a revolution that undermined religion as they understood it.

[6] It also seems to surprise non-Canadians to whom I present this material.

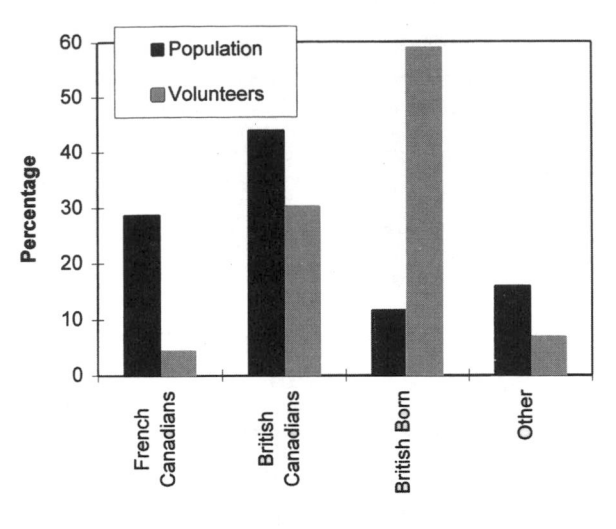

Figure 6.1. Percentages of population and volunteers by group, 1916 (see Table 6.1).

A comparison of Quebec's contribution with those of other provinces provides another indicator of relatively low francophone volunteering[7] (Table 6.2 and Figure 6.2). Military-age men from Ontario actually volunteered at higher than the national average under Militia, Patriotic, and total recruiting. Ontario, and indeed all of Canada, look poor only in contrast with the target figure and with the level of volunteering by British-born Canadians.

Once conscription was introduced, Quebec's relative contribution of men to the war effort increased (Brown and Loveridge 1982: 65 and Chart F: 78) (Table 6.3). However, the gap remained large. Quebec had approximately 70 percent as many men between 15 and 44 as Ontario but only about half as many serving in the CEF. It had approximately 75 percent as many of that age group as the Western Provinces but only about 45 percent as many in the CEF. Although the demand for exemptions was high throughout Canada, reaching an average of 93.7 percent nationally when conscription was introduced, it was higher still in Quebec (Canada 1919: 138–40, 145–8; Brown and Loveridge 1982: 63–4). According to one report, all but 400 of the total registrants in Quebec applied for exemptions (Canada 1919: 3, in Duff letter). By all accounts,

---

[7] The military did keep statistics by the province of residence, but these are complicated by the fact that English-speaking units were raised in Quebec and French Canadians were often assigned to English-speaking units raised in other provinces. With these caveats in mind, the provincial breakdown nonetheless demonstrates a substantial difference in attracting volunteers in Quebec than in other regions.

Table 6.2. *Volunteers for infantry of Canadian Expeditionary Forces, 1914–17, as percentage of 15–44 male age group*

Region	Males 15–44[a]	First contingent[b] (%)	Militia recruiting[c] (%)	Patriotic recruiting[d] (%)	Total volunteers (%)
Maritimes[e]	208, 803	0.4	3.6	6.0	10
Quebec	442,703	0.7	2.4	1.6	4.7
Ontario	638,709	0.9	5.4	8.1	14.4
West[f]	591,852	1.6	6.3	7.7	15.6
Canada	1,888,825	1.0	4.7	6.6	12.3

Note: All figures are rounded to the nearest one-tenth of 1 percent.
[a] These figures are based on the 1911 figures. The source is Brown and Loveridge (1982: Chart F, 78), who took them from *Canada Yearbook 1913* (82–4).
[b-d] Brown and Loveridge (1982: Chart F, 78). These are the percentages of the regional male population, ages 15–44, who volunteered in the region.
[e] The Maritimes refers to New Brunswick, Prince Edward Island, and Nova Scotia.
[f] The Western Provinces include Saskatchewan, Alberta, Manitoba, and British Columbia.

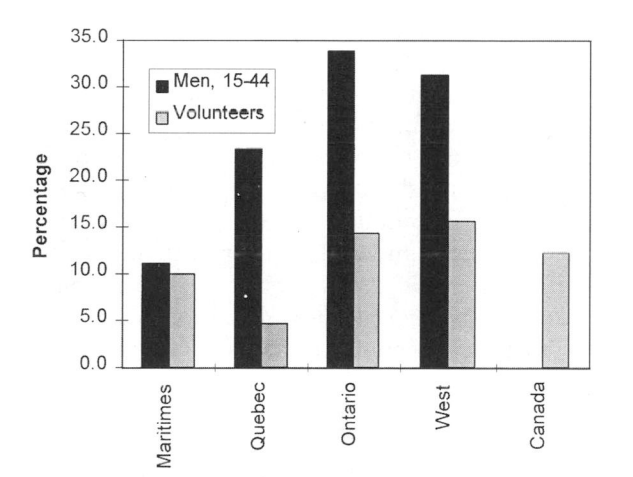

Figure 6.2. Percentages of men aged 15–44 in population and as volunteers in Canadian infantry, 1914–16 (see Table 6.2).

Table 6.3. *Operation of the Military Service Act, 1917–19*

Region	Total registrants, ages 20–32[a]	Total registrants (%)	Registrants in CEF[b] (%)	Registrants exempted-deferred[c] (%)	Registrants exempt farmers[d] (%)	Registrants exempts canceled[e] (%)
Canada	401, 882		20.7	81	28	13.4
Ontario	124,965	31	21.7	76	24	12.3
Quebec	115,602	28	16.5	89	22	18.1
Maritimes	47,019	12	31.7	79	21	14
West	114,296	28	23.3	80	42	10

Note: These figures are all drawn from a summary of the information available in Canada, Sessional Paper 246, "Report of the Director on the Operation of the Military Service Act, 1919." NAC, RG 24, Vol. 1842, File GAQ 10-44, GAQ 10-47, Vol. 1. The percentage calculations are ours.
[a] Sessional Paper 246: 42,56, 76, 94, 102, 118, and 121.
[b] The percentages are calculated from figures in Department of Militia and Defence, European War Memorandum No. 6. Respecting Work from the Department of Militia and Defence, 1919. NAC, RG 24, Vol. 1842, file GAQ 10-47.
[c] The percentages are calculated from figures available in Sessional Paper 246: 100.
[d] The percentages are calculated from figures available in Sessional Paper 246: 103.
[e] The percentages are calculated from figures available in Sessional Paper 246: 17 and 54.

defaulting and draft evasion were higher in Quebec than in the other provinces.

A major disparity in military enlistment rates clearly existed among French and English Canadians. What needs to be explained is why the British-born were so likely to volunteer, why so many English Canadians chose to volunteer instead of free-riding, and why so many French Canadians refused their compliance to the war in the form of failure to enlist. A review of economic and social incentives, on the one hand, variation in perceptions of trustworthiness of government and ethical reciprocity, on the other, should provide an explanation – if either the opportunistic obedience or contingent consent hypotheses are correct.

Economic factors

Throughout most of the war the wages paid to military recruits were below those available in the industrial and agricultural sectors. The opportunistic hypothesis predicts that the rate of volunteering should be highest among those citizens most likely to accrue economic gains by joining the military and lowest among those most likely to suffer economic losses. This latter group should also be the most likely to resist conscription, assuming the costs of resistance were not too high. It follows that those groups with lower wages, higher unemployment rates, and less stable jobs should exhibit a higher proportion of individuals willing to enlist than those with higher wages, low unemployment rates, and stable employment.

From 1911 to 1917 in Canada, this was not the case. The Province of Quebec was less wealthy and had higher unemployment rates than predominantly anglophone provinces (Marr and Paterson 1980: 425; Brown and Cook 1974: 128). A comparison of the industrialized sectors reveals that wages were relatively low in Quebec. Indeed, Quebec had long been and continued for some time to be a low-wage and high-unemployment society (Noel 1992). Workers were more likely to be laid off and to remain unemployed for longer periods than workers in Ontario (Marr and Paterson 1980: 442).

A purely opportunistic hypothesis would predict higher enlistment and less active opposition to conscription among those populations suffering the highest unemployment levels. This is also a possible explanation of the high percentages of volunteers among recent immigrants, especially the British-born, who were particularly susceptible to unemployment (Brown and Loveridge 1982: 56–7) and of the high volunteering in the West, where a large percentage of the British born had gone searching for work. For French Canadians, unemployment and low wages are not sufficient explanations of behavior. They would predict above average, not below average, rates of volunteering – at least early in the war.

Nor can demographics fully explain the difference. Although French Canadians tended to marry earlier and have more children (Coates 1929: 34; Kuczynski 1930: 201, 207) and, therefore, more dependents (Marr and Paterson 1980: 443) than English Canadians, 24.4 percent of the total single, 15+ male population resided in Quebec. This contrasts with 32.4 percent in Ontario and 31.4 percent in the West. Yet the percentage of volunteers in both Ontario and the West was nearly three times the percentage in Quebec. Moreover, the percentage of men between 20 and 32 who registered was almost exactly the same in the West and in Quebec and only 3 percent higher in Ontario (Table 6.3).

Another possibility is that Quebec and other francophone areas had a higher proportion of military-age men engaged in farm labor. Farmers were generally reluctant to enlist and expressed serious reservations about conscription, fearing they would not have the hands to bring in the crops. Moreover, farmers were benefiting from the high prices generated by the war economy. Among those who registered after 1917 under the Military Service Act, there was a slightly lower proportion of farmers in Quebec than in other regions.[8] The highest percentage was in the Western Provinces, where there was also the highest enlistment. Using other figures, 31.4 percent of Quebec's, 31 percent of Ontario's, and 28.1 percent of Nova Scotia's labor force was employed in agriculture; only the prairie provinces of the West were higher (Marr and Paterson 1980: 430). Ontario was significantly more urban, however; only a minority of Quebecois lived in Montreal or Quebec City, the focus of most recruiting (Brown and Loveridge 1982: 64).

One hypothesis is that those least likely to be exempted among the employed would be more likely to oppose conscription. The probability of receiving an exemption was highest for farmers and for those employed in essential industries. Was support of conscription relatively higher within those occupations and lower among those in other occupations?

For farmers, the answer seems to be yes. To a large extent, their support of conscription depended on assurances of exemptions, and a promise made just before the election of 1917 gave them confidence their occupation would receive one of the few blanket exemptions. Farmers' sons who were "honestly" employed in foodstuff production would be discharged even if their local tribunal failed to exempt them (Granatstein and Hitsman 1977: 75). This promise may help explain the overwhelming support of the highly agricultural prairie provinces of the West for Union government in that election and for conscription policies more generally. It does not help explain the variation in eastern and middle Canada, where roughly one third of the population was in the agricultural sector.

Another ground for exemption was employment in occupations essential to the economic war effort (Armstrong 1974 [1937]: 201). In December of 1916 the government had conducted a national registration of male Canadians to determine if a pool of potential volunteers still existed. Of the approximately 80 percent who registered, 36 percent were considered "critical" to the war economy (Granatstein and Hitsman 1977: 46). Workers employed in such industries reasonably expected to be exempted.

Essential industries, namely iron, steel, and heavy manufacturing, were those that could help meet the demand for shells and planes (Easterbrook and Aitken 1988: 488). Although the percentages of the labor force employed in mining, manufacturing, and construction were virtually the same in Ontario (33.4 percent) and Quebec (33 per-

---

[8] These figures are based on farmers who registered. Defaulting and draft evasion were higher in Quebec, making for lower registration relative to its population.

cent)(Marr and Paterson 1980: 430), heavy industry was concentrated in Ontario because of its proximity to American energy sources (Marr and Paterson 1980: 441). Industry in Quebec tended to be small-scale manufacture of "textiles, gloves, flour milling, cigar and cigarette manufacturing and bakery products" (Brown and Cook 1974: 129). If employment in industries critical to the war effort was the basis for exemption, industrial workers of Quebec had a lower probability of exemptions than the industrial workers of Ontario and thus greater reason to oppose the draft. On the other hand, given the probability of exemptions and given the availability of increasingly well-paid employment in the industrial sector (Brown and Loveridge 1982: 55), an economic calculation seems to suggest a lower rate of volunteering by young men from Ontario than occurred.

This is not the whole story, however. What makes it particularly difficult to assess the calculations concerning the likelihood of exemptions is the fact that the Military Service Act gave local tribunals almost complete discretion over the granting of exemptions, as long as they justified their decision as "in the national interest" (Willms 1970: 13). It is hard to determine whether potential francophone conscripts even knew of this fact, let alone had confidence that "their" tribunals would be liberal in the granting of exemptions. In fact, the Quebec tribunals were far more willing to grant exemptions than were the tribunals of other provinces. On the other hand, Quebecois were more likely to have their exemptions canceled (Table 6.3).

A recent study of volunteers among employees of the Canadian Pacific Railway (CPR) (MacKinnon 1994) provides further and extremely compelling evidence that economic factors cannot account sufficiently for the variation in volunteering behavior. MacKinnon finds that the percentages and timing of British-born, anglophone, and francophone recruits mirrors the national averages. The beauty of this study is in its sample: these are employed, urban workers whose occupation would be considered "essential" with the introduction of conscription. CPR did encourage volunteering, and it offered pay and pensions to those who joined up, benefits available to all equally, be they British-born, francophone, or anglophone.

The other fact that stands out in MacKinnon's research is that francophone employment at the CPR rose with anglophone volunteering. Thus, at least some francophones clearly saw economic advantages to staying out of the military and benefiting from the high wages of the military economy. The British-born and anglophones, too, could have made such a calculus; some did but on average were less likely to than their francophone colleagues. A model of opportunistic obedience would predict the same behavior in all three groups. Why is it that the franco-phones seemed to have preferred jobs and the anglophones contribution to the war effort?

Perceptions of the trustworthiness of government

Anglophones and francophones distinctly differed in their perceptions of the extent to which the federal government was capable of making credible commitments. One important account of the conscription crises is entitled *Broken Promises* (Granatstein and Hitsman 1977), summing up precisely the view many French Canadians had of the history of the state's and anglophone majority's relationships with their people.

Francophones did not have to reach far back in history for evidence of broken promises. The Ontario bilingual Schools Controversy of 1914–16 coincided with the declaration of war. In 1914 the Ontario Department of Education passed Regulation Seventeen, which effectively limited the teaching of French in first form elementary school to those schools in which it was already being taught. French Canadians believed this provision was a deliberate attempt to prevent the opening of new French Roman Catholic (separate) schools in Ontario (Armstrong 1974 [1937]: 93). Morton claims the regulation did "choke off" French lan-guage education for nearly 10 percent of the population (Morton 1980: 62).

The charismatic Henri Bourassa, who was also the editor of the Montreal-based newspaper *Le Devoir,* and his Nationalist party began to campaign against Regulation Seventeen and, ultimately, against further Canadian involvement in the war – but at the price of the cozy relation-ship the Nationalists had earlier enjoyed with the Conservatives. French Canadians in Quebec, Manitoba, and New Brunswick joined the battle against the policy. The issue was so heated that all the press, English and French, nationalist, liberal and conservative, gave the Ontario Schools Controversy almost daily attention during 1915 and 1916 (Armstrong 1974 [1937]: 109).

Although there was debate within the House of Commons and within Borden's cabinet, the regulations came under provincial jurisdiction, not federal. The Ontario government refused to back down, appropriately fearful that it would be voted out if it was perceived as giving in to the francophones (Granatstein 1969: 5). Bourassa's campaign challenged the legitimacy of both the Ontario and federal governments by maintaining that the school laws were in direct violation of the principles of confeder-ation. The Nationalist attacks on the government climbed in frequency and intensity through 1915 and 1916, coinciding exactly with the slow-ing of the French Canadian war effort. The Nationalists used the schools question very effectively during that period and were able to use it to foster opposition to the war effort.

The Schools Controversy was a provincial problem, but the military clearly came under federal control, and the military, both historically and in its World War I recruitment efforts, did little to inspire confidence among francophones that draftees, let alone voluntary recruits, would be treated fairly. Traditionally, the military was an institution monopolized and enjoyed primarily by Scottish Canadians. By the advent of the 1914–17 war it was ill prepared to recruit and train francophones. The military even placed an Anglican priest in charge of Quebec's enlistment drive. It took considerable pressure by a number of influential citizens to overcome the resistance of Colonel Sam Hughes, the Minister of Defence, and Sir Robert Borden to the creation of the now famous *le 22me bataillon*, the first francophone battalion (Gagnon 1986: 27–32). However, *le 22me bataillon* attracted only a small fraction of the francophone enlistees. The majority of francophones from outside the major French Canadian areas of the country and many from the francophone regions of New Brunswick were often placed within English-speaking units. Those who did get placed in French Canadian units initially, except for those in *le 22me bataillon*, were likely to be split up and the men used as reinforcements elsewhere. Soon after the war began, French recruits began to write home complaining of being assigned to English-speaking units (Armstrong 1974 [1937]: 126). The social costs of joining the military were lower for anglophones. There was no language barrier, and anglophones were often able to enlist with friends and family. Such companionship and stability were less likely for French recruits (Morton 1980: 60).

Militant enlistment practices affected both considerations of cost and perceptions of government impartiality. There was no official discrimination against francophones in the military, but it is nonetheless the case that francophone servicemen felt and were often made to feel uncomfortable. The effect overall was a higher social cost to enlistment for francophones than anglophones. Equally importantly, the military was a symbol and concrete evidence of the federal government's inability to implement military service nondiscriminatorily.

The federal government engaged in other acts that undermined its trustworthiness during this period. When the war began, it transferred part of the legislative power of parliament to an emergency committee. This council followed the British wartime system, often passing "Order-in Council" laws by decree. In 1916, the number of such laws rose dramatically (Armstrong 1974 [1937]: 142). The government also showed its ineptitude and possible corruption during a 1916 war supplies scandal in which members of the ruling party were accused of illegal activity (Willms 1970 [1956]: 2). Perhaps the most important delegitimizing action of the Conservative government was its manipulation of elections. First, it postponed federal elections during the war. Second, it gerrymandered the election itself.

Government actions alone might cause any Canadian to reevaluate his willingness to consent. When combined with the growing knowledge of the length of the war and its death toll, the reluctance of even English Canadians to enroll is understandable. Many anglophone Canadians may have come to distrust Borden's government, as evidenced by their votes in the 1917 election, but on the whole they retained confidence in the federal government as a bulwark of anglophone interests.

For the French Canadian, Borden government actions were additional pieces of evidence of general government untrustworthiness relative to francophone interests. The French Canadian expected the government to provide for both the individual and the French Canadian culture. Over the two years of the Ontario Schools Controversy, the federal government had demonstrated its inability and, from some perspectives, unwillingness to protect French culture or even democratic procedures. Nor had the government paid adequate attention to the intense francophone opposition to conscription.

Social pressure and ethical reciprocity

At the crux of the conscription controversy during both world wars was the question of what constituted loyalty to Canada. Much of the francophone population believed loyalty required military service only in the defense of actual Canadian territory. This understanding was embodied in the various pieces of legislation and agreements between Britain and Canada surrounding Confederation in 1867 (Laurendeau 1962: 25–32; Wade 1968, *passim*) and was sanctified by *la théorie du Pacte*.[9] Its terms were extremely clear, at least on one point: francophones could be called upon to defend only Canadian – and not British – interests. Quebec did not consider itself an immigrant colony of Britain; its loyalties were to Canada as a self-contained unit, not Britain or the Empire.

For many English Canadians, when Britain was at war, every citizen in the Empire was at war. Defense of Canada included defense of Britain, wherever in the world the Empire was threatened. For nearly all English Canadians, whatever they felt about Britain, loyalty implied active participation in the war effort, including military service.

Anglophones and francophones thus had distinct views of what con-

[9] See discussion in Chapter 3.

stituted ethical reciprocity during World War I. To some degree, this sense of ethical reciprocity was reinforced with concrete social sanctions. Enlisting for the military is a public act. Unlike voting, done in the privacy of a booth, joining the military (or not) is a declaration of one's position. In anglophone Canada, such an act generally brought economic and social benefits and the removal of social sanctions. The decision to enlist was more likely to have the opposite effect in francophone Canada.

The militia tradition was strong, especially in Ontario. Community pressure and, potentially, community ostracism reinforced recruitment of local militia. The francophones also took considerable pride in their battalions, especially *le 22me,* but there were relatively few such efforts compared to anglophone Canada. White feather campaigns existed in Toronto but not in Montreal. So did large-scale campaigns to encourage enlistments, including speaker bureaus, organized efforts to exert personal pressure on potential recruits, and promised benefits from employers and communities (Wilson ed. 1977).

There was, at least, initially some activity in Quebec in support of the war effort, but both the Catholic Church and, increasingly, the nationalist organizations mobilized francophone public opinion against conscription. There is little evidence, however, of monitoring and sanctioning, formal or informal, to enforce what they considered the appropriate behavior relative to the war effort. Although the Catholic Church may have had the capacity to monitor and sanction, it did not. The Nationalists and other groups may have been eager to enforce refusal to consent, but there is no evidence that they had the capacity.[10]

The French Catholic Church was the most important organizational actor in French Canada at the outset of the war. The French Church was conservative religiously and socially, and it urged the francophones to support the war. The Archbishop of Quebec admonished French Canadian soldiers to remember:

England has protected our liberties and our faith. Under her flag we have found peace, and now in appreciation of what England has done, you go as French Canadians to do your utmost to keep the Union Jack flying in honor to the breeze (*Canadian Annual Review* 1914: 287 quoted in Armstrong 1974 [1937]: 58)

The Church lent its support to the general war effort by actively encouraging contributions to war relief, but even early in the war the Church

---

[10] Catherine Fieschi invested considerable time trying to track down organizational memberships and other indicators of social capital (Putnam 1993) in the francophone and anglophone communities during both world wars. Little information is currently available, however.

hierarchy was split about the proper role for French Canadians (Armstrong 1974 [1937]: 61). A few in the Church hierarchy advocated sending men, but most encouraged French Canadians to support Britain with loyalty and cooperation, primarily consisting of praying for the success of Britain (Armstrong 1974 [1937]: 9).

Church support waned between 1914 and 1917, partially due to the influence of Bourassa (Gravel 1974a: 14). It did not oppose Canada's war policy and continued to claim loyalty to the Empire, but it never wholeheartedly supported the war effort. Moreover, it publicly questioned the policy bargain in other arenas. A potential loser in the Ontario Schools Controversy, the Church hierarchy assailed the injustice of the policy in formal pastoral letters to parishes and through the Church-controlled press, *Action Sociale* and *La Croix*. A content analysis of the articles in this period reveals that the Church remained politically conservative but was defensive in response to any perceived attacks on its prerogative (Jones 1973).

Although the Church continued to give verbal support to the war effort, its actions and published statements could not help but signal to French Canadians that this organization, the embodiment of their culture, was questioning the legitimacy of English Canadian authority and laws. The Borden government's withdrawal of the exemption for clerical students further cemented antagonism of the Catholic Church to conscription.

By 1917 enlistment in Quebec fell drastically (Armstrong 1974 [1937]:167, 135; Morton 1971: 101). Military units were being stoned in Montreal – in rather sharp contrast to their treatment in Toronto. Henri Bourassa was openly labeling as "fools" those who served in the military. There is considerable evidence of social pressure or, at least, social norms against enlistment and, certainly, against conscription.

Many English Canadians seemed to have felt that able-bodied francophone men should answer the call for military service in the same proportions as able-bodied anglophone men. The low rate of French Canadian volunteering was evidence to anglophones of francophone refusal to meet their obligations as Canadian citizens. At least some part of the support of conscription in English Canada was an effect of wanting the state to provide assurances that others, and most particularly the francophones, contributed their share. According to Granatstein (1969: 5):

By 1916, French-English relations were at their lowest point since . . . 1885. The French Canadians were assailed in Ontario and west as a cowardly race who would not fight. Racial and religious slurs were hurled at the Province of Quebec, and even moderate English Canadian opinion was reaching the boiling point. Demands were beginning to be heard for a system that would equalize sacrifice at the war fronts – conscription. If the French would not volunteer, they should be forced to fight.

1939–1945

At first glance the conscription crisis of World War II is but a reprise of the earlier events. Anglophone support and francophone opposition were once again articulate and intense. The government, however, responded very differently to the demands of manpower procurement from 1939 to 1945.

In 1921 a Liberal government headed by Mackenzie King took office. The election regained for the Liberals many of the English Canadian seats lost to the Union government in 1917. Quebec, voting overwhelming Liberal, became an important province in the fortunes of Canada's Liberal party. The Liberal government was reelected in 1925, replaced by a Conservative government in 1930, but returned in 1935. The Liberals remained in power throughout the duration of the war.

By the late 1930's, leaders from both major parties were publicly renouncing conscription. Mackenzie King, perhaps because his parliamentary majority depended on Quebec, believed that national unity should not be sacrificed for conscription. During the 1940 election campaign he promised the Canadian people that he would not allow conscription as long as his party retained power (Granatstein 1969: 16). This pledge, reinforced by Ernest Lapointe, the Minister of Justice, was instrumental in securing the largest parliamentary majority in Canadian history while winning every seat from Quebec (McNaught 1988 [1969]: 266).

In 1939, when war was declared, there was no shortage of volunteers for the military because of the persistence of high unemployment associated with the Depression (Granatstein and Hitsman 1977: 134). Manpower problems would not materialize until late 1940, when both the army and war industry expanded.

In 1939, shortly after the declaration of war, the Premier of Quebec, Maurice Duplessis, called for provincial elections. Duplessis led the Union Nationale, a nationalist-conservative party adamantly opposed to conscription, the war more generally, and Liberal leadership in Ottawa. Both Prime Minister Mackenzie King and Ernest Lapointe, the Minister of Justice, feared that if Duplessis was reelected, English Canada would interpret the election as a signal of Quebec's unwillingness to assist in the war effort.

The federal government presented voters with a choice. If the Union Nationale won, the Quebecois members of the Liberal cabinet would resign. This move might bring down the government, which would likely be replaced by a Union government similar to the one that administered the 1914–18 war and introduced conscription. Ottawa offered the following choice: defeat Duplessis or prepare for conscription.[11] The Quebec Liberals received 53 percent of the popular vote and 69 of 90 seats (Granatstein and Hitsman 1977: 136).

The elections of 1940 were held in March, during a lull in the war. After the defeats of Belgium and France in May and June of 1940, King's promise became difficult to keep. The Conservatives began calls for national registration, and organizations such as the Canadian Legion began advocating outright conscription (Granatstein and Hitsman 1977: 141). The Liberals responded with the National Resources Mobilization Act (NRMA). This legislation authorized immediate registration of all males over the age of 15 and conscription of unmarried males for 30-day military training periods. Later these training periods were expanded into long-term service, establishing a permanent force stationed only on Canadian soil. Overseas military duty remained strictly voluntary.

By 1941 manpower needs became pressing and conscription was again under discussion. Given wavering opinions within in his own party, King decided to call a plebiscite on the question of conscription. At issue was the release of King and his party from their earlier no-conscription pledge. The question asked of the electorate was:

Are you in favour of releasing the Government from any obligations arising out of any past commitments restricting the methods of raising men for military service?

Despite a campaign funded by the federal government to convince them to vote yes, 72.6 percent of Quebec's voters said "no." Deleting the predominantly English speaking districts of Quebec, the "no" tally among francophones rises to 85 percent (Pariseau and Bernier 1987: 117; Linteau 1989b: 148). "No" was also returned in six heavily French populated districts outside of Quebec. Approximately 80 percent of English Canada voted to release the Liberals from their promise[12] (Table 6.4).

---

[11] There were of course other reasons as well for the Duplessis defeat. The population of Quebec had lost confidence in his ability to cope with unemployment, were disturbed by the escalating provincial budgetary crisis, and were offended – at least some were – by his autocratic style and conservative ideology. Furthermore, many were attracted by the reformist stance of his rival for office, Adelard Godbout (Wade 1968: 930–1; Linteau et al. 1989a, I: 152–5).

[12] "In Prince Edward Island 82.4 per cent voted 'yes,' in Ontario 82.3, in Alberta 70.4, and in New Brunswick, the smallest 'yes' percentage, 69.1. The overall results showed that 2,945,514 Canadians voted 'yes' and 1,643,006 had marked their ballots 'no.' There is no doubt, however, that the results were a . . . clear demonstration of the differences in attitude and emotive feeling toward the war, England, and the duty of a citizen that co-existed in Canada" (Granatstein and Hitsman 1977, p. 171).

Table 6.4. *Plebiscite of 1942*

Province	Voting yes (%)	Voting no (%)
Prince Edward Island	82.4	19.6
Nova Scotia	77.9	22.1
New Brunswick	69.1	31.9
Quebec	27.4	72.6
Ontario	82.3	17.7
Manitoba	79.1	20.9
Saskatchewan	71.2	28.8
Alberta	70.4	29.6
British Columbia	79.4	20.6
Yukon	68	32
Total Canada	64	36

Notes: All figures are rounded to nearest one-tenth of a percent. Figures are drawn from Granatstein and Hitsman (1977: 171); Granatstein (1969: 47); *Montreal Daily Star* (April 28, 1942: 2); *The Canada Gazette* (June 23, 1942: no. 413, vol. LXXV: 1–6).

Following the plebiscite, the Ministry of External Affairs authorized a secret Gallup poll of opinion in Quebec (Hoy 1989: 16–17). One hundred "intensive interviews" revealed that 68 of 72 respondents believed Canada was controlled by English Canada, 63 of 66 believed French Canadians were not treated as equals, and 48 of 57 felt Canada would not be endangered by the fall of England. Among the 65 respondents to the question "Why does Canada want conscription?" only 18 felt it was to win the war while 33 answered because "they are against French Canada" and 14 believed it was to defend England. Saul Rae, the official in charge, advocated "counter-propaganda" to convince French Canadians that conscription was not a punitive action against them; it was not primarily to aid England; it was a policy that other countries, such as the United States, employed successfully; and it would earn French Canadians goodwill with the Americans and with other Canadians.

King, probably aware of the poll and certainly sensible to francophone opposition, delayed conscription. The parliamentary motion that sent conscripts overseas carried on December 8, 1944. Mackenzie King had worked hard, with mixed results, during the preceding two weeks to convince Liberal French Canadian MPs that the policy change was necessary, even unavoidable. Even so, one French Canadian minister resigned. The measure passed by a vote of 143 to 70 with 32 Quebec members voting against (Wade 1968: 1068). As notable as the number of negative francophone votes was the split in the francophone vote. It was, after all, their governing party that proposed the policy. After the decision, there were protests and rallies (Wade 1968: 1071–4), but only according to one unsubstantiated observer did they approach the reactions of 1917 (McNaught 1988 [1969]: 267).

The government initially made no attempt to send conscripts overseas. The NRMA continued to be sufficient to meet manpower needs until 1944. If not for a forecasting error made by the army, conscripts might never have left Canada. Unfortunately, the Army grossly underestimated its infantry casualties relative to those in other assignments and by 1944 was short on reinforcements. The reinforcement crisis compelled the government to send 16,000 conscripts overseas in the final months of the war.

As in the First World War, there is evidence that French Canadians, especially in Quebec, did not voluntarily enlist for military service at the same rate as their English Canadian counterparts. Figures are once again inexact, but a former Conservative Prime Minister, Arthur Meighten, produced the following figures in 1941 (Table 6.4).

One official estimate placed French Canadian enlistment per capita at 60 percent of English Canadian enlistments. Another calculation, covering the entire war period, claimed that, "25.69 per cent of the male population of Quebec aged 18 to 45 enlisted, as compared to 42.38 to 50.47 per cent for the other provinces" (Pariseau and Bernier 1987: 117). In an unofficial comparison of enlistments in the Canadian Army by place of birth, Quebec contributed 14 percent of enlistees and Ontario 32 percent[13] (Table 6.5).

Quebec may have lagged behind Ontario in the proportion of its eligible population in uniform, but its enlistments were higher than in the earlier war (Wade 1968: 935). According to yet another estimate, Quebec provided 19 percent of the servicemen, up from 12 percent in World War I (Linteau 1989b: 149).

Economic factors

World War II began in the midst of the Great Depression. Unemployment was high throughout Canada, but the economic conditions of

---

[13] Of course, the Army represents only a portion of Canada's fighting forces.

Table 6.5. *Enlistments in the Canadian Army by place of birth, 1939–1945* [a]

Place of birth	Number of enlistees	Total enlistees (%)
Quebec	85,931	14.1
Ontario	193,164	31.8
Maritimes	81,935	13.5
Western Provinces	145,214	23.9
Total Canadian	506,244	83
British countries	68,058	11.2
American countries [b]	17,283	2.9
France	310	0.1
Germany & Austria	1,091	0.2
Other European countries	13,305	2.2
Asian countries	358	0.1
Miscellaneous countries	1,785	0.3
Total	608,434	100 [c]

Note: All figures are rounded to nearest one-tenth of 1 percent.

[a] The raw figures come from "Canadian Army–War 1939–45, G.S. Appointments and Enlistments by Place of Birth," two pages of typed statistics. NAC RG 24, Vol. 18824, file Station CDN Army 133.065 (D634). The percentage calculations are ours.

[b] 17,077 of the American enlistment are from the U.S.

[c] The numbers do not add up to exactly 100% because of rounding to nearest one tenth of 1 percent.

Quebec were particularly bad. At the beginning of the war, Quebec was still below the national average in personal per capita income and higher in unemployment rates. Quebec's 1939 personal per capita income was 85 percent of the national average, compared to 124 percent for Ontario. Quebec's unemployment rate remained slightly higher than average during the war, roughly 2 percent higher than in Ontario (Marr and Paterson 1980: 426–7). These facts alone indicate a material interest in enlistment. In fact, many Quebecois and francophones did enlist although at numbers still below what might be expected, given the prevalence of economic hardship (Table 6.5).

Using the figures from Table 6.5 and population figures from the 1941 census, nearly 4 percent of Ontario's population enlisted in comparison to less than 2 percent of Quebec's. This is an improvement from the nearly 4 to 1 ratio of World War I, but it still represents a significantly greater contribution by Ontario than by Quebec (Figure 6.3). The evidence does not indicate, however, that Quebecois should necessarily have enlisted in the same numbers or even same proportions as their neighbors in Ontario. In 1911 Quebec's population was approximately

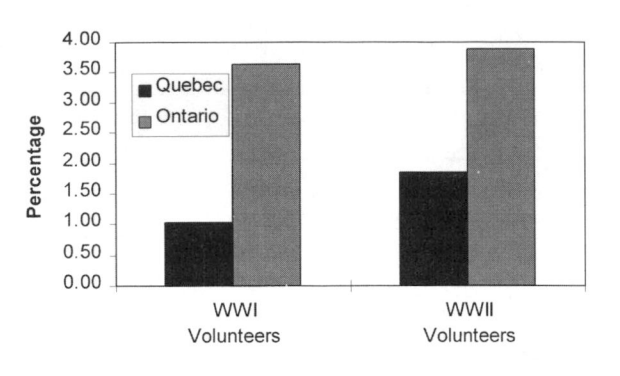

Figure 6.3. A comparison of volunteers in Quebec and in Ontario, World War I and World War II (Granatstein and Hitsman 1977: 160). All figures are rounded to the nearest one-tenth of 1 percent.

79 percent of Ontario's; by 1941 it was 88 percent. However, Quebec remained slightly less urbanized than Ontario, 59.5 percent versus 63.1 percent. During the war, dependency, defined as the percentage of the population under 15 and over 64 year of age, remained higher in Quebec than in Ontario (the only province for which comparative data are available), with the percentage of the dependent population falling from 43 to 40 percent in Quebec and remaining constant at 36 percent in Ontario (Marr and Paterson 1980: 443). Thus, one might expect slightly lower enlistment rates in Quebec than in Ontario but not the great discrepancy the statistics reveal.

As in World War I, the revival of industry and the advantages of civilian employment became apparent over the long run. However, once again, if economic benefits were the motivation for choice, one would expect more or less the same behavior across Canada. Quebec and francophone enlistment generally should have been, at least at the start of the war, close to, if not above, the national average. As the war progressed, given the absence of conscription for overseas duty, volunteering in Ontario should have been lower than it was, given the location of key industries in the province.

Perceptions of the trustworthiness of government

The King government lost some credibility everywhere by proposing the introduction of conscription, despite promises not to. The plebiscite did much to regain the trust of anglophone Canadians, as evidenced by their strong, positive vote. It fueled the flames of francophone mistrust, however.

The opposition to conscription in Quebec had several strands. There were religious and other conservatives who feared changes in the traditional francophone way of life (Jones 1973, 1981; Wade 1968). Others were pro-fascist. Still others were social democratic. There were those who did not understand the war as a world conflict or as a major threat, and they were confirmed in their view by the neutrality of the United States (Laurendeau 1962: 36–9). According to one important observer, the large "no" vote was a protest, not against the war, but against the idea of imperialism. (Scott 1942: 72) What was true for virtually all the opponents, whatever their social ideology, was that conscription represented a violation of *la théorie du Pacte*.

The federal government lost further credibility by its failure to reform the Canadian military after World War I. The military establishment had done little to alleviate the linguistic cleavage experienced during the first war. Language barriers continued to inhibit francophone training and promotion (Pariseau and Bernier 1987, especially pp. 109–42). The perception of inequality of treatment raised serious questions for some Quebecois about the commitment of Canada to equality of sacrifice (Gravel 1974b; Linteau et al. 1989b: 149).

There are important distinctions, nonetheless, between the Borden and the King governments. Borden's indifference, if not actual antagonism, to francophone concerns was evident in both his policies and his negotiations. King, on the other hand, did all he could to uphold his promises and to regain francophone trust. His government included important francophone ministers, and his plebiscite was worded so as to make it clear that his commitment to nonconscription had been real and could be changed only with large-scale popular support. After the plebiscite, he tried to appease those who had voted against releasing him from his earlier promise. Given the immense international and national pressures on his government and the intensity of francophone feeling about conscription, his success was far from total in convincing French Canadians that his government was trustworthy. Nonetheless, he retained most of the Quebec backing for his party at the national level in contrast to the desertions of the Nationalists from Borden's government and the complete shift of Quebec from his party.

Social pressure and ethical reciprocity

Nationalist organizations had become, if anything, stronger by World War II, and anticonscription sentiment reigned among groups as ideologically diverse as the Union Nationale, the Liberal Party of Quebec, and le Bloc populaire canadien. Undoubtedly, social sanctions existed among some segments of the community.

Giving and refusing consent: Canada

The election results of 1939, the plebiscite of 1942, and the voting records of MPs from Quebec during the 1944 recruiting crisis offer strong evidence of francophone opposition to overseas conscription in World War II. Leaders of both major parties in the Quebec provincial elections of 1939 pledged to fight conscription. A new organization, the Ligue pour la Défense du Canada, mobilized against conscription and organized the defeat of the plebiscite in Quebec (see esp. Laurendeau 1962; Granatstein 1973). Much of the Catholic Church, virtually all ultranationalists, and many liberal dissidents, some of whom went on to form the Bloc populaire, also campaigned to defeat the plebiscite.

On the other hand, there seems to have been less antagonism to voluntary enlistment. The differences in francophone social pressures and social norms concerning enlistment and conscription between World Wars I and II are best captured by two famous Canadian novels both set in Montreal and both published in 1945: *Two Solitudes* by Hugh MacLennan (1990 [1945]) and *The Tin Flute* by Gabrielle Roy (1980 [1945]). The first describes a nationalist draft resister from a well-off family with lands in the countryside in 1917–19, and the second the choices of a father and eldest son in a poor, urban family, for military service as a means out of their devastating economic situation of the Great Depression.

In anglophone Canada, war fever was high. Opposition to conscription was largely the position of small, ideological groups, at least by the time of the plebiscite.

ANALYSIS

It is now time to return to the questions posed at the beginning of this chapter: What accounts for the variation among Canadian groups in their voluntary enlistment patterns and responses to conscription, and what accounts for the increased enlistments of the francophones in World War II relative to World War I?

The case for the opportunistic explanation

Opportunistic obedience and disobedience is the most parsimonious explanation of compliance. Thus, to the extent that economic or social incentives explain variation in volunteering, voting, or protest, we need look no further. However, economic incentives fail to account for the extent of volunteering by anglophone Canadians and arguably predict higher rates of enlistment and acceptance of conscription among francophone Canadians than we observe. On the other hand, the social costs imposed by the military were higher for francophones than an-glophones.

One factor that should clearly influence decisions about joining the military are the social and other costs imposed by local cultural organizations, such as churches and nationalist associations. During World War I, there is little evidence that francophone cultural organizations imposed effective sanctions, although there is some evidence that an-glophone organizations, at least in Ontario, did. There is somewhat more evidence of the capacity of francophone organizations to sanction in World War II, but there is also a higher rate of francophone enlistment.

While social pressures created by anglophone organizations for enlistment and francophone organizations against volunteering may play an important role in accounting for the difference in enlistment, a public act, they are not as satisfying in explaining differences in voting behavior, a private act. Moreover, the recognition of the importance of social pressure only raises other questions: What explains why social sanctions were used to encourage enlistment in anglophone Canada and to discourage it in francophone Canada? In other words, what explains the difference in the attitudes toward the war and conscription? The ability of local cultural organizations to impose sanctions does not account for the ethical concerns they are enforcing.

Cost–benefit calculations are likely to have influenced some decision making, but the variables often work in opposing directions. They cannot be brought together into a unified explanation of behavior. Nor does opportunistic obedience offer much insight into the intensity of feeling in francophone Canada, especially Quebec, in opposition to conscription and the intense support of so many anglophones for the war effort.

Other possible explanations

Another possible explanation is patriotism, that is, some form of ideological commitment to serve. Only the British-born volunteered in percentages significantly higher than their percentage of the population, however, and they were also the group suffering the most from high unemployment. Nonetheless, MacKinnon's study (1994) suggests that something other than economics was motivating them; among individuals in virtually the same economic circumstances, the British-born were still the most likely to volunteer among the three groups. Thus, at least for this group, patriotism – at least toward Britain – seems a possible explanation of at least some of the observed behavior.

The case for contingent consent

Anglophones and francophones clearly possessed different views of the mutual obligations of individual citizens and the state. Moreover, the dominant francophone view was that the federal government and the anglophone majority consistently broke their promises regarding protection of francophone culture. Finally, the policy bargain on conscription was itself under dispute among francophones. The press, existing governmental institutions, and the cultural beliefs stimulated by cultural organizations meant that most potential recruits had sufficient information to evaluate the conscription bargain, calculate the costs and benefits of following their preferences, secure credible information about the behavior of others, and ascertain the likelihood of the government keeping its side of the conscription policy bargain. The information revealed made it broadly rational for many Canadians to encourage volunteering and then support conscription in principal. In the case of most francophones, with their deep distrust of government and a widely shared ethical stance against conscription, contingent consent was less likely. Government might compel obedience; it could not, without convincingly demonstrating its trustworthiness, achieve consent.

The factors hypothesized as necessary to produce contingent consent were obviously absent for many francophones and present for many anglophones during World War I:

(a) Government's behavior, especially during the Ontario Schools Controversy, offered little assurance of government trustworthiness to uphold its side of a bargain or an equitable draft. On the other hand, anglophone Canada had a history of promises kept by the federal government.

(b) Cultural organizations stimulated cultural memories already aggravated by government behavior in the case of francophone Canada and created an ethical reciprocity around the positions of not volunteering and opposition to conscription. In anglophone Canada, cultural memories played a positive role, encouraging loyalty to both the federal government and the Empire and ethical reciprocity concerning enlistment and support of conscription.

(c) To the extent that government invested resources in persuading Canadians of government trustworthiness or ethical reciprocity in support of the war, the information disseminated in French Canada was based on mistaken assumptions about francophone loyalty to France. On the other hand, oppositional groups invested considerable resources in disseminating information about instances of gov-

ernment untrustworthiness and of oppositional actions among francophones.

. (d) The low rates of volunteering among the francophones seems to
have increased anglophone support of conscription.

What distinguishes World War I from World War II is the behavior of
government actors. The contrast between the strategies of Borden and
King is sharp. Borden was basically indifferent to francophone concerns.
He manipulated the electorate and parliament so as to impose his preferred policies without serious concessions to opponents. King did all he
could to appease the francophones and to rebuild their trust. He did not
simply break his no-conscription pledge; he did so with the authority of
a general plebiscite. His government compelled as few men as it could
into overseas duty. Although the same factors were at work to reduce
contingent consent among the francophones, the actions of the King
government helped increase the level of volunteering.

Additional evidence for this perspective lies in the reaction to the
actual introduction of conscription. To the extent that underenlistment
within a population group reflected free-riding by individuals who actually supported the war effort, we should expect approval of or at least
resignation to conscription. To the extent that failure to enlist was
caused by a refusal to consent, we should expect opposition to both the
proposal of conscription and its implementation. In French Canada,
where the population had become sentient to government insensitivity
to their language and culture, the reaction was violent but considerably
more so in 1917 than in 1944. In English Canada where acceptance of
the government's justification of the war was more widespread, the
reaction was more positive. Draft evasion and desertion rates were also
higher for francophones than anglophones. Again they were much lower
among French Canadians in World War II than in World War I, in part
perhaps because so few francophones were conscripted to fight overseas.

CONCLUSION

In 1914–18 the Canadian government attempted to evoke consent to its
recruitment and conscription policies despite the objections of a large
segment of the citizenry. Canadians had conflicting interpretations of the
extent to which government policy was consistent with the policy bargain on military service and conflicting evaluations of government trustworthiness. There was greater skepticism among French than English
Canadians that the war was one of defense. From the French Canadian
perspective, recruitment and especially conscription represented unjusti-

163

fied attempts by a government already failing to keep its promises to impose additional citizen responsibilities and costs. To most English Canadians conscription was simply the fairest policy for ensuring compliance with the already existing responsibilities of every Canadian in a war that they supported.

Canadian institutions meant that the anglophone majority could impose its will on the francophone minority. Thus, universal conscription was introduced despite the strong opposition of the majority of the francophones. The immediate result was repression of the draft resisters, but the long-term effect was the continued and increased distrust of the federal government and of the anglophone majority by the francophone minority.

The francophone and anglophone positions were broadly similar in World War II, and once again the majority imposed its policy preference on the minority. However, the Liberal Party and the King government did far more than Borden in trying to make their commitments credible and in winning the trust of at least some proportion of the francophone population. To an extent, they succeeded. Volunteering was higher and resistance to conscription lower in World War II than in World War I.

Coercion through conscription was the answer of the Canadian government – and indeed of almost all the governments fighting in the Great War – to manpower procurement problems. Among those who approved the war but were free-riding, conscription did not stir resentment. Among those who disapproved the war and felt betrayed generally by the government, the introduction of conscription, especially in 1917, left a lasting scar. The major impact of the conscription crisis was to deepen the rift between francophones and anglophones.

7

A *weapon against war: Conscientious objection in the United States, Australia, and France*

What I have to do is to see, at any rate, that I do not lend myself to the wrong which I condemn.
>   Henry David Thoreau, "Civil Disobedience"

His disciples went to visit Rabban Yochanan ben Zakkai as he lay ill. They said: "Master, give us your blessing." He replied: "May you fear God as much as you fear human beings." They said: "No more than that?" He replied: "That is more than enough, believe me! Do you not know that when we are about to commit a transgression we dismiss God from our minds and hope that no human eye may notice us!"
>   *Talmud* (quoted in Gates of Repentance: 231)

Conscientious objection is a weapon of protest. It is not, however, a collective protest. It is an individual, but socially informed, act of resistance. It requires no organization, no mobilization of others, no group process. It is an action undertaken by single individuals albeit, generally, individuals who are part of self-conscious groups of war protesters.

Conscientious objection bears an obvious family resemblance to civil disobedience. Where it differs is that it has become a legal act of resistance. It was not always, so, however. Historically the term referred to opposition to war and conscription on grounds of conscience whether one consequently received a legal exemption from military service or whether one resisted the law by refusing to be conscripted. Conscientious objection and civil disobedience share another quality: rarely is the decision to engage in either act done in the absence of a social or political context that raises questions about the government's actions and policies.

Conscientious objection is neither the only nor necessarily the most prevalent form of refusing consent during war. Applications for draft

This chapter is based on an earlier paper co-authored with Stephen DeTray (1993).

exemptions and deferments may also reflect dissent; certainly the illegal acts of draft evasion, draft resistance, and emigration to avoid conscription are other examples of refusing consent. Unfortunately, the data on those behaviors are very poor; there is simply no way to make comparisons across countries or even across wars for the same country. There are better data on desertion, but this is a decision made once a man has joined the military and after he has experienced its real costs.

Although conscientious objection may be an act of very few, there appears to be a positive correlation between reliance on conscientious objection and other forms of dissent. Moreover, conscientious objection, unlike other forms of refusing consent, requires an explicit and public statement of opposition to government demands. Finally, it is not easy to use conscientious objection as a means to free-ride;[1] manipulating the exemption system is a far easier route. Thus, conscientious objection does provide a fairly good indicator of the extent of noncompliance with the war effort.

The existence of conscientious objection raises at least three questions for the model of contingent consent. The first is whether acts of conscientious objection constitute a kind of moral behavior that an account based on ideological motivations can totally explain. The second is why governments that are presumably trying to achieve citizen consent to and participation in a war permit the establishment of an institution that permits citizens to legally refuse consent. The third is how the institution of conscientious objection not only reflects but also engenders ethical concerns. The final chapter discusses the third question; most of this chapter focuses on the first and the second.

The bulk of the chapter explores variation over time and among countries in the reliance on conscientious objection as a means of registering refusal to consent to a given country's declaration of war and method of conscription. In particular, it considers the history of conscientious objection in the United States, Australia, and France. These three countries all experienced the two world wars and, subsequently, politically unpopular "little" wars involving conscripts. France fought

---

[1] Stringent requirements for being a c.o. make it difficult, if not impossible, to manufacture a history of pacifist social values, however, and thus reduce the likelihood that those without any normative stance will choose this option. Moreover, the costs of being a c.o. relative to some other options can be relatively high. Opportunists were likely to be a null set in France during all three wars and in Australia and the United States during World War I when c.o.s experienced severe punishments and were more likely than not to be put on the front lines, albeit in a nonmilitary capacity. Thus, nothing was gained and much lost by being a c.o. During Vietnam and Korea, there were easier options. Only during World War II in the United States (since Australia did not have overseas conscription) was there any real possibility of opportunistic c.o.s, but they would have to have been drawn from the ranks of the Jehovah's Witnesses or traditional peace churches, an unlikely scenario.

the war in Algeria and the United States and Australia the war in Vietnam. Moreover, they vary in regard to factors posited as affecting compliance: the costs of using conscientious objection; the evaluation of the government's trustworthiness; and the evaluation of the government's war and conscription policies.

HYPOTHESES

Whereas the Canadian case presented an opportunity to contrast the model of contingent consent to the model of opportunistic obedience, conscientious objection offers a contrast between models of ideological disobedience and contingent refusal to consent. To rephrase the hypotheses derived from the model of contingent consent in these terms:

> *(rev. 1)* *The less trustworthy citizens perceive government to be, the more likely they are to refuse to contingently consent to its policies and, therefore, comply.*
>
> *(rev. 2)* *The larger the proportion of citizens refusing to contribute from a given population, the more likely others from that population will also refuse to contribute.*

Alternatively, conscientious objectors may be individuals whose choices are not reducible to rational calculations of cost. They have such strong moral positions that they refuse to participate in the military under any conditions. To rephrase the hypothesis derived from the ideological model in these terms:

> *(alt. 2)* *The more strongly and widely held are ideological positions in opposition to a particular policy, the more non-compliance.*

In either case, intensity of opposition to the war or government increases the proclivity to refuse consent. There may also be opportunistic conscientious objectors who perceive that becoming a c.o. is the best way to avoid military service, but the requirements of becoming a c.o. generally make this difficult. Conscientious objectors are not totally insensitive to cost; of interest here, however, are those who are paying a price rather than avoiding a cost. Contingent conscientious objectors distrust government and are concerned about doing what they perceive as ethically right within their reference group, but they are more cost-sensitive than ideological objectors. However, if the costs of being a conscientious objector are too high, even those who take serious exception to government policy may find themselves in the army or seeking other ways to avoid the draft. Strong ideological commitment does not necessarily involve martyrdom.

A weapon against war: Conscientious objection

The major claim here is that contingent conscientious objectors are those whose ethical concerns inform their calculation of costs and benefits. They calculate whether the price to be paid for dissent is too high, but their evaluations of the trustworthiness of government and the fairness of the conscription policy make the price they are willing to pay higher than would be paid by an opportunistic conscientious objector but lower than that borne by a moral absolutist. Moreover, they are strategic actors who wish "to do the right thing," to engage in ethical reciprocity with others in their relevant subgroup. Thus,

> (I) *Contingent conscientious objection will increase with increases in:*
> *(A) distrust of government;*
> *(B) evidence of dissent against the war in the relevant subgroup; and, given the above,*
> *(C) reduction of the costs of being a conscientious objector.*

If ideology is the determinant motivation, variation in the costs of being a c.o. should have significantly less influence on the choice of being a c.o.:

> (II) *Ideological noncompliance will increase with an increase in membership in pacifist religions or the Jehovah's Witnesses.*

The greater the intensity of opposition to the war or to conscription, the more young men will choose to be c.o.s, even if the price remains the same. The existence of the institution of conscientious objection makes this possible not only by lowering the costs of such a choice but, equally importantly, by altering social expectations, that is by affecting beliefs regarding what others are likely to do and about the effects of one's own action. The institution of conscientious objection legitimates objection to war, provides a stimulus for public discussion and debate about the war itself, and delimits the bounds of legal objection by sanctioning those who misuse the process. The effect can be to increase objection to the war and the government, to provide information about where to search for allies for one's ethical concerns, and to mobilize public sentiment both for and against the war, the government, and those who refuse consent.

This analysis behaviorally distinguishes among the strongly ideological and contingent conscientious objectors by evidence about their involvement in pacifist groups versus organizations mobilized against a particular war. The second indicator, the price each is willing to pay for his ethical commitments, lies on a continuum. Moral absolutists are the least cost sensitive and the most evidently motivated by ideological,

168

usually religious or political, values. At the extreme, they are willing to pay any price to uphold their religious and political convictions, and they tend to belong to religious or political groupings that proclaim these views. Contingent conscientious objectors are demonstrably opponents of the war or of conscription, but they engage in this form of refusal to consent only when the costs are sufficiently low. Opportunists are also influenced by cost, but there is nothing to indicate any strong ethical concerns.

It is not possible to distinguish behaviorally between moral absolutists and contingent conscientious objectors who are unwilling to pay any price but willing to pay a very high price, such as going to jail for their beliefs.[2] It is possible to make the inference that an increase in conscientious objection among individuals who do not belong to the Jehovah's Witnesses or to other religions whose continued membership requires conscientious objection represents an increase in contingent conscientious objection. Historically conscientious objection, as purely ideological refusal to consent, should vary with membership in those churches.[3] A greater proportion of nonmembers becoming c.o.s, on the other hand, suggests an increase in contingent refusal to consent.

VARIATION WITHIN COUNTRIES OVER TIME

United States

The issue of conscientious objection was first raised in reference to service in the militias of the American colonies. In 1658 in Maryland Richard Keene engaged in "pacifist resistance" and was, consequently, "fined and 'abused by the sheriff' for refusing to be trained as a soldier" (Kohn 1986: 6). During the American Revolution some localities had provisions for exemptions from compulsory military service on grounds of conscience, but no such exemptions existed in the Federal Militia Act of 1862 or subsequent Union drafts for the Civil War until 1864. In the interim, Quakers, Mennonites, and other pacifists paid for their religious beliefs by spending time in military jails. When objections on religious

---

[2] One draft resister I spoke to described how he weighed the consequences of his decision: He was willing to (and did) go to prison for a year or two but only if he was fairly certain that he would subsequently suffer no serious professional or social stigma.

[3] A greater proportion of members relying on conscientious objection may be an indicator of contingent refusal to consent rather than of a more absolutist ideology; to evaluate this claim will require fairly detailed knowledge of the membership. For example, the Quakers often make the decision to be a c.o. one of individual conscience rather than a requirement of membership.

grounds became legal in 1864, religious exemptions were granted liberally. Most objectors were sympathetic to the abolition of slavery and accepted noncombatant assignments.

The issue of conscientious objection did not again become a matter of serious public debate until World War I. With U.S. entry into the war, Congress limited c.o. exemptions to members of traditional and "well-recognized" pacifist religions whose beliefs prohibited them from participating in war in any form. However, lack of a specific policy by the Selective Service authorities led to arbitrary rulings by local boards concerning which denominations qualified. In December 1917 the law was liberalized to recognize nonreligious opposition to war in general. No absolute exemption from military service was legally possible (Chambers 1987: 215–17).

Qualified c.o.s, required to perform noncombatant duties, were sent to army training camps before being reassigned. There they were segregated and, often, subject to verbal and even physical abuse. Out of some 24 million registrants, 64,693 men (0.27 percent) filed claims for c.o. status, 56,830 were certified by local boards as c.o.s, 29,679 of these passed the physical exam, and 20,873 were inducted into the army. This experience led approximately 80 percent to soon abandon their stand as objectors (U.S. Secretary of War 1919: 17).

Ultimately, 3,989 draftees, out of a total of 2.8 million inducted, claimed to be c.o.s unwilling to serve in the military in any capacity. The majority belonged to historic pacifist churches, Quakers, Mennonites, and Moravian Brethren, but perhaps 15 percent were religious objectors from nonpacifist churches and 10 percent nonreligious, "political objectors" (Chambers 1987: 216–17). Of these, 450 were court-martialed and imprisoned for their refusal to engage in any kind of service, combatant or noncombatant. Another 940, who similarly refused, were segregated within army camps (U.S. Secretary of War 1919: 25). Together the statutorily acceptable and the civilly disobedient conscientious objectors comprised 0.15 percent of all inductions.[4] The 1,390 who refused any kind of service were labeled "absolutists," and they clearly were absolutists in that the price they paid was very high indeed. There is considerable evidence of brutality and mistreatment in the camps. Given that resistance was considered treason, 17 of those who were court-martialed were sentenced to death, 142 to life imprisonment, and 73 to twenty years in prison. The death sentences were commuted, but 17 of those imprisoned died in jail (Kohn 1986: 28–9). Among these resisters were Mennonites, Dunkards, members of the Industrial Workers of the World, Seventh Day Adventists, and Jehovah's Witnesses. The

[4] These percentages were compiled from U.S. Selective Service System (1950a, b).

members of this last sect would accept only ministerial exemptions, which they were routinely denied.

The Selective Service and Training Act of 1940 included new and slightly more liberal provisions for c.o.s than had been available in early legislation (Sibley and Jacob 1962: 45–52). It exempted any person from "combatant training and service in the land or naval forces of the United States who, by reason of religious training and belief, is conscientiously opposed to participation in war in any form" (Sibley and Jacob 1962: 50). Local boards were to decide on c.o. claims and place those whom they certified as c.o.s either in noncombatant training in the military or assign them to "work of national importance under civilian direction" (Sibley and Jacob 1962: 50). There was no provision made for absolutists or for nonreligious objectors. However, Congress gave complete exemptions to ministers of religion and theology students but without defining a "minister."

During World War II c.o.s were once again a tiny proportion of the American draft-age population. Of 34,506,923 who registered for the draft, approximately 72,354, or about two tenths of one percent, initially requested exemptions on grounds of conscience. Out of approximately 9,600,000 inductees, some 25,000 registered c.o.s served as noncombatants, 11,950 did alternative service in civilian work camps, an estimated 20,000 applicants failed to receive official c.o. status, and 6,086 went to prison for violating the Selective Service Act by refusing to serve the military in any capacity (U.S. Selective Service System 1950a). The official figures of the numbers who served as noncombatants in the armed forces is probably too low; according to Sibley and Jacob (1962: 86–7) the numbers may have been as high as 50,000. Their explanation of why so many c.o.s entered the Army and Navy instead of joining the new Civilian Public Service include factors such as groups, most importantly the Seventh Day Adventists, who actively encouraged noncombatant service; the belief that work in the Army or Navy would more directly alleviate the human suffering caused by war; and the requirement that those who entered the Civilian Public Service pay their own way while those who served as noncombatants received Army or Navy wages (Sibley and Jacob 1962: 88–90).

Unlike in World War I, absolutists were tried in civilian courts, not court-martialed as traitors. Moreover, the Selective Service System administrators, aware of the excesses of World War I, sought to find the line between "the harsh treatment of c.o.s, on the one hand, and their overly liberal treatment, on the other" (U.S. Selective Service System 1950a: 1). Consequently, c.o.s who had violated the Selective Service Act were still confined to prison but to federal rather than military prisons. Maximum sentence was five years, and the average sentence peaked at

171

32.4 months in 1944 (U.S. Federal Bureau of Prisons 1947: 19). These improvements did not stop all abuse, however. Kohn cites reports of c.o.s being beaten, denied food and medicine, and being placed in cells with "sodomists and homosexuals with the obvious inference and implications" (1986: 53). One c.o. claimant was remanded to a mental institution for no apparent reason other than a refusal to fight the Japanese. He was not released until 1970, some 28 years later (Sibley and Jacob 1962: 53).

Only a minority of imprisoned c.o.s dissented from the war effort on nonreligious grounds. The largest proportion of those imprisoned, almost 4,500, were Jehovah's Witnesses, 316 admitted no religion, and 255 made political or philosophical claims (U.S. Selective Service System 1950b). As in World War I, members of traditional peace churches and Jehovah's Witnesses accounted for approximately three quarters of convicted absolutist objectors.

On January 6, 1951, the Universal Military Training and Service (UMTS) Act was passed, replacing the Selective Service Act of 1948. The law lowered the age of liability to $18\frac{1}{2}$. C.o.s were permitted to perform specified civilian tasks as alternative service. The period of service in both military and alternative service was increased from 21 to 24 months. Under the UMTS Act 1,560,000 men were inducted and processed for the Korean conflict. The percent of c.o. exemptions jumped, with three times the percent of inductees receiving c.o. status in 1952 than had even applied for objector exemptions during World War II. In 1952 1.64 percent of inductees were classified as c.o.s.[5]

In the late 1960s and early 1970s, a growing U.S. involvement in Vietnam brought dramatically increased inductions. The increase was threefold between 1965 and 1966. There was also an increase in mass disobedience in the form of raids on local draft boards to destroy draft records. Destruction of draft records initially met with severe penalties, but, over time, sympathetic juries in some locales tolerated such practices.[6] The U.S. invasion of Cambodia in May 1970 and the deaths of students at Kent State and Florida State provoked massive nationwide antidraft activities. More than 10,000 draft cards were returned following the deaths of the students, with this number increasing to 25,000 by November 1970.

Conscientious objection also increased during this period. The ratio

[5] These figures differ somewhat from those presented by Kohn (1986: 70, 93). He has apparently misread at least one of the tables from Selective Service records for his World War II ratio, confusing registrants with inductees. The figures presented here are compiled from U.S. Department of Commerce (1973: 55, appendices 12 and 13); and U.S. Selective Service System (1950a: 314).

[6] Especially dramatic was the case of the "Camden 28" in early 1972.

of objector exemptions to inductions leapt from 5.6 percent in 1968 to 14.2 percent in 1970.[7] The rise in c.o. applicants partially reflected the fact that the basis for claiming a conscientious objection had become more liberal. The Supreme Court decision in *Seeger* v. *United States* (1965), upheld in the *Welsh* v. *United States* (1970), found that conscientious exemption no longer required a belief in a supreme being. The Supreme Court in the *Gillette* v. *United States* (1971) did, however, confirm the rejection of claims on the basis of what was labeled selective conscientious objection. Objection had to be to all wars, not a particular war.

The rules regarding c.o. applications and the attitudes toward those claims by local draft boards also underwent modification during the course of the war (Davis and Dolbeare 1968: 89, 93, and esp. 108–10). Consequently, the costs of becoming a c.o. decreased. Statutory revisions of the UMTS Act accompanied the extension of the draft in 1967. These revisions mandated no change in the short window of time in which to register as a c.o., but they did eliminate previous provisions for a thorough third party investigation of the case upon appeal against a negative board decision. The reduced costs of acquiring and providing information by both applicant and draft board were somewhat offset, however, by the fact that appeal boards made decisions on more limited information. Moreover, if a claimant persisted in refusing to be inducted following a negative decision of the appeal board, he was subject to nearly immediate prosecution. If the court determined that there was a "basis in fact" for the board's decision, the claimant was convicted and sentenced to five years in prison and/or a $10,000 fine. As the war progressed, however, there is evidence that the draft board members were more likely to grant c.o. status and less likely to impose such heavy penalties.

The costs of becoming a c.o. declined significantly between the declaration of World War I and the conclusion of the war in Vietnam. Civilian authority replaced military authority for both those who were given c.o. exemptions and those who violated the Selective Service Act on grounds of conscience. Sanctioned discrimination and brutality decreased, and alternative forms of service increased. It became easier both to apply for and to be accepted as a c.o.

Between World War II, Korea, and Vietnam there was a large jump in applications for and granting of c.o. status (Figure 7.1). One factor that distinguishes World War II from Korea and Vietnam was that the first required full mobilization and the other two did not. This fact in and of

---

[7] Compiled by the authors from U.S. Department of Commerce (1973: appendices 12 and 13, 55).

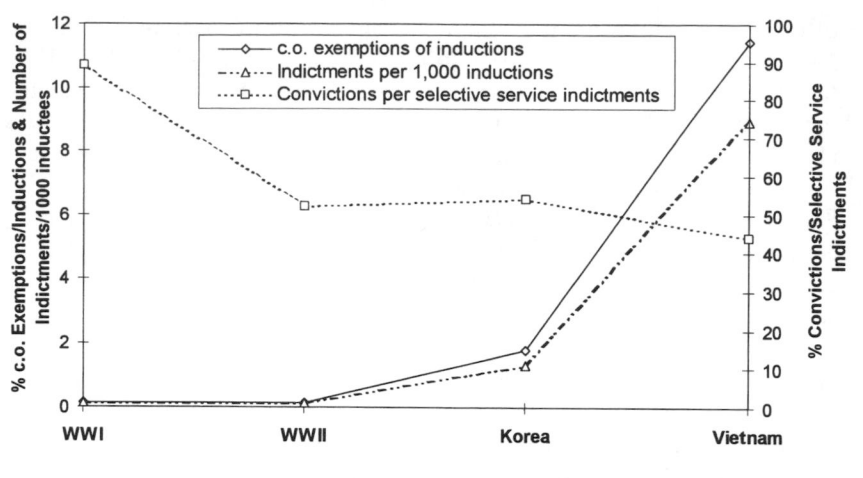

Figure 7.1. Conscientious objection in the United States (U.S. Department of Justice 1973: table H-10; 1950–3, table D-4; 1941–5: tables 12 and D-4. U.S. Secretary of War 1919: 25. U.S. Selective Service System 1950: (Mon. #11)315, (Mon. #14)16; 1973: Appendix 12).

itself may have increased tolerance for c.o. applications by draft boards. Tolerance of the right to object increased considerably by the time of the war in Vietnam. The grounds for becoming a c.o. had widened. There was also a greater likelihood of defendants winning in cases involving all kinds of selective service violations, including those by c.o.s.

By inference a high percentage of the defendants in draft violation cases during Vietnam were contingent conscientious objectors. Of the 3,275 selective service violators sent to prison in the Vietnam era, "many could have easily avoided any penalty but chose instead to bear witness against the war by submitting themselves to punishment" (Baskir and Strauss 1977: 15). Given the nature of the rules governing exemptions on the basis of conscience, it is not surprising that, up through World War II, most conscientious objectors were members of traditional peace churches or Jehovah's Witnesses (Figure 7.2). Nor is it surprising that most of those who went to jail for their absolute refusal to serve, even in noncombatant categories, were either religious absolutists or individuals with strong political affiliations, such as anarchists and socialists. As long as the institutional arrangements levied a high price for moral convictions, the convictions had to be extremely strong.

Further support for interpreting these figures as an increase in contingent conscientious objection is the fact that World War I was a far less popular war than World War II, yet the applications, exemptions, and convictions related to conscientious objection were significantly fewer.

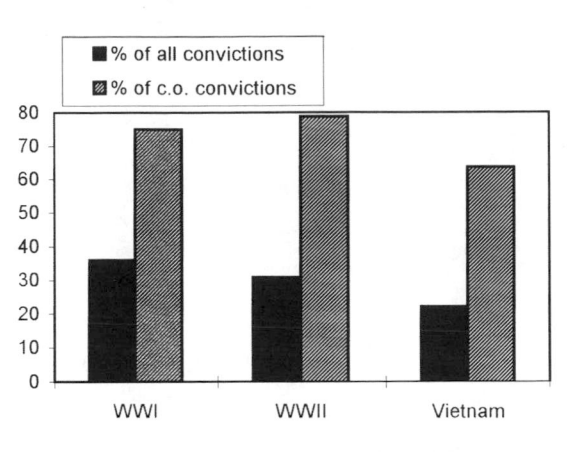

Figure 7.2. Violations of Selective Service laws by members of traditional peace churches and Jehovah's Witnesses (Baskir and Strauss 1977: 15; Chambers 1987: 216; U.S Selective Service System 1950: (Mon. #14)15–16).

In World War I, most of the 2,599 who served as civilian c.o.s, as well as the 940 relegated to army camps and the 450 convicted of treason and related crimes for refusal to serve, should, I believe, be considered absolutists. They suffered considerably for their beliefs. They were under military authority and, on the whole, treated abominably. The contingent and opportunistic conscientious objectors tended to abandon their stand as they realized the stigma of being a c.o. was too high relative to that of doing their military service. The costs of being a c.o. had decreased by World War II, and the proportion of those engaging in contingent conscientious objection went up – even though the war was more generally approved. The 6,086 who went to jail were clearly absolutists, as were those from traditional pacifist religions and avowed pacifist organizations; the rest of the nearly 37,000 granted c.o. status were, arguably, contingent conscientious objectors.

Conscientious objection was highest, in percentage terms, during the Vietnam War. Certainly the liberalization of c.o. requirements in the 1950s, the further modifications during the Vietnam era, the Supreme Court decisions, and tolerant draft boards lowered the costs of being a c.o. On the other hand, less individually costly alternatives were more widespread than in previous wars. The probability of being conscripted was lower than during World War II and medical and student exemptions easier to obtain. Nor is it at all evident that it was less costly to apply for conscientious objection than to seek some other forms of exemption. There are three possible interpretations of this increased reliance on conscientious objection despite the existence of alternative

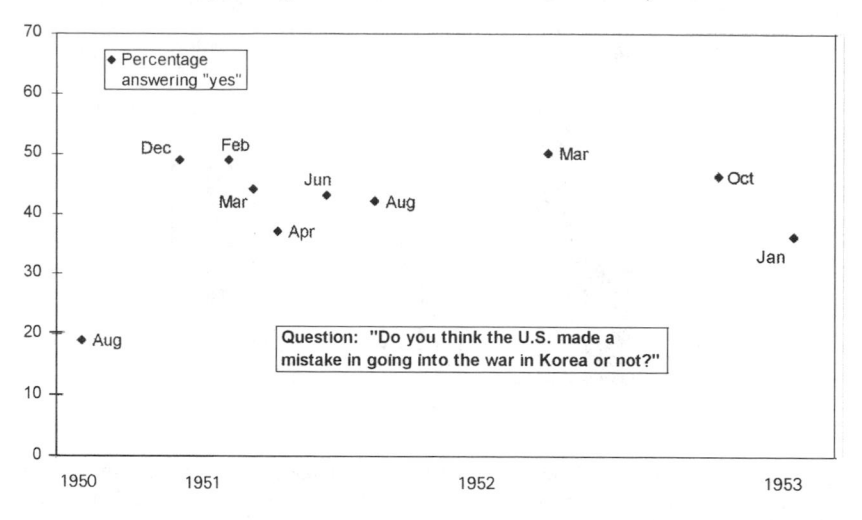

Figure 7.3. U.S. opinion polls and Korean War, 1950–3 (Niemi, Mueller, and Smith 1989: 69).

and less costly means of avoiding military service. First, as was the case, all forms of refusing consent went up. This begs the question, however, of why so many bothered with conscientious objection. Second, conscientious objection may have been the strategy of choice for those who could not succeed in obtaining exemptions. Unfortunately, the data do not exist that would permit proper evaluation of this hypothesis. There is impressionistic evidence, however, that at least some proportion of the c.o. applicants chose this option rather than seek a deferment. This suggests the third possible explanation: conscientious objection permits an individual to express ethical disapproval of the war effort and government policy without going to prison or leaving the country, two more individually costly alternatives.

If contingent conscientious objection is at least partially a reflection of the popularity of a war, there should be a correlation between levels of citizen approval and the amount of conscientious objection. Unfortunately, there are no extant surveys of public opinion on World War I or II.[8] Disapproval ratings of the Korean War (Figure 7.3) and of the

---

[8] Opinion polling did not exist during 1914–19. It did exist in the 1940s, and there is a survey taken by *Fortune* magazine in 1940 that indicates considerable ambivalence of the U.S. citizenry concerning possible entry into the war (Supplement to *Fortune,* July 1940). There are indications in the literature that President Roosevelt authorized Gallup polls during the war, but the polls have never been released. One extant Gallop poll from July 1940 showed 86 percent against entering the war. See Niemi, Mueller, and Smith (1989: 231).

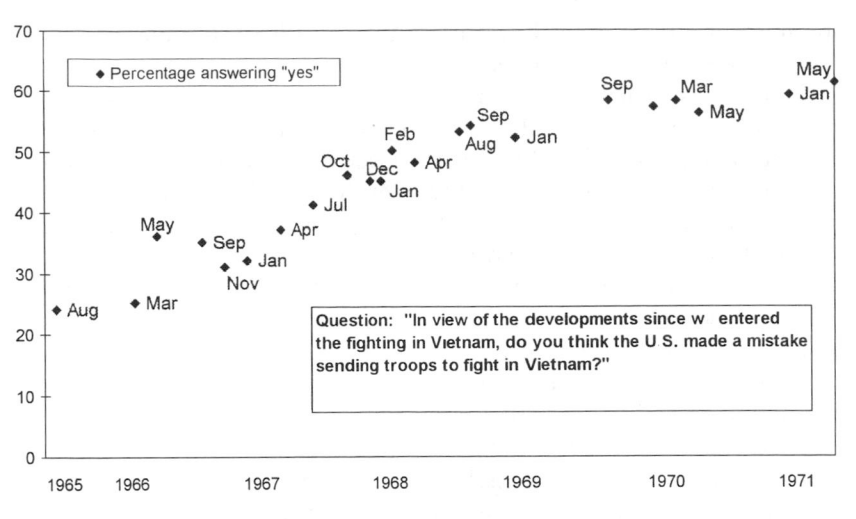

Figure 7.4. U.S. public opinion on the war in Vietnam, 1965–71 (Niemi, Mueller, and Smith 1989: 71).

Vietnam War (Figure 7.4) indicate both that Vietnam was more unpopular and that dissatisfaction with government policy increased markedly during the Vietnam era. At least some of this opposition was translated into contingent refusal to consent in the form of contingent conscientious objection, especially given the increasingly low costs of this strategy.

The data do not permit exact determination of how much of the increase in the reliance on conscientious objection, especially during Vietnam, resulted from perceptions of the illegitimacy of military service and how much from reduction in the costs of being a c.o. What the data do clearly suggest, however, is that: one, both factors were at work; and, two, given dissatisfaction with the government and the war effort, conscientious objection is used only if the costs are sufficiently low.

Australia

Australia shares with the United States an Anglo-Saxon tradition of law, and it, too, sent conscripts to fight in Vietnam. Unlike the United States, however, Australia has, since 1909, a continuous history of compulsory military training. In this respect, it is more like France. Where it is distinct from both of the other countries in this study is that only with Vietnam was the government empowered to send conscripts overseas. Australia's institution of conscientious objection is largely a set of rules

177

administering legal refusal to engage in compulsory training or in national defense during wartime.

Although conscientious objectors were few in number and their direct effect on combat minimal, they arguably play an important symbolic role in Australian politics. The history of conscientious objection in Australia is a history of citizen obligations and rights, especially the national service obligation and the right to dissent. Conscription itself was always controversial in Australia. During World War I, conscription for overseas duties had been roundly defeated in two national referenda. Conscription for overseas duty had been introduced only for the last two years of World War II and only in certain areas of the South Pacific. No conscripts had served in Korea. Thus, the issue of sending conscripts to fight in Vietnam was politically touchy, as, of course, was the war itself.

Australia made provision for conscientious objection in 1903, just two years after constituting itself as a federated and independent Commonwealth country. Indeed, its Defence Act of 1903 was "the first national legislation to grant total exemption from military service on the grounds of religious belief" (Smith 1989: 13). Initially, exemption was permitted only for members of certain churches, the traditional peace churches. The question of conscientious objection was moot, however, until 1909 when compulsory military training was introduced.

In 1910 the Defence Act was amended to include "conscientious belief" against the bearing of arms. Such a belief was presumed to have a religious basis, but the legislation did not explicitly say so (Jordens 1989b: 3). The amendment further provided for determination of exemptions by civilian courts and limited objection to the act of bearing arms. This was interpreted to imply that noncombatant military service might be required during wartime (Smith 1989: 16).

Australia conscripted men for military service only within Australia during World War I. It extended the area where conscripts could serve to the Southwest Pacific during World War II, which effectively extended duty only to Papua New Guinea. Thus, conscientious objection was hardly at issue in 1914–1918. Even so and despite the stigma attached, some members of traditional peace churches, notably the Christadelphians, Seventh Day Adventists, and Quakers (Plymouth Brethren), petitioned parliament to excuse them even from the domestic forces on the grounds of religious objection (Gilbert and Jordens 1988: 343).

The issue of conscientious objection began to take on significance only in 1939. In that year parliament, following British precedent (Gilbert and Jordens 1988: 343) amended the Defence Act to clarify that conscientious objection was not limited to members of the traditional peace churches and to permit appeals to the supreme court of a state or territory (Smith 1989: 17). The amendments stopped short of total exemption and required noncombatant service. Excluded, moreover, were Communists, Jehovah's Witnesses, and others believed to represent a threat to the state (Hasluck 1965 [1952]: 600; Gilbert and Jordens 1988: 343–4).

Those liable to military service had the right to apply for conscientious objector status. Applications were heard by "a court of summary jurisdiction, that is, one constituted by a police, stipendiary or special magistrate" (Hasluck 1965 [1952]: 602), and appeals were possible. If the court granted exemption, it could take either of two courses of action: make the individual liable for noncombatant work in the Citizen Forces or for civilian work. These procedures made the costs of application relatively low for sincere objectors.

The magistrates were not always as tolerant in practice as in principle, however. While they tended to be gentle with those willing to accept noncombatant duties, they were often quite harsh in their prosecution and jailing of those who sought total exemptions. The prosecutions and jailings intensified after 1941. A significant rise in applications precipitated the change in implementation. The 260 claims in December 1940 represented the highest monthly total in the war, and the 1,712 claims from August 1940 through March 1941 represented two-thirds of the total applications for the whole war (Hasluck 1965 [1952]: 600). Authorities were indulgent until 1941, when the large rise in applicants seems to have led the courts to increasingly reject claimants. Fear of opportunism, on the one hand, and of illicit applications by Jehovah's Witnesses, on the other, seems to account for the tougher actions by the courts. There were more prosecutions and more convictions, which carried jail sentences of two weeks to six months.

Caught in the net of prosecutions and convictions were sincere objectors. Their plight was the subject of lobbying efforts by pacifist groups and Parliamentarians. In July 1941 the Minister of the Army proposed to the War Cabinet an amendment of the Defence Act to provide for total exemption. No amendment followed, but in July 1942 National Security Regulation S.R. 80 did extend total exemptions and encourage liberal implementation of the act (Jordens 1989b: 4). Even with the reduction of prosecutions, there were nonetheless conscientious objectors who were forced to serve and consequently suffer in the army for their continued refusal to obey orders (Gilbert and Jordens 1988: 345).

There were approximately 500,000 volunteers and 250,000 conscripts for World War II. One percent of the conscripts applied for c.o. status (Smith 1989: 17). There were 2,791 applications of which 636, or nearly a quarter, were rejected; 1,076 or approximately 40 percent of those accepted were assigned noncombatant duties; 973, or approximately 35 percent, agreed to approved civilian work; 41, or approximately 1 percent, were granted unconditional exemptions; and 65, or approximately 1 percent, were still pending determination at the end of the war.[9]

The amount of conscientious objection recorded between 1939 and 1945 was numerically and statistically insignificant, but it did have some slight political impact on the government, which was persuaded of the case for total exemptions (Hasluck 1965 [1952]: 599–602; Gilbert and Jordens 1988: 343–5). However, the government was not eager to amend the Defence Act so soon again and tried to liberalize the granting of total exemptions through administrative action.

Australia did not send conscripts to Korea, Malaya, or Borneo, where it was militarily involved during the 1950s. The issue of conscientious objection did arise, however, in relation to the compulsory military training scheme of 1951–59. Between 1951 and 1953, there were 329 claims for total exemption, of which 52 percent were granted, 29 percent given noncombatant status, and 19 percent refused, and there were 238 applications for noncombatant duties, of which 92 percent were granted and 8 percent refused (Jordens 1989b: 5).

The reintroduction of conscription in 1964 brought in its wake a renewed public debate on conscientious objection (Jordens 1989b: 5–8; Smith 1990). There were provisions for conscientious objection on both religious and nonreligious grounds by those already in the army as well as those facing conscription (Jordens 1989b: 7). Upon registering, which was required, a young man could fill out a special form on which he declared himself a c.o. He only had his case heard before a court of summary jurisdiction if, in fact, he was balloted in (i.e., his name was drawn in a lottery) and then passed the medical examination. The claimant could hire legal assistance at his own expense and bring in witnesses to testify concerning his beliefs. The Registrar was also entitled to counsel. Appeals of the magistrate's decision could be made by either the Registrar or the applicant.

These provisions came under increasing criticism as the war progressed. By the late 1960s, the Anglican Church and the Australian Council of Churches joined with the traditional peace churches in expressing opposition to the war. They advocated the use of conscientious objection and pressured for liberalization of the conscientious objection provisions. In 1966 the General Synod of the Anglican Church even went so far as to declare that Anglicans could in conscience refuse to bear arms (James 1968: 266–7). The most complete endorsement of reform of the Defence Act was offered by the Australian Council of Churches in a 1968 report. They advocated a very thorough liberaliza-

[9] The numbers are drawn from Hasluck (1965 [1952]: 598–602). We derived the percentages. There seems to exist no other record of the number of applicants and their disposition.

Variation within countries

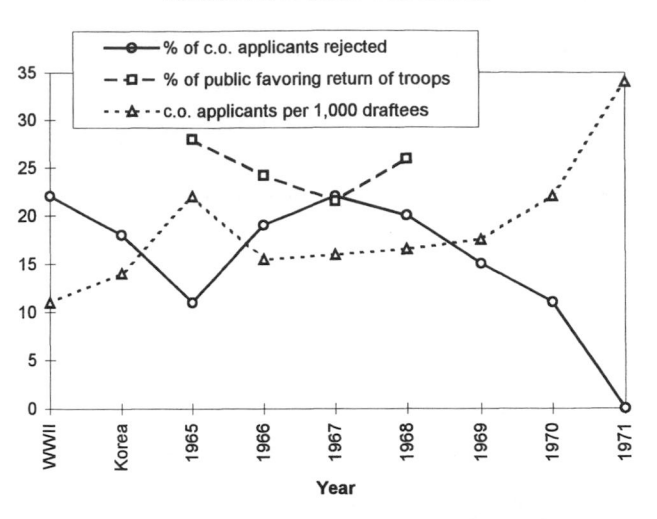

Figure 7.5. Public opinion and conscientious objectors in Australia during World War II, the Korean War, and the Vietnam War (Hasluck 1952: 598–602; Jordens 1989b: 5; Australia 1970a: 1730; 1972a: 622).

tion of the provisions affecting conscientious objectors. Many of these would significantly reduce the costs of applying. For example, under the unamended act, individuals registered for conscientious objector status only after registering for the military and thus were liable to an examination or call-up while their cases were still pending. Of equal concern were those cases of individuals whose applications had been rejected but who did not then voluntarily agree to military service. The Australian Council of Churches were eager to prevent indefinite detainment in military prisons, for the law did not count these prison terms as part of the two years' required military service (James 1968: 269–72).

Nor did the law, as defined by section 29A of the National Service Act, permit conscientious objection against a particular war. This was reaffirmed in the famous William White case in 1966 and reaffirmed in 1968 in the Thompson case (Smith 1990: 122–4).

The evidence of the link between changes in institutionally imposed costs and the variation in the rate of conscientious objection during the Vietnam War is fairly compelling. Figure 7.5 reveals what appears to be a nearly perfect inverse correlation between the number of claimants and the level of rejection. As the tolerance of applications goes up, the applications go up. As the tolerance of applications decreases, the applications go down.

Figure 7.5 further indicates that as public opposition increases, appli-

Table 7.1. *Conscientious objectors in Australia as determined by courts*

Years	Number of objectors
1965[a]	80
1965–66[b]	241
1965–68[c]	368
1965–70[d]	550
1965–71[e]	875
1965–72[f]	1,133

If these figures are correct, then the jumps were as follows:

1965 (1st reg.) to 66	+161
1965–68	+127
1968–70	+182
1970–71	+325
1971–72	+258

[a] McMahon (1965: 3637).
[b] Jordens (1989b: 9, note 38).
[c] Smith (1990: 129).
[d] Snedden (1970: 2).
[e] Jordens (1989b: 69). Also, see Australia (1971b: 279).
[f] Australia Ministry for Labour (1972).

cations and tolerance both increase noticeably. Other evidence supports this view. An increase in protest against the war in Vietnam appears to correspond with a rise in applications for conscientious objection. Cases determined by the courts went up significantly from 1965 to 1970, the moment of greatest mobilized opposition (Table 7.1).

Cases were not handled the same way in all states, however. The implementation of the institution of court decision making varied significantly (Table 7.2). In New South Wales one magistrate decided all the cases, and he held strong and narrow views (Jordens 1989b; Smith 1989). Consequently, an applicant was three times as likely to be refused in New South Wales or Queensland than in Victoria, for example. The other states also experienced differences in attitudes among magistrates as well as different influence by protest groups.

In the case of Australia as in the case of the United States, the major factors producing contingent conscientious objection increased during the Vietnam War. There was a reduction in the costs of applying for and becoming a c.o. at the same time that there was significant public

Variation within countries

Table 7.2. *Regional variations in Australian court decisions*

	NSW	Vic.	Qld.	SA	WA	Tas.	Total
As of 15 May 1968:[a]							
Granted total exemption							
Number	19	51	39	28	22	3	162
(Percent)	(19)	(29)	(40)	(40)	(42)	(33)	
Other provision							
Number	79	124	58	41	31	6	339
(Percent)	(81)	(71)	(60)	(60)	(58)	(66)	
Total Number	98	175	97	69	53	9	501
As of August 1971:[b]							
Granted total exemption							
Number	119	342	87	87	83	15	733
(Percent)	(54)	(79)	(66)	(83)	(81)	(79)	
Granted noncombatant status							
Number	55	63	14	2	5	3	142
(Percent)	(25)	(14)	(11)	(2)	(5)	(16)	
Refused							
Number	45	30	30	16	15	1	137
(Percent)	(21)	(7)	(23)	(15)	(15)	(5)	
Total Number	219	435	131	105	103	19	1,012

[a] Australia 1968: 1442
[b] Australia 1971b: 279

questioning of the war, the government, and the conscription policy. Between 1965 and 1968, there was little change in the public opinion concerning the war; most Australian citizens believed the fighting in Vietnam should continue, although they tended to disapprove sending conscripts there (Table 7.3).

After 1969 the Australian opinion polls indicated that the war was generally unpopular (Curthoys 1990: 151). The "moratorium" on May 8, 1970, involved 120,000 people demonstrating in all of Australia's capital cities (Gilbert and Jordens 1988: 356). This was a large number in a country of only about 15 million. Moreover, as the war progressed, the issue of objection to particular wars, on the one hand, and forms of alternative service, on the other, continued to be debated (Jordens 1989b; Smith 1990). A majority of Australians were against sending conscripts to Vietnam even when a majority supported the war per se (Curthoys 1990: 151; Goot and Tiffen 1983: 142–3). Such popular opposition to overseas conscription further fueled the argument for a right to object to a particular war. Additional evidence is in Tables 7.1 and 7.2. They indicate a steady rise in the number of applications and upward trends in approval of c.o. applications and the granting of total exemptions in comparison with noncombatant exemptions.

183

Table 7.3. *Australian public opinion on war and on conscription, 1962–1968*

Question: Continue to fight in Vietnam?

Date	Continue (%)	Bring back (%)	Undecided (%)
September 1965	56.4	28.0	15.6
February 1966	70.5	22.5	7.0
September 1966	61.5	25.9	12.5
March 1967	72.6	21.5	5.9
April 1968	68.4	25.9	5.7

Public opinion polls on conscription[a]

Date	For (%)	Against (%)	Undecided (%)
June 1962	67	27	6
August 1963	69	27	4
November 1964	71	25	4
April 1965	68	29	3
September 1965	69	23	8
May 1966	63	31	6
July 1966	68	26	6
November 1966	63	33	4
June 1967	57	40	3
December 1967	70	25	5

Public opinion polls on sending conscripts to Vietnam

Date	For (%)	Against (%)	Undecided (%)
December 1965	37	52	11
February 1966	33	56	11
May 1966	38	49	13
July 1966	38	52	10
August 1966[b]	36	63	1
November 1966	38	51	11

[a] Forward (1968: 128) notes that the April 1965 and June 1967 polls were taken of a sample of 15–20 year olds. The others were taken of a sample of adults.
[b] This poll was taken by Australian Sale Research Bureau from a random sample of 16-25 year olds. It is reproduced in Forward (1968: 129).
Source: From Australian Gallup polls.

There was a marked rise in c.o. applications from World War I to World War II and an even more marked rise during the Vietnam War. Smith (1989: 17) calculates that about 1 percent of all who served as conscripts applied for c.o. status in World War II. Of the 51,272 of those who were balloted in and enlisted during Vietnam, it was closer to 2 percent who applied.[10] This clearly represents an increase in contingent conscientious objection since there is little evidence of any significant jump in membership in pacifist churches. Institutions are part of the story, but equally important must be the opportunity costs of service in the military relative to the costs of objection. While there was some threat to the Australian continent during World War I, it was minimal. There were actual bombings of Australia during World War II, and the probability of being in combat increased for those who stayed home. Only during Vietnam was conscientious objection an objection to near certain combatant military duties. Thus, it is no surprise that the percentage of applicants for conscientious objection during Vietnam was nearly twice that of World War II, and that it was more of an issue in World War II than in World War I.

At the same time that the costs of service went up, the costs of conscientious objection went down. They were not uniform, however, across Australian states during Vietnam, and the reliance on conscientious objection tended to reflect the differences. What is even more interesting is the variation in reliance in conscientious objection over the course of the war in Vietnam. If changes in cost cannot account for this variation, then perhaps shifts in ethical evaluations of conscription or the war itself can.

France

France has a very different tradition of military service than the other countries in the study and a quite distinct history of conscientious objection. The linked concepts of the "nation in arms" and the citizen-soldier make universal military service not only a legal obligation but a mark of citizenship. For nearly two hundred years national military service has been a rite of passage for virtually every French male. Nor were there debates over the introduction of conscription at the commencement of each war; conscription was already firmly in place.

The relative lack of controversy over universal military service did not mean, however, the absence of dissent. Self-inflicted wounds, draft dodging, insubordination, desertion, and protests in the streets constituted the traditional French repertoire of weapons against war and military service. What was missing was conscientious objection. The French legal tradition had little place for such an individual expression

---

[10] The figures are rough in both cases. Smith (1989) uses Hasluck's figures on c.o.s and his own estimates of approximately 250,000 enlistees. The Vietnam figure is crafted from statistics provided on actual enlistment in Australia House of Representatives (1970a: 73, 1971c: 279). The figures on conscientious objection are drawn from Tables I and II for the years 1965–mid 1971.

of conscience, and traditional peace church members were few and relatively weak politically in this largely Catholic country.

Universal conscription was first introduced in France under the French Revolution. There were exemptions on religious grounds, but these were granted only to Anabaptists. Quakers were refused exemption. Napoleon I, on the other hand, regularly provided exemptions to members of a variety of dissenting religions in countries conquered by France. There was, however, no legal recognition of the status of conscientious objector. Nor did any such recognition in law take place until 1963. Consequently, the use of this means to refuse consent is relatively low compared to the United States and Australia.

Prior to 1920, there was no serious discussion of conscientious objection in France. *Insoumis,* rebels and insubordinates, and *réfractaires,* draft dodgers, were a serious problem for the government at times (Auvray 1983; Meyer-Spiegler 1969: 100–3). There were also serious problems with desertions and mutinies during World War I (Pedroncini 1968). Despite some significant opposition to World War I by parts of the union moment,[11] the issue of conscientious objection was not a matter of public discussion until lobbying for a law commenced in the 1920s and 1930s (Auvray 1983: 174; Martial 1984: 15). Ingram's excellent accounts (1991a, b) of this early debate reveal that the concept of conscientious objection was so foreign that the French did not even have the concept in their vocabulary until the 1920s or in their dictionaries until the 1930s. Moreover, he argues, while government officials feared the sabotaging effect of conscientious objection on the "nation in arms," leaders of the pacifist movement also expressed concern about this individualist and "negative" course of action. During World War II, there were perhaps a dozen c.o.s (Sablière 1963: 21) before France was occupied.

To the extent that there was a movement for conscientious objection during wartime, it existed in the 1950s and early 1960s. France engaged in two wars of note, the war in Indochina (1949–52) and the Algerian War (1955–62). Opposition to the war in Indochina was organized by the Communist Party and the Mouvement de la Paix, who led large demonstrations against it. The only significant act of conscientious ob-

---

[11] The Confédération Générale du Travail (CGT), composing approximately 6 percent of the potentially unionized workforce (Horne 1991: 15), maintained its prewar position of opposition to a national mobilization until 1914. Its 1912 congress proclaimed that the CGT "does not recognize the right of the bourgeois state to dispose of the working class" (cited in Horne 1991: 27). However, upon the declaration of war, the leaders of the CGT and the Parti Socialiste immediately aligned themselves with the nationalist republican traditions of France and with the "nation in arms"; they identified the defense of democracy with the progress of trade unionism (Horne 1991: 43–7).

jection, however, was by one Henri Martin, who became a martyr after being accused of and condemned for sabotage, demoralizing the army, and so on (Meyer-Spiegler 1969: 313–33; Verlet 1967: 29).

The war in Indochina was fought primarily by professionals and the Foreign Legion, rather than conscripts (Silver 1994: 18; Meyer-Spiegler 1969: 292). Thus, it is not totally surprising how little conscientious objection there was during this period. Meyer-Spiegler reports a total of fourteen c.o.s in 1950, of whom nearly all were Jehovah's Witnesses (1969: 233–4).

The Algerian War was more controversial and did involve sending conscripts to serve in Algeria. There was political opposition but nowhere near on the scale provoked by U.S. or Australian involvement in Vietnam. The French protests began as early as 1955, when those who had completed their military service were recalled (Meyer-Spiegler 1969: 337–54; Auvray 1983: 216–19). These first protesters were vocal but generally stayed within the bounds of legality. Over the course of the war, however, there seems to have been a marked increase in draft dodging, desertion, and other forms of noncooperation with the military. According to some accounts, three to four thousand youths deserted or fled to Switzerland (Martial 1984: 20–1; Verlet 1967). The alternative was to serve in a wartime army or spend time in prison. The noncooperators were generally allied with the "Jeune Résistance" started by maybe a dozen draft dodgers around 1959 but becoming a significant political force by 1962 (Auvray 1983: 222–3; Verlet 1967).

There were people who called themselves conscientious objectors throughout the 1950s and early 1960s, but few chose this difficult route. In the absence of a statute legalizing and regulating conscientious objection, there was no way for an individual to object legally to participation in military service. This meant the only alternative was some act of disobedience against the military. The determination of the offense and punishment was by the military with no consideration to be given to motive. The most frequent offenses were failure to report for duty and refusal to carry out orders, usually the order to don the uniform or to engage in weaponry training. Failure to turn up carried a sentence of one to two months in military prison during peacetime and two to ten years during war; officers were dismissed (Sablière 1963: 41–2). Disobedience was punishable by one to two years (Sablière 1963: 42–3). Disobedience seems to have been the more frequent, perhaps, as Sablière claims (1963: 60), because most individuals desired to indicate their submission to the state, if not to military service. It may also have had to do with the considerably lesser amount of prison time during war.

None of the time spent in the brig awaiting trial or serving one's sentence was credited as time in the military (Sablière 1963: 60, 65). The military could return to prison a man who once again refused to report for duty or to obey orders. Recidivism was reduced somewhat by discharges granted after the first imprisonment for reasons of health and by forfeiture of French citizenship. Ninety-three objectors were discharged, and seventeen forfeited citizenry in the post–World War II period (Sablière 1963: 76–7).

There were, at the most, no more than 500 c.o.s altogether between 1950 and 1962 or not quite 0.02 percent of approximately 3 million young men called up.[12] Approximately 80 percent of those who have been labeled c.o.s. were Jehovah's Witnesses.

The numbers did go up sharply in the late 1950s, but at the highest point, 1961, only 65 went to court, of whom 50 were Jehovah's Witnesses (Meyer-Spiegler 1969: 233–6; Sablière 1963: 51–4). Even during the Algerian War, most of those who sought recognition as conscientious objectors were members of traditional peace churches, Jehovah's Witnesses, and anarchists. These last two groups tended to be absolutists. They denied the right of the state to require their service in any form.

During the period of the Algerian War there was a movement to introduce a statute on conscientious objection as well as to improve the abysmal conditions for those already convicted. Anarchists, particularly Louis Lecoin, played a crucial role in these campaigns. In 1957, he founded *Liberté,* which was the organ of the Committee to Help Objectors (Martial 1984: 19). His actions are credited for the institution, in 1958, of a five-year limit on prison terms for c.o.s and the release of nine out of ninety c.o.s currently in prison who had already served five years (Sablière 1963: 155–206; Martial 1984: 19–20).

When the war ended, there was still no statute on the books. In June 1962 Lecoin, then aged 74, commenced a highly publicized hunger strike. In 1963 the first French statute authorizing conscientious objection finally appeared.[13] It had some peculiar features, however. It required c.o.s to spend twice as much time in noncombatant or civilian service as the length of service required of those who did not object. It also made it illegal to propagandize, that is inform others, about the existence of the statute. Finally, it required a written explanation of one's reasons for requesting exemption, and this explanation had to be

---

[12] These figures are compiled from a single onion-skin sheet entitled *"ETAT de renseignements statistiques: Effectif appelés sous les drapeaux."* The sheet was found in an unnamed file of materials on conscription provided to Margaret Levi by the Service Historique Armée de la Terre when she visited their archives in Vincennes in July 1990. It lists the young men called up in the various services and the totals for 1945–65. Other figures are from Martin (1993: 84), who estimates that there were less than one hundred c.o.s between 1945 and 1955 and only about two hundred in the early 1960s.

[13] For a discussion of the 1963 and subsequent laws, see Martin (1993: 80–97).

submitted within a very short and precise time. The determination was then done in a closed session by a juridical committee, half of whose members were from the military. Neither the c.o. applicant nor his counsel could present oral argument (Martial 1984: 22–6).

The problems of implementation and the increasing number of applications led to renewed political pressure to liberalize the statute. The 1970 transformation of the universal and compulsory military obligation to an obligation to serve the nation in one of a variety of ways added a further pressure.[14] The Jehovah's Witnesses increased in size during this period and also increased in terms of their members making requests to be recognized as religious objectors, but the largest increase was among those who framed their conscientious objection in political and ideological terms (Martin 1993: 88). The year 1983 represents the most recent liberalization of the law affecting c.o.s. They can now be part of a civilian service. The result is greater legal tolerance of c.o.s and a significant increase in their numbers. They still have to perform a longer length of service than those who join the military, but it has become easier to apply, easier to get one's application approved, and easier to actually engage in alternative service. Moreover, it is now legal to publicize the possibility of being a c.o.

Even in France, where it was so difficult to be a conscientious objector, there was a rise in reliance on its usage during the post–World War II period, the only period for which there are data. The numbers are small, but there is nonetheless a fairly steady rise (Table 7.4). The historical narrative suggests that two factors probably contributed to this rise. The first was the unpopularity, among some, of the Algerian War. The second was the liberalization of the treatment of c.o.s, particularly in the wake of Louis Lecoin's 1957 campaign.

Consideration of the numbers of applications and exemptions since 1971 highlights the importance of institutional arrangements (Figure 7.6). There is a particularly big jump in both applications and acceptance following the legal changes of 1983. In 1987 the number accepted as c.o.s went to 2,616 (République Française SIRPA 1989: 16) and in 1988 to 2,379 (République Française SIRPA 1990: 16). Since these figures represent national service during peacetime, it is not possible to gauge the effect of an unpopular war. However, should some future war begin to use conscripts and be the object of protest, there should be a corresponding and fairly significant rise in applications for conscientious objection.

---

[14] Interview with Geneviève Pietri, Chef du bureau, Protocole, Armée Jeunesse, Ministère de la défense, Paris, 2 July 1990.

Table 7.4. *Conscientious objection in France, 1945–62*

Year	Number of c.o.s imprisoned	Number of men called	Percentage c.o.s imprisoned
1945	0	244,907	0.000
1946	0	166,637	0.000
1947	0	211,931	0.000
1948	3	264,686	0.001
1949	5	203,680	0.001
1950	16	233,117	0.007
1951	11	227,231	0.005
1952	19	224,424	0.008
1953	15	179,456	0.008
1954	20	233,196	0.009
1955	15	236,519	0.008
1956	21	365,072	0.006
1957	23	248,003	0.009
1958	40	234,989	0.017
1959	45	249,589	0.018
1960	30	201,929	0.014
1961	65	262,202	0.025
1962	49	265,111	0.018

Source: Calculated from the Ministère de la Défense (France), "Bilans Officiels," found in the files of the Service Historique de l'Armée de Terre, Vincennes; and Sablier (1963).

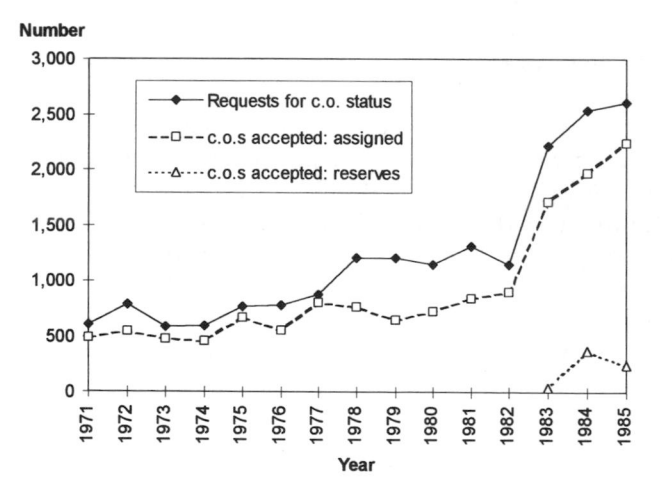

Figure 7.6. Conscientious objectors in France, 1971–85 (France Ministère de la Défense 1985: Bilan C12).

VARIATION AMONG COUNTRIES

There is not only variation in applications for and acceptance of conscientious objection over time. There is also considerable variation among countries for the same or similar wars. Both the United States and Australia sent conscripts to fight in Vietnam, and from 1954 to 1962 France sent conscripts to Algeria. All three of these wars evoked serious protest movements in their home countries, and the use of conscientious objection rose relative to its use in previous wars. The reliance on this weapon against war varied quite widely among the three countries, however. During the Vietnam War, the percentage of U.S. registrants who applied for c.o. status has been estimated as slightly over 0.4 percent while the percentage of the Australian registrants was slightly over 0.1 percent.[15] In France, of course, there was no legal way to be a c.o., and the number of illegal c.o.s was tiny.

To what extent might this variation be accounted for by (1) differences in institutional arrangements that affected the costs of being a c.o.; (2) differences in perceptions of the legitimacy of the war; and (3) differences in perceptions of the fairness of conscription? On all of these dimensions, France raises the greatest obstacles to contingent conscientious objection, the United States the fewest, and Australia lies between them (although closer to the United States than to France).

What most clearly distinguishes France from Australia and the United States is the extent to which its institutional arrangements created disincentives to apply for c.o. status and become a c.o. The costs were considerably lower in the United States and Australia. Both countries had statutes that legalized conscientious objection and permitted objections on nonreligious grounds. It was, however, somewhat more difficult to apply and qualify in Australia.

Institutional factors may also account for the difference between rates of conscientious objection in the United States and Australia. In the United States a young man could apply and was best off applying for c.o. status upon registering for the draft. Australians applied only after being drafted, that is balloted in, and passing the medical exam. Thus, one should expect that a smaller percentage of Australians would apply, *ceteris paribus*. Moreover, in the United States, the initial determination

---

[15] Approximately 2 percent of those who actually served were c.o.s, but only 0.1 percent of the total pool of registrants. Of those who were balloted in, that is actually drafted, the percentage was closer to 0.6 percent. Unfortunately, however, we do not yet have comparable figures for the United States. The Australian statistics are drawn from available numbers on c.o.s through 1972, as presented in Table III, available figures on registrants (Australia House of Representatives 1972a: 3443–4), and available figures on numbers balloted in through 1970 (Australia House of Representatives 1971a: 623–4).

was made by the applicant's local draft board, and the draft boards varied in their tolerance and in their susceptibility to influence. In Australia all applicants had to go to court from the very beginning.

It is not the case that there were more alternatives available to Australians. Deferments were harder to get, and leaving the country carried similar costs in both countries. There was a large number of individuals who joined the Citizen Military Force (Jordens 1989b: 20–1), but there was a large number of Americans who joined the National Guard.

Australia did experience a rise in violations of their military service requirements. Nearly 12,000 youths failed to register between 1965 and 1971, with an average annual number of prosecutions being 202 until a crackdown in 1971–72 that produced 723 prosecutions (Australia House of Representatives 1972a: 3443–4; Jordens 1989b: 21). According to the Minister of the Department of Labour and National Service, there were 1,625 prosecutions for failure to register between 1968 and the middle of 1972, but only thirteen were imprisoned out of about 38,000 enlisted.[16] In addition between 1965 and 1971, an average of sixteen persons per year failed to attend their medical (Jordens 1989b: 70).

The extent of national service violations indicates that there may have been some serious reluctance about being part of the military effort. The data also suggest, however, a relative paucity of institutional disincentives. There were few prosecutions and even fewer jail sentences. While it is clear that there was a decline in punitive action in the United States during Vietnam relative to the past (Figure 7.1), it is not clear whether U.S. or Australian institutions were more tolerant of these violations. Thus, the only clear-cut distinction is in the institutional arrangements that facilitated applications by Americans relative to Australians.

In all three of the countries, c.o. applications increased with an increase in distrust of government, if unpopularity of the government's war effort can be taken as an indicator of growing loss of confidence in government. Certainly, unpopularity of a war indicates that citizens do not trust the government sufficiently to take the word of its spokespersons that war is worth fighting. The countries varied on this dimension as well as in their institutional arrangements. French protests during the Algerian War never reached the proportions of those against the Vietnam War in Australia, whose protest movement rivaled that in the United States. However, opinion polls indicate that Australians were more likely to approve the war than American citizens (Figure 7.4 and Table 7.2).

[16] Australia Ministry for Labour and National Service (1972: 1). The figures provided, although official, are not consistent with some of the other official figures, which suggest that out of 761,854 young men who turned twenty during this period, 53,315 failed to register between 1965 and 1972. See Australia House of Representatives (1972a: 3443–4).

Analysis

It is hardly the case that the French are less contentious than the Australians or Americans. What may enter in here, along with institutions, are very different perceptions of the fairness of conscription. A curvilinear perception of fairness emerges from the narrative.[17] The least antagonism to conscription occurred in France, where the obligation for military service is a relatively unquestioned part of growing up a French male. U.S. citizens expressed the strongest sense of the violation of the norms of fairness. Deferments were rampant and class-biased. Many felt the draft lottery, which was in use for part of the war in Vietnam and earlier, was a trivial and unfair basis for being sent to war, especially when it was revealed to be nonrandom. In Australia there were also issues of fairness regarding conscription but not nearly so many as in the United States. It is simply a matter of bad luck if your year comes up when there is a war. Australian young men have had to engage in compulsory national training since the beginning of the century. However, until the war in Vietnam, it was an individual's choice whether to participate in overseas combat. Vietnam marked a significant change in conscription policy. In terms of acceptance of national service, Australia falls in the middle between France and the United States. Although the eligible in both Australia and the United States had reasons to raise questions about the fairness of the system, the inequities of the American system were more clear-cut.

ANALYSIS

The hypotheses that follow from the model of ideological disobedience suggest that the most important factor in accounting for a rise in conscientious objection should be membership in traditional pacifist religions. There is no question that the United States has a larger population of members of dissenting, including pacifist, religions and that France has the smallest. This is undoubtedly part of the explanation in the variation among the countries. Moreover, in all of these countries, the membership in the Jehovah's Witnesses did experience a rise. In France, an increase in the numbers of Jehovah's Witnesses accounts for some of the rise in c.o.s since 1963, but the secularization of conscientious objection appears to be the more important determinant of the overall rise in applications (Martin 1993: 88–9). In Australia, membership in the Jehovah's Witnesses more than doubled between 1961 and 1971 (Vamplew 1987: 427) and continues to rise (Australian Commonwealth Bureau of Statistics 1965: 290, Table 74; 1974: 149; 1983: 12, Table 13; 1990: 373), but Jehovah's Witnesses were barred from being c.o.s and so

---

[17] Russell Hardin suggested this point.

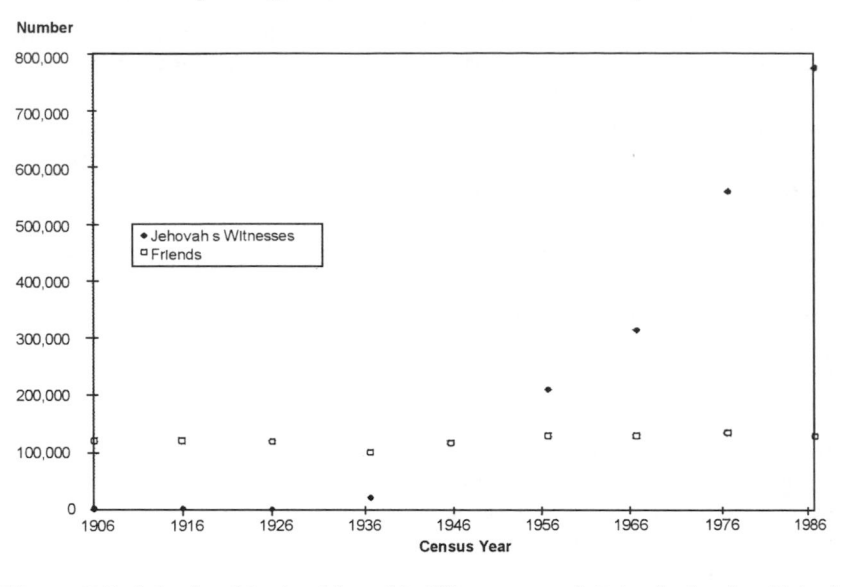

Figure 7.7. Membership in Jehovah's Witnesses and Friends in the United States, 1906–87 (U.S. Census 1906: 25, 343; 1916: 20, 350; 1926: 86; Armitage 1919: 199; Stelzle 1931: 260; Weber 1939: 15, 94; Landis 1958: 60, 261; Whitman 1969: 45, 172–4. Jacquet 1989: 241–3).

cannot account for the increase in conscientious objection in the 1960s and early 1970s. In the United States the Jehovah's Witnesses did experience a rise in membership, but, as was already demonstrated (Figure 7.2), they still account for only a small proportion of the conscientious objectors. Only the United States has figures on Quakers, and none of the countries has adequate figures on other possible peace churches. There was virtually no increase between 1957 and 1967 in the United States among those who identified themselves as Quakers and only a slight increase after those years (Figure 7.7). Thus, neither the literature nor the statistics attribute to religious affiliation the dramatic increases in conscientious objection during the war in Vietnam in either Australia or the United States.

Some skeptics might argue that all contingent conscientious objection can ultimately be reduced to egoistic motivations and egoistic cost–benefit calculations. One reason why some individuals were willing to pay such a high price is that they would have paid a higher price for joining the military. Indeed, if we push this line hard enough, even the absolutists are narrowly rationalist in that they tend to reside in communities that may make it more costly for them to engage in military action than to spend time in jail resisting the service. Both religious and

194

political pacifists actually are affected by two, often competing, reference groups, one national and one local. If they highly prize their association with a particular religious or political group that requires conscientious objection, expulsion from the group may represent a higher cost than the jail sentence imposed by the state. The Christadelphians, for example, "defellowshipped" any member who failed to reject all service. On the other hand, the Quakers, Brethrens, and most other religious and political groups that encouraged conscientious objection made even conscientious objection a matter of individual conscience (Sibley and Jacob 1988). Moreover, evidence of social pressure does not negate the intensity of the ideological commitments of pacifists, Jehovah's Witnesses, and those with intensely held political allegiances, especially in liberal democracies where there are considerable opportunities for exit from groups that demand more than their adherents are willing to supply (Hechter 1987).

More interesting is how few conscientious objectors there are, how few individuals are willing to pay such a high price for their convictions. This lends credence to the argument that most individuals, most of the time, are rational in the sense that they choose the option with the highest net benefit.

In considering the cross-time and cross-country variation in the use of conscientious objection, it is apparent that when the costs of being a c.o. are extremely high, as they were in all countries during World War I and in France until the 1960s, only those who are moral absolutists are willing to pay the price. As the costs go down, more of those who are contingent dissenters become contingent conscientious objectors. Between World Wars I and II, there were both institutional liberalization and an increase in the perceived acceptability of the war. It was easier to become a c.o. during World War II, but there was less reason to. Even so, conscientious objection went up, and it went up even more in subsequent wars – in all the countries under study. There is no precise way to determine whether conscientious objection rose less than one would expect given the lower costs. Clearly the reduction in institutional barriers contributes to the rise in this form of dissent.

Institutional change

There are several possible arguments that might account for the changes in institutional arrangements that lowered the costs of contingent conscientious objection. One argument that may account for origins but not change is religious culture. There is no denying that religious differences are crucial to an explanation of the origins of the institutional arrangements affecting conscientious objection. Nor can one deny the importance of the rights tradition. France, with its predominantly Catholic population, does not have the same history of pacifist churches and dissenting religions as does the United States; Australia lies in the middle. The effects of such a cultural factor, however, are mediated through institutions. It is the rules, the material incentives and disincentives – not socialization – that are doing most of the work. Even in France, with its citizenry's commitment to "the nation," its statism, and its relatively high degree of Catholicism, a lowering of the costs of becoming a conscientious objector (or doing other kinds of alternative service) significantly increased the numbers who applied and qualified, even controlling for the increase in the membership of the Jehovah's Witnesses.

Another form of the political culture argument has to do with the steady increase in the extension and consciousness of rights throughout the Western world during the twentieth century. Certainly the direction of change in all three countries, and in most others (see Moskos and Chambers eds. 1993), is toward reduction of the costs of being a c.o. Undoubtedly, greater legal and administrative tolerance of c.o.s is one effect of a secular trend, but the general revolution in rights cannot adequately account for the timing of the changes in the rules nor for the variation among countries. Consciousness of rights may be an important factor in accounting for the willingness to express dissent in general and to claim conscientious objector status in particular, and certainly an increased tolerance of such expressions and claims considerably reduces the costs of behaviorally refusing consent. However, consciousness of rights becomes relevant only if there is a sense that rights are being violated. The existence of what some perceive as an unjust war, a noncredible government, or an unfair conscription system must also be part of the model.

Another explanation would emphasize social control.[18] The rules and the implementation of the rules almost always change in wartime. That is when the institution of conscientious objection becomes most salient for conscripts, but the timing also may reflect government attempts to promote public support for the war effort. Since so much of the increased tolerance for c.o.s was produced through administrative implementation rather than actual legislative change, the government retained its ability to be more repressive or to buy off discontent as needed. Neither the Korean nor Vietnamese wars required full mobilization, and thus the government could afford even more exemptions from combat during these conflicts. Of course, the government response may not have reflected social control at all but rather simple expediency. Given that only a relatively small proportion of potential draftees were necessary to

---

[18] Fred Block suggested this argument.

Analysis

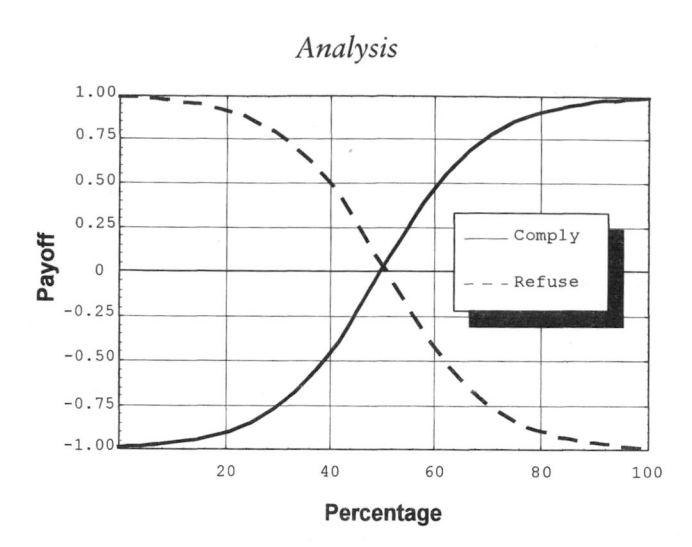

Figure 7.8. Schelling diagram of ethical reciprocity. (Diagram developed by Kjell Hausken as part of our jointly authored paper [in progress].)

the war effort, it was less politically and financially costly to exempt dissenters or give them alternative service than to let them continue as troublemakers, in the army or out. Although a social control argument or an administrative expediency argument can account for the correlation between institutional change and war, these arguments cannot account for either the precise timing or the content of the change.

The model of contingent consent offers a somewhat different interpretation and the one most consistent with the evidence. According to the model, when there is less contingent consent, there are fewer who comply. The percentage complying has some effect on the extent of social pressure to conform with the given norm of a reference group, but it has an even stronger effect on ethical reciprocity. Evidence of noncompliance increases the probability of contingent refusal to consent, which in turn further decreases noncompliance. The Schelling diagram has the form shown in Figure 7.8.

Institutional change in conscientious objection is in response to increased political pressure on government by constituents and actors with moral clout and good publicity campaigns. Crucial to this effort is the existence of individuals who are willing to proclaim themselves conscientious objectors and, if necessary, go to court or jail as a consequence. The effect is to use the existing institution of conscientious objection to create a social expectation that refusal to consent to conscription as mandated is a legitimate and normatively acceptable act. Those who suffer punishments for being conscientious objectors illuminate an unattractive government policy and subsequently mobilize media and public opinion against it. Arguably, the moral absolutists and even the first of the contingent conscientious objectors play the role the initial activists in the Civil Rights Movement played: their combined actions produce the threshold at which others are then willing to join the movement (Chong 1991). The considerable popular agitation against the war in Vietnam and the well-publicized and widespread draft resistance presented clear evidence that many young men were not supporting the war effort. This evident breakdown in contingent consent probably encouraged even more refusal to consent, and conscientious objection was one of its forms.[19] This in turn created pressure on government to develop policy more in keeping with what had become the popular ethical concerns.

When the attack on government could be mollified by administrative reinterpretation of the rules or by an amnesty, this was done, leaving the rules themselves intact. When public agitation could be assuaged only by actual rule modification, that was the course of action chosen. In all cases, however, the change follows a major publicity campaign and is incremental in nature.

The evidence suggests that there were both ethical concerns and egoistic calculations of the costs and benefits in the decision to become a conscientious objector. This is, possibly, a case where both moral commitments and egoistic motivations operate in the same direction. The institution of conscientious objection is both a reflection and a source of the ethical concerns that promote conscientious objection. Its very existence legitimizes this weapon against war. Its publicized use by even a few may make others aware of ethical arguments against the war and conscription and may make others more willing to refuse their consent.

CONCLUSION

What is particularly noteworthy in this chapter is how few individuals are willing to sacrifice so much for their beliefs and how many individuals are willing to sacrifice something. The investigation of conscientious objection permits some insight into the changing relationship between citizen and the state and, especially, into the changing concept of the citizen soldier in democracies.[20] Conscientious objection, at first glance,

---

[19] Fred Block noted that a certain amount of social learning probably went on during the course of wars, especially the Vietnam War. The parents of boys and the boys themselves learned that years before registration, they should start establishing their credentials as c.o.s. Thus, by the late 1960s and early 1970s more potential contingent dissenters were prepared to become c.o.s.

[20] See Moskos and Chambers (1993) for an illuminating discussion of these changing relationships and concepts. Also, see Cohen (1985) and Silver (1994).

seems an unambiguous expression of morality, a clear-cut example of moral convictions as the dominant element in the individual's decision calculus. The existence of conscientious objectors seems to falsify the claim, made by some neoclassical economists (e.g. Stigler and Becker 1977), that virtually all action can be explained by the calculation of costs and benefits. It may undermine even the weaker claim that ideologies play a role in decision making but are cost sensitive (Brennan and Lomasky 1989; North 1990: 44).

Although institutional tolerance of both dissent and conscientious objection significantly lowered the costs of contingent conscientious objection, it still required a considerable commitment. Moreover, there remained some forms of dissent for which there was little tolerance and very high costs. Jeopardizing citizenship by leaving the country is an example. If a reduction in costs was the only element in the calculation, then there were far less costly forms of action, especially in the United States during Vietnam, when various deferments and exemptions were possible. Even a short jail stint was probably less costly than eternal exile. Nonetheless, during Vietnam nearly 40,000 Americans chose very high costs indeed when they emigrated to Canada or Sweden; there was no reason to anticipate the subsequent Carter amnesty (Baskir and Strauss 1977: 14). In France three to four thousand military-eligible youths may have deserted or fled to Switzerland during the Algerian War (Martin 1993: 20–1; Verlet 1967).

Variation in requests for conscientious objector status is one indicator, albeit a rough indicator, of the perceived legitimacy of government and the fairness of the conscription system. Its use as an indicator, let alone as a weapon against war, is largely determined, however, by the institutional arrangements that delimit its availability. Such an institution affects the costs of becoming a conscientious objector. Equally importantly, it shapes the ethical concerns and reciprocity that make possible its further use and that encourage legal dissent against war.

8

The democratization of compliance

. . . science started and ended in observation, and theory should always be
endangered by it.
   Norman Maclean (*Young Men and Fire:* 137)

All history is written backwards. . . . We choose a significant event and
examine its causes and its consequences, but who decides whether the
event is significant? We do, and we are here; and it and time, they are in
our hands. . . . We make them fight their battles over again for our
edification and pleasure, who fought them once for entirely other reasons.
   Margaret Atwood (*The Robber Bride:* 123)

Governance by consent is extremely demanding of both governments
and their citizens, but it is less costly and less dangerous than governance
by coercion. While there is a strong coercive element to all governments,
whatever the regime form, democracy's maintenance requires, as well, a
significant degree of voluntary and active compliance. This is not the
once-and-forever consent to a social contract that Hobbes elaborated,
nor is it the generational and large-scale contract renewal of Locke. It is,
instead, the felt and activated obligation to cooperate with the demands
of government in those domains that are constitutive of citizenship and
citizenship rights.

These are among the lessons of the historical events and struggles
recounted here. The model of contingent consent has been endangered
by observations and alternative explanations. It survives the test of
plausibility and sheds considerable light on compliance and consent in
democracies.

This last chapter reviews the dominant theories of consent and obligation within democracies and their relationship to the model of contingent consent. It then turns to what the investigation of military service
policies teaches about normative and institutional change and to the

200

extent that other research supports or contradicts these findings. The final section reconsiders the relationship between rationality, ethics, and consent within democracies.

THEORIES OF CONSENT AND OBLIGATION

Political consent is an act granting permission to a government to proceed in making and implementing laws. It implies some commonality of interest between those giving and those receiving consent, but it does not necessarily connote approval of particular laws and policies. Some group or another seems always to be taking exception to the way in which government intervenes in their members' lives. The question of when antipathy to government translates into a justifiable right to resist government continues to vex political theorists. Most classical political theory concerns itself with consent to a regime, but more recent theorists include in their compass both general consent and consent to a specific course of action.

The linked themes of consent and resistance to government have been major subjects in political theory since John Locke's *Two Treatises on Government* (1965 [1690]). Locke not only posits consent as essential to legitimate government but also claims that citizens have the right to rebel against unjustified authority. For Locke dissent embodies rebellion, but consent is tacit and implied. Continuing to live in a community or even crossing one of its public highways constitutes acceptance of the regime that maintains that highway. Writing long before the ballot and other forms of legal participation by citizens in politics, Locke did not concern himself with ongoing active consent. At the heart of both his notion of consent and that of Hobbes are explicit and voluntary social contracts between the citizens and their governors.[1]

Discussions of the role and meaning of citizen consent continued through the centuries (see esp. Green 1967 [1907]), but the recent debate began in the 1960s. The interest in consent is an analogue to the independence movements of colonial peoples, the Civil Rights movement in the United States, the repression experienced by those living under dictatorial regimes, and the war in Vietnam. Contemporary theorists generally follow Locke in arguing that consent requires evidence of benefits from membership in the polity and that acceptance of those benefits obligates citizens to perform the duties expected of members. However, they also argued that consent has different characteristics in democracies than it did in the period in which Locke lived. Crossing the

---

[1] Hardin (forthcoming) argues that such a social contract is empirically nonsensical.

street or even remaining in the country are problematic criteria that fail to capture the intention of the actor.

Among those who argue for a theory in which obligations are attendant on express consent are Tussman (1960) and Walzer (1970). As Tussman (1960: 36) put it:

There is a necessary condition which must be satisfied *whatever* is proposed as a sign of tacit consent. That is, the act can only be properly taken as 'consent' if it is done 'knowingly,' if it is understood by the one performing the act that his action involves his acceptance of the obligations of membership.

For Walzer (1970: 111–12) express consent implies an explicit act best proclaimed through "meaningful participation" or some other indicator of active support of the government and intention to become a full citizen.

Many other contemporary theorists are less than sanguine about the possibility of developing a consent-based theory of political obligation – even if its purpose is to justify dissent. Plamenatz (1968) questions whether consent is the sole basis for duty, and Simmons (1979) finds incoherent the arguments that link the two concepts of consent and obligation. To Pateman (1979) the term consent has no real meaning; she argues that coercion is the defining characteristic of the modern state and, therefore, citizen action is coerced and not consensual. For Herzog (1989) at issue is the morality of the relationship that consent entails. His metaphor of the "happy slave" raises the concern that individuals can agree to participate in a social system that is morally unacceptable. It is difficult to live in the shadow of Nazi Germany or Pol Pot's Cambodia or Apartheid South Africa and not recognize the all too numerous instances in which members of a polity have actively participated in and generally consented with a horrific regime.

Lack of intention, philosophical incoherence, the belief that government is force, and the immorality of particular governments are powerful arguments against consent as the basis for political obligation. As inspiring as these authors are, however, they take us away from the task at hand: identifying behavioral consent and explaining its variation. The enterprise of these theorists is to provide the basis for moral action. The purpose of this book is to provide an empirical political theory to account for the how, when, and why of action. The question here is not whether moral principles and ethical evaluations should motivate behavior but whether they do.

Max Weber, as is often the case, comes to the rescue. His combined interest in explanation and institutional design allows him to consider what accounts for variation in behavior and, in addition, evaluate the effectiveness of certain institutional arrangements against the standards of normative criteria such as democracy and efficiency. For Weber, willing obedience to law is most likely when the law emanates from "a voluntary agreement of the interested parties" or is imposed "by an authority which is held to be legitimate and therefore meets with compliance" (1968: 36).

To identify the attributes of legitimate authority is the daunting task Weber lays before us. He himself dedicates considerable space in *Economy and Society* (1968) to this project. Political theory also offers guidance as to the criteria citizens might, and probably do, use. Pitkin (1966: 39–40), for example, argues that, "Your obligation depends not on whether you have consented but whether your government is such that you *ought* to consent to it [her emphasis]." She offers both procedural and substantive criteria for assessing whether a government deserves consent (1966). Klosko (1992) emphasizes the requirements of a presumptive benefit and an arrangement of mutual cooperation; for him the criterion is the fairness of the policy in its extractions and distributions.

The most relevant argument for empirical theorists concerned with assessing when government might expect more or less compliance comes from Brian Barry's *Justice as Impartiality* (1995). Inspired by recent theorists of justice, especially Thomas Scanlon (1982, 1988), Barry (1995: 11) argues for "principles and rules that are capable of forming the basis of free agreement among people seeking agreement on reasonable terms." He eschews substantive criteria in favor of procedural requirements that presume the superiority of no particular view. His is an account of rational individuals who seek to be able to defend their actions to others by an appeal to having behaved fairly; and of institutional arrangements that give them confidence that they, in turn, have been treated fairly by the government demanding their compliance.

Barry offers a standard for evaluating government authority (1995: 164): "To the extent that the major institutions conform to the demands of justice as impartiality they are legitimate. This means that the members of the society can justifiably demand the cooperation of others in maintaining those institutions." What it means for a government to conform involves procedures that ensure adequate dispersal of information about the effects of a policy, recognition and due consideration in the decision-making process of the interests of all concerned actors regardless of social identity, and impartial implementation. Essential are educational, media, voting, and other institutions that ensure the possibility of good information and relatively equal access to government.

Justice as impartiality is not available to every society as an operative criterion for institutional design. Where social war rages, might – and not justice – defines policy. Where a powerful group can enforce rules that enslave or disadvantage individuals on the basis of ascriptive or cultural characteristics, injustice prevails. The prerequisites of a society that meets the high standard of justice as impartiality are widespread commitments not only to the avoidance of conflict, and, if possible, the achievement of consensus but also to equality among citizens. A society that lacks these conditions may be operating according to prevailing beliefs about the meaning of justice but not according to justice as impartiality (1995:113–14).

Just what does all this have to do with explaining behavioral consent? A central argument in *Of Rule and Revenue* (Levi 1988) is that compliance by citizens is a quid pro quo for services provided by government. A major argument of this book is that voluntary compliance in democracies requires that quid pro quo plus fair and impartial treatment by government actors and by citizens of each other. How to evaluate this claim is the subject to which we now turn.

Initially, it seemed reasonable to assume that citizen approval of a policy was crucial to evoking a sense of obligation that would promote consent;[2] in earlier formulations of the problem, approval of the policy was a necessary precondition of contingent consent (Levi 1993). The cases reveal that sometimes approval is important, but even more important is the perception that government actors and other citizens are behaving according to widespread notions of fairness. More concretely, this study suggests what is required for citizens to have confidence in the fairness of government. To trust government to be fair is to possess the expectation that government decisions will result from a process that represents and seriously considers all of the relevant interests; that government actors will keep the spirit of their policy promises; and that government actors will implement the policy nondiscriminatorily. Thus, citizens have in fact developed a standard quite similar to Barry's ideal "justice as impartiality."

This is not the whole story, however. Citizen obligations are activated only where compliance produces what Klosko (1992: 39) calls "presumptive goods," indispensable goods "necessary for an acceptable life for all members of the community." This is a narrower category than Rawls's primary goods (1971: 62); for Klosko (1992: 40) the list is restricted to collective goods such as "national defense and law and order, protection from a hostile environment, and provisions for satis-

---

[2] Plamenatz (1968: 13) makes the distinction between consent and approval, but I had not fully understood this nicety until I undertook the historical research.

fying basic bodily needs."[3] Free-riding on the bus or tram, jay-walking, smoking in a nonsmoking underground station, speeding, and other such offenses, while indicative perhaps of a certain breakdown of social order, are not necessarily indicative of a decrease in consent. On the other hand, noncompliance with conscription, taxation, and social security regulations most definitely are. Interestingly, the case studies reveal a greater propensity toward behavioral consent when the presumptive benefit is clearer; as a rule, wartime armies evoke volunteering at a much higher rate than do peacetime armies.

Second, there is an implicit understanding among citizens as well as between citizens and government. The concept of ethical reciprocity attempts to capture this relationship. Contingent consent requires that an individual believe not only that she is obliged to comply but also that others are or should be obliged to comply. When she has evidence of widespread noncompliance, she has two possible responses. She herself may no longer feel obligated to comply, or she may feel she has the right to compel the compliance of others. The cases have provided evidence of both reactions. The first reaction may be consistent with the logic of the iterated prisoner's dilemma (Taylor 1987 [1976]), but it is inconsistent with Hobbesian and even Lockean consent theory, which brook little noncompliance. Both reactions conform, however, with obligations that derive from principles of fairness. Fairness becomes the normative justification for both individual noncompliance and, equally important, for calling on central government to enforce the compliance of others.

NORMS OF FAIRNESS

If a norm is defined as an informal rule that defines appropriate behavior in a particular context so as to promote collective benefits (Ensminger and Knight 1997),[4] then contingent consent depends on two different norms of fairness. The first establishes the standards of fairness for government trustworthiness. The second defines when members of a community should ethically reciprocate with each other.

The standards of fairness by which a citizen evaluates the behavior of government, on the one hand, and fellow citizens, on the other, varies

---

[3] Even this list may be too broad to suit libertarians or even Kateb (1992) who argues for a contract based on democratic individualism that depends on and supports an extremely limited government.

[4] Most sociologists take norms as axiomatic, but when and how they play a role in influencing action has only recently become a subject of major empirical attention. There is now an extensive discussion of norms in rational choice theory. See, e.g., Ullmann-Margalit (1977), Taylor (1982), Sugden (1986), Axelrod (1986), Hechter (1987), Elster (1989), North (1990), Coleman (1990: 241–99), Baron (1993), Denzau and North (1994), Crawford and Ostrom (1995), Ensminger and Knight (1997).

among groups within the polity and over time. Justice as impartiality may be the reigning standard among much of the population, but it is neither the only standard nor the historical standard. Norms change over time. For example, Adam Smith (1982 [1759]: 209–11) observes that even such humane philosophers as Aristotle and Plato accepted and even justified infanticide. More recently, the women's movement precipitates demands on husbands by women once seemingly satisfied or at least not actively dissatisfied with their marriages.

The norms of fairness that affect consent and compliance also change. In feudal societies, the set of mutual obligations between lord and serf determined when the lord was trustworthy and thus had a right to expect the compliance of his subjects. A similar norm existed in the rural villages of Southeast Asia prior to the Green Revolution (Scott 1985). The European, American, and Antipodean state building of the nineteenth and twentieth centuries involved the creation of democratic citizens, which itself depended on the evolution of equality before the law. "Justice as impartiality" (Barry 1995) began to emerge as the norm by which citizens evaluated their state.

The research in this book on military service policy reveals several instances of norm change. The two of immediate interest are the late-nineteenth-century elimination of the practice of buying out from the draft in France and the United States and the gradual popular and governmental acceptance of conscientious objection in the twentieth century. A third, acceptance of conscription as a democratic practice, receives attention in later sections.

Buying out appears to fit a bargaining model of normative change in which norms are presumed to have distributive consequences and in which relative bargaining power among relevant actors with different norms determines the dominant norm (Ensminger and Knight 1997). Commutation, substitution, replacement, and other devices for purchasing exemptions served the interests of the propertied who could afford the going market price and who had electoral or other influence with policymakers. Nor, initially, was there much opposition. Buying out was Pareto optimal; those men who chose to became replacements or substitutes preferred military service to the alternatives. However, in France, the price of substitutes and replacements fluctuated widely, in response to regional labor markets and the number of troops required. When peasant proprietors could no longer afford to buy their sons out of the army and when more fathers gained the vote, a demand for change emerged. In the United States during the Civil War, substitution was retained because it served rural interests with clout in Congress, but commutation was abolished when draft riots crippled New York.

Although relative bargaining power long maintained the norm of

206

purchase and although change in relative bargaining power led to the eradication of the norm, the bargaining model does not quite capture the full story. A competitive pressure enforced the change in France. As a consequence of its ignominious military performance against Prussia, the French sought a better model and turned to the more successful Prussians who had eliminated buying out. At the same time, the republican ideology of equality of sacrifice began to swamp the norm of special elite privileges. This is an instance of ideological commitments by a few creating focal points that enlarge the set of alternatives until that point in time when the alternative better serves the interests of those with bargaining power (see Ensminger and Knight 1997).

A bargaining model may account for most of the change in the norm of buying out, but it cannot possibly provide the explanation of the acceptance of conscientious objection. Conscientious objection has never served the direct interests of any but a small minority. Moreover, it requires a popular norm that seems to violate the very definition of a norm given by Ensminger and Knight (1997). It requires tolerance of those who seem to choose not to cooperate in the "collective social interactions" of fighting the common enemy. Conscientious objection appears to violate the principle of equality of sacrifice, the very norm that had defeated buying out. Hostility was particularly strong in France, where the government prohibited it by law until 1962. In the Anglo-Saxon democracies, with their histories of dissenting religions, conscientious objection has almost always been legal. Nonetheless, c.o.s were often subject to brutality and punishment. The current tolerance of conscientious objection did not really emerge until the middle of World War II.

The development of a norm of tolerance for conscientious objection seems to be an example of moral suasion by the few willing to pay the price for their convictions. However, other factors also contribute to the evolution of this more pluralistic norm. First, government officials came to realize that the relatively few conscientious objectors would not produce a groundswell that would inhibit their efforts to build an efficient fighting force. Second, supporters of conscientious objection used the media, the churches, and other forms of bargaining power to create public pressure to accept conscientious objection.

Consideration of conscientious objection reveals that the interests of those who bargain for a norm need not be material or selfish. It also highlights the importance of fear of noncompliance with a prevailing norm. Sanctions are evoked to inhibit increasing deviations and, thus, an unraveling of the social cooperation a norm is meant to sustain.

The study of the history of military service in democracies reveals critical elements of the relationship between citizens and the state. Military service is one of the obligations constitutive of citizenship. In democracies, however, this citizen obligation carries with it a corresponding obligation of government toward its citizens. Military service can only be demanded, conscription can only be required, when the war is "just." What makes a war just is neither clear-cut nor self-evident.[5] It is, however, incumbent upon democratic governments to somehow persuade the citizenry that the war serves the interests of the nation as a whole. When they fail to do so, distrust of government increases and so, too, does contingent refusal to consent.

It is further incumbent upon democratic governments to use a system of conscription which is fair, or at least is perceived as fair. Inequities in the system may be understood as a failure on the part of government officials to keep their side of the conscription bargain and, thus, license for citizens to withdraw their cooperation.

Over the centuries documented in this book citizens in democracies have raised the standards for judging the fairness, impartiality, and trustworthiness of government actors in picking and waging wars. Achieving contingent consent is both more necessary and more difficult. If a significant minority voices dissent, it is likely to contribute to a breakdown in ethical reciprocity, and if government extracts its compliance too forcibly, the government may be perceived as behaving illegitimately.[6]

THE ROLE OF DEMOCRACY

Empirically, political obligation rests on the citizen's perception that government actors and other citizens are trustworthy. The activation of obligation implies institutional arrangements that make promises and commitments credible, but it may also require extraordinary acts of compensation to overcome distrust based on past experiences. It implies government decision-making bodies that are not only representative but actively considerate of the diverse wishes of the population. It implies membership in a community of citizens who possess some common norms and standards about what it means to reciprocate with each other.

Attempts to empirically document the relationship among ethical concerns, cost-benefit calculations, institutions, and behavior are rare.

---

[5] Walzer (1977) offers a useful perspective on this issue.

[6] Such problems of domestic mobilization may be the crucial factors in accounting for the "democratic peace," that is, the observation that democracies do not wage war against each other. It is simply too difficult for a government to obtain popular contingent consent to such a war effort. I hope to explore this issue further in a separate paper.

Role of democracy

The rational choice literature has made some progress in specifying the conditions under which "ideology matters" or might matter (see esp. Brennan and Lomasky 1989; Levi 1988; Mansbridge 1990; Margolis 1982, 1990a, b; Ostrom 1990; Nelson and Silberberg 1987; North 1981, 1990), but the work tends not to be empirical. Sociologists and political psychologists have made some important theoretical and empirical contributions, but the range of cases remains small (Tyler 1990; Ayers and Braithwaite 1992; Pinney and Scholz 1995; Monroe 1996). There are two principal reasons for the relative paucity of empirical work. The first is that the theory itself is still in the process of development. The second, and equally important, issue is the difficulty of obtaining data adequate for testing the hypotheses derived from the theory that does exist.

As the cases demonstrate, the implicit bargains between citizens and their government and among citizens are subject to repeated reinterpretation, renegotiation, and transformation in the nature of the obligations to which citizens are asked to consent. The research in *Consent, Dissent, and Patriotism* identifies at least four major catalysts for change in the expectations citizens have of their governors and of each other: (1) the extension of democratic institutions, particularly the enlargement of the franchise; (2) the accumulation of experience with particular policies; (3) significant levels of noncompliance; and (4) institutional facilitation of rational and ethical behavior.

The extension of democratic institutions

Throughout the two hundred years covered by this study, Britain, France, Australia, New Zealand, Canada, and the United States significantly extended the spheres of political, civil, and economic rights. Increased democratization facilitates the ability of citizens to act and fundamentally changes the constraints on governmental actors. Two game trees illustrate the difference between democratic and nondemocratic institutions (Figures 8.1 and 8.2).

Note the difference in the number of moves. In the nondemocratic game tree, the game has only three moves. First, the government chooses between a conscription policy that the polity views as fair or one the polity views as unfair. Second, the populace chooses to comply or to refuse to comply. Third, the government chooses to uphold its agreements if the polity complies or to punish the refusers who do not comply. In the democratic game tree, there are four moves. The electorate can sanction the government if it disapproves its second move.

By providing citizens with a variety of effective means for sanctioning government actors, democratic institutions create a new basis for coop-

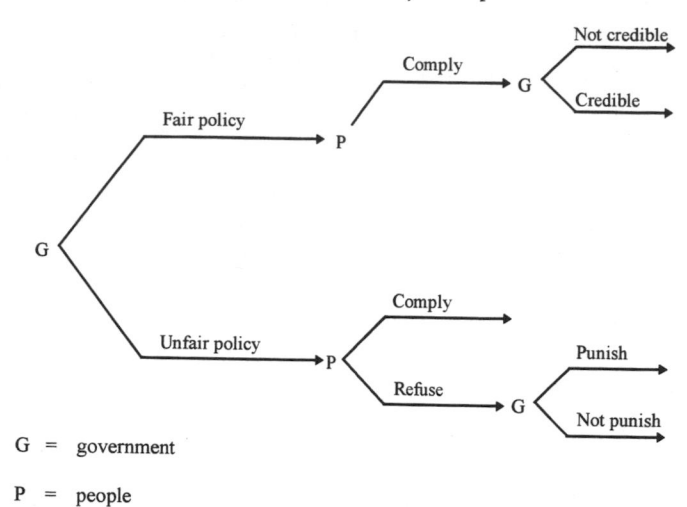

G = government

P = people

Figure 8.1. Nondemocratic game.

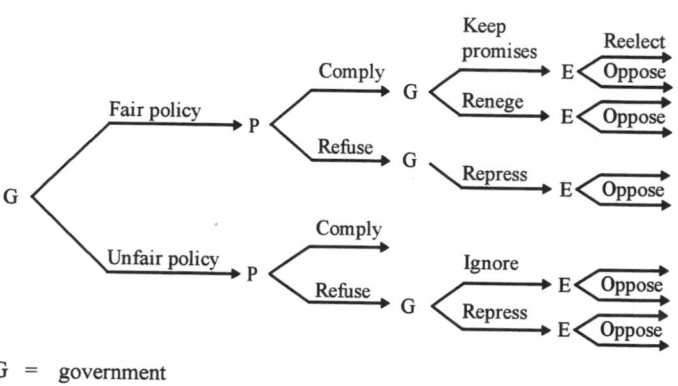

G = government

P = people

Figure 8.2. Democratic game.

eration between government officials and citizens. They make possible credible commitments by government actors and thus reduce citizen concerns that government actors will break their policy promises. The effect is to increase the probability that citizens will approve governmental regulations and obey them. As Dasgupta (1988: 50), points out, you will not trust government "to do on balance what is expected of it if you do not trust that it will be thrown out of power . . . if it does not do on balance what is expected of it."

210

Role of democracy

The threat of citizen sanctions are not enough, however, to produce policy change compatible with citizens' interests. In numerous countries in quite recent years, antagonism toward various economic austerity measures has produced campaign promises but not necessarily policy delivery – and without severe consequences for those elected officials who broke the promises (Stokes 1996). It may be the case that the elected officials have succeeded in gaining citizen trust by persuading citizens that the policy in fact reflects a common interest (see, e.g., Bianco 1994). If so, then something more is involved than the institutional arrangements permitting sanctions. Signaling, persuasion, and other acts by politicians are making a difference. The ability of the prime minister to win some trust from the francophones was certainly a factor in accounting for their increased compliance in World War II, and the reverse may have been a factor in the number of votes against conscription in Australia during the World War I. Thus, politics as well as institutions matter.

Experience

The introduction of new actors into the political process changes the location of the median voter and the median legislator and thus may lead to alterations in policy without any overt pressure. However, democratic institutions and democratic ideology may actually mold preferences. At the least, democratic ideology establishes grounds for evaluating perceived government actions and the actions of other citizens. At the most, democratic institutions constrain behavior until the available alternatives become what people effectively demand. Once-common American practices such as slavery, discrimination against women, smoking, and gun-toting have become either beyond the pale or, at the least, socially questionable. Consequently, certain possibilities become unthinkable; there develop what Tetlock, Peterson, and Lerner label "taboo trade-offs" (in press) and Walzer calls "blocked exchanges" (1983: 99–103). For example, the sale of human beings, the sale of offices, and the purchase of substitutes for military service or jail time are no longer within the realm of legal, ethical, or even cognitive (except possibly for economists) possibility. The democratic element in democratic institutions may have the effect of changing preferences in regard to what constitutes fair influence over government, equitable policies, or standards of behavior for governmental actors. What begins as a norm of the few becomes the norm for the many. What is becomes what ought.

Experience with a policy and evidence of its distributional impact are not always sufficient to create a demand for change. In the absence of an altered standard of fairness, no reform is likely to emerge. However, sometimes experience reveals and, in the process, even alters the norms of fairness themselves. Thus, voluntary military service appeared fair to most of the populace of Anglo-Saxon democracies at the onset of World War I until it became evident that it produced little equality of sacrifice. Severe punishment of conscientious objectors appeared reasonable until a few principled martyrs revealed the illiberalism of such legislation.

Experience is most likely to produce change when an individual believes he is being asked to pay a high price when others do not. This was an explicit concern of those who rioted against the Civil War drafts. There is also evidence (cited in Chapter 4) that French recruits perceived unfairness during the *levée en masse*, the Napoleonic conscriptions, and after 1848. In both cases, the ideology of democracy at the least reinforced and may even have contributed to the creation of these perceptions.

What is particularly interesting in several of the cases is how the standard of fairness that emerges produces a demand for institutions designed to enforce this standard. In situations in which the majority, or at least a large percentage of the population, feels it should comply and a significant minority do, the majority is more likely to demand rules that compel universal obedience. This was the case in Canada, where anglophone support of conscription was in part a function of their desire to evoke equal sacrifice from the francophones. Indeed, the belief in military service as a citizen obligation and the desire to ensure equality of sacrifice provided a basis for support of conscription throughout the democracies. On the other hand, the study of conscientious objection illustrates how a moral minority, willing to pay the costs of noncompliance, can influence the rules by influencing democratic standards of fairness to permit certain forms of principled dissent.

Noncompliance

One of the major findings of this study is that noncompliance is an important resource of political change, that "inherent in the defiance of many rules is not only a threat to social order, but a challenge to the particular pattern of domination on which that social order rests" (Piven 1981: 489). Individuals who find themselves badly served by an institution will try to change it, if they can, but not all individuals have the economic, political, or organizational resources that would enable them to engage in successful bargaining with or collective action against the state. Often, individual – but collectively informed – noncompliance is their best strategy.

Noncompliance can and demonstrably does lead to institutional change. However, even when it is self-conscious withdrawal of or refusal to give contingent consent, it does not always produce the changes sought by the noncompliant. Perceptions of low volunteering more often became a justification for conscription of these groups rather than a reason to cease demanding their services. Widespread draft evasion generally leads to a tightening of the rules and an increase in administrative capacity rather than an abandonment of the draft. On the other hand, armies have reformed in response to the costs of implementing discriminatory policies. The notion of individual rights has been expanded by conscientious objectors. United States and Australian foreign policy is still influenced by the effects of the Vietnam War experiences; fear of citizen resistance is a strong constraint on war-making and international interventions.

Facilitating ethical behavior by rational actors

Much of the philosophical and sociological literatures treat egoistic interest and ethical standards as in conflict, although there are some important exceptions (e.g. Sen 1977; Margolis 1982, 1990a, b; Hardin 1988; Mansbridge 1990; Ostrom 1990; Baron 1993; Scharpf 1994).[7] Motivations based on egoistic interest are claimed to drive out motivations based on ethical standards or affect. This may be true in some circumstances and for some ethical standards, but in many instances of political relevance, ethical standards and egoistic interest are in fact both compatible and mutually reinforcing. Under certain conditions, coercion strengthens ethical standards. For example, revelation of the explicit enforcement pyramid by regulators seems to encourage agents to act upon ethical standards or to value goals other than egoistic interest (Ayres and Braithwaite 1992). Third-party enforcement ensures that *others* are complying; an individual can then choose to comply with more certainty that she is not a sucker (see Levi 1988). In Margolis's view (1990a: 832) coercion strengthens norms when the enforceable rule makes a mandated behavior more commonplace and acceptable, such as was exemplified by the effects of Civil Rights legislation. The expected behavior becomes both a "statistical" and a "pragmatic" norm, to use Margolis's terminology (1990a: 821). It is behavior that becomes, on the one hand, more usual and, on the other hand, the standard whose violation evokes disapproval.

Positive incentives may have the same effect. Young men volunteer to fight in wars because they are patriots, but this is not to deny the influence of coercion in the form of conscription or incentives in the

---

[7] See the important review essay by Crawford and Ostrom (1995). For a perspective that is clearly antagonistic to the rational choice approach, see Etzioni (1988).

form of pay and educational benefits. Single parents and the unemployed comply with the regulations governing extra income because they fear losing benefits if they do not, but their willingness may be strengthened by the belief that it is their obligation to do so (Weatherley 1991). Even effective tax systems rely on both auditing and voluntary compliance derived from a sense of duty (Pinney and Scholz 1995; Scholz 1994).

Certain kinds of reductions in the costs of compliance or volunteering can further facilitate the mutual reinforcement of ethical standards and egoistic interest. For example, the removal of restrictions on voting registration brings more people to the polls. The recruitment of soldiers as a Pals' Brigade, as was done in Britain at the start of World War I, encourages young men to volunteer as a group. The relaxation of tough rules affecting outside employment or the economic role of partners has positive effects on the compliance of welfare recipients. A decrease in the paperwork involved in taxpaying, voting, unemployment insurance, welfare, or military enlistment all encourage more voluntary compliance.

OTHER STUDIES OF COMPLIANCE

The numerous and various studies of compliance with and obedience to law provide out-of-sample sources of data for considering the power of the model of contingent consent. These studies deploy a wide range of methods: experiments, surveys, original archival work, and participant observations. Rereading this extensive research suggests that contingent consent is a useful way to integrate and make sense of many of their findings.

Several people suggested consideration of desertion from the military as a measure of contingent consent. Luckily, others have looked at this behavior, most notably Pedroncini (1968) and more recently Bearman (1991) and Smith (1994). Bearman, focusing on the Civil War, argues for the importance of group norms in affecting individual decisions about desertion. Smith's Foucaultian account of the authority relationships within a French infantry division during World War I uncovers a variety of forms of noncompliance and disobedience. He concludes that soldiers, therefore, possessed the means to engage in struggle with their commanders and were more empowered than most analysts of the military generally recognize. The soldiers were not always obedient, but neither did they mutiny: "Consent to the Third Republic and its institutions set the outer limits of French soldiers' resistance to authority during World War I. They internalized this consent in ways that prevented the French army mutinies from going the way of the Russian army mutinies – at a time when no external use of power could have" (Smith 1994: 258).

Other studies of compliance

Another account of noncompliance as a political resource is James Scott's wonderful *Weapons of the Weak* (1985), a book also influenced by Foucault. Scott's is a detailed investigation of the power relationships within a single Malaysian village. He argues that when the landlords broke the implicit social contract to provide for the landless peasants, they rebelled in the only way they could, with shirking and vandalism. Their motivation was injustice, but their concept of what represented fair and just behavior by the landlords was very much an effect of the experience of their village life. They did not demand equality, but they did expect the social insurance of the moral economy to which they had become accustomed.

Scott (1985) and Smith (1994) both argue that the use of noncompliance is bounded by the extent to which its users find the overarching institutional arrangements fair or just. However, they have little to say on the politics of compliance; their empirical focus is resolutely on acts of defiance, resistance, or nonconformity. Burawoy (1979) and Przeworski (1985), on the other hand, focus on consent. Working within a Marxist tradition, their aim is to understand why workers do not rebel against and even support exploitative capitalist relationships. For Burawoy, the answer lies in the politics of the shop floor and in the participation in choices concerning the organization of production (1979: 27). Participation also helps generate consent for Przeworski (1985), but it is democratic political participation by workers who believe that they are profiting and will continue to profit from capitalist economic arrangements while influencing some aspects of social distribution.

One of the most significant studies of compliance and obedience is Tom Tyler's *Why People Obey the Law* (1990). His investigation of responses to court decisions concludes that the perception of the decision making process as fair is more important than the actual outcome. To the extent that individuals believe the process was fair, they can bear to lose. To the extent that they believe it was unfair, they are not even happy about winning.

Other and very different kinds of research lend support to the arguments that, one, noncompliance is a power resource in the political struggle between the relatively weak and those who exercise authority over them, and, two, participation and relative material well-being are the keys to consent. Recent studies of variation in compliance with contemporary government policies suggest that a sense of obligation to comply arises when individuals believe themselves engaged in reciprocal – and reciprocated – contractual relationships. Evidence that the regulators wish to command obedience rather than achieve consent is likely to increase noncompliance. Scholz (1984) on corporate regulation,

Handler (1987) on dependent clients and consumers of modern state services, Miller (1992) on principal-agent relationships within firms, and Ayres and Braithwaite (1992) on "responsive regulation" in a variety of administrative spheres are among the authors who provide strong empirical grounding for the positive role of cooperative regulatory relationships. Research carried out under the auspices of the Administration, Compliance, and Governability Program of the Research School of Social Sciences adds further weight to the claim that citizens are more likely to comply and contingently consent when they perceive reciprocity in their relationships with those who have authority over them. Braithwaite (1995) on "games of engagement" in policy arenas as diverse as nursing homes and affirmative action, Weatherley (1991) on compliance with social security regulations, and Peel (1995) on the relationships between the residents of a working-class suburb and the state provide compelling and detailed accounts of the bases of both compliance and noncompliance.

Experimental work on cooperation represents yet an additional kind of research on compliance. In earlier experiments Hoffman and Spitzer (1985) learned that their subjects preferred joint profit maximizing even when it contradicted individual profit maximizing, that they acted " 'as if' they distribute the payoffs in accord with their perceptions of fairness (260)." Delving further, they concluded that individuals tend to use a Lockean "just deserts" model. Dawes, van de Kragt, and Orbell (1990) sum up their findings in their title: "Cooperation for the Benefit of Us – Not Me, or My Conscience." They discover that solidarity, based on group identity, is what drives cooperation. After conducting a series of experiments among North American and Polish subjects, Frohlich and Oppenheimer (1992) conclude that when individuals make decisions about distribution without knowing what their individual shares will be, they consistently choose a floor constraint principle, ensuring a minimum income to the worst-off individual. Moreover, once the principle is chosen, it remains stable due to a combination of continued individual satisfaction and increased individual productivity. Both the initial choice and its stability depend, however, on a democratic decision process involving discussion and participation.

Economists and many rational choice scholars are more skeptical about the explanatory utility of such concepts as fairness and ethics. They find reputational and institutional mechanisms sufficient to explain agent compliance in a variety of historical settings (see, e.g., Greif, Milgrom, and Weingast 1994; Milgrom, North, and Weingast 1990; Greif 1989). Hechter (1987), for example, has a powerful model of solidarity and cooperation that is totally grounded in incentives and sanctions. Other economists and rational choice scholars, however, argue that incentives by themselves cannot explain enough of the observed compliance. Those who stray least far from the conventional neoclassical paradigm emphasize the expectations that develop as a result of iterated games (e.g. Kreps 1990, Calvert 1992, 1995; Greif 1994a). However, there are also those who explicitly concern themselves with fairness and other norms (e.g. Jones 1984; North 1990; Huang and Malueg 1994; Rabin 1993; Thaler 1991 and his co-authors, e.g. Kahneman, Knetsch, and Thaler, 1991 [1986]a,b). All, in one way or another, are searching to understand the basis for the commitments Sen (1977) so eloquently claims as crucial in transforming the "rational fools" of neoclassical economics into recognizable but still rational agents.

All of the research cited above addresses some part of the problem studied; none, with one exception (Scholz 1994), actually uses the model of contingent consent. Using a combination of survey materials and an extraordinary data set made available to him by the Internal Revenue Service, Scholz (1994) finds that the best explanation of variation in taxpayer compliance is contingent consent, operationalized as a duty heuristic. Taxpayers who feel they have an obligation (or duty) to pay in return for benefits received overestimate the probability of being caught for noncompliance, a fear that reinforces their sense of obligation to comply.

The numerous studies on compliance and cooperation have no single common conclusion. Nor do they share a common normative position about a "good" state, the "best" relationships of authority, the appropriate principle of justice, or the contributions of group solidarity to a humane society. What emerges from most of the research, however, is the importance of expectations that make possible commitments, on the one hand, and reciprocal and participatory relationships, on the other. Reading this material in light of the model of contingent consent, the evidence appears overwhelming that contingent consent (or something remarkably like it) exists and motivates large numbers of people.

RATIONALITY, ETHICS, AND DEMOCRATIC CONSENT

One measure of the strength of a democracy is its capacity to undergo institutional change while remaining democratic. To do this the government must be one that its people largely trust and to which they are prone to give their consent. In other words, the state must be perceived as legitimate. Political theorists have offered several views of legitimacy, but the ones that resonate best with the historical materials investigated here all depend on the relative responsiveness of government to its populace. This has several aspects. The first is material; the state produces presumptive goods for which citizens – in principle – are willing to give their compliance in exchange. The second is procedural; the government adequately involves the citizenry in the decisions about the policy. The third is normative; the government meets the standards of fairness that are prevalent at that time and among the relevant population. There is no explicit consent by means of an agreement to a social contract; nor is there an overt and generalized acknowledgment of acceptance of political obligation. Nonetheless political obligation is a very real phenomenon and motivator of compliance.

Obligations and consent that are grounded in fairness have their limits, limits against which committed democrats must always be on guard. Perhaps the most serious of these is the tendency to seek the imposition on others of the obligations one is willing to take on oneself. Both a religious majority that requires others to abide by its norms and a leadership that brooks no dissent are clear examples of violations of democratic liberties. However, so, too, can be the requirement by a plurality of voters that equality of sacrifice requires military service even by those with principled objections or that fairness implies excessive monitoring of citizens who are being asked to comply with government demands.

A second danger is the extent to which the standard of fairness may be manipulated to serve particularistic rather than universal ends. Citizens in democracies have multiple opportunities to express their preferences and to attempt to shape government policy in light of those preferences, but government actors, the media, and other powerful institutions also have opportunities to alter or even construct those preferences. Are democratic citizens in fact, the "happy slaves" Herzog (1989) discusses, individuals who believe they are getting what they want only because they do not know how to think about the alternatives? Is conscription actually enslavement, taxation theft, and welfare social control?

This book suggests that there is unquestionably an historical and political context to preferences, but it equally suggests that the plurality of preferences and interests democratic institutions permit is a palliative against allowing alternatives to remain unthinkable or particularistic for too long. First, not all citizens perceive government in the same way. Not only are there individual variations in beliefs, information, economic incentives, ideologies, and other factors that influence compliance, there are also systematic variations by groups that have distinct experiences with the fairness of government or distinct differences in their standards of fairness. Second, not all citizens use the same strategies to achieve their ends. Some citizens will refuse their consent to the extent possible. Others will try to impose their will on the rest. There are also important instances where members of the group attempt to demonstrate even

218

greater commitment to the state than the majority, perhaps as a way to signal loyalty and to win improved rights for their group within society.[8] Blacks and Nisei Japanese in the United States, the Druse in Israel, and the Sikhs in India are among the most notable instances. The effect of diverse strategies is, over time, a multitude of pressure points on democratic institutions to change and respond.

The existence of contingent consent provides stability for democracies. The process of establishing – or reestablishing – the conditions for contingent consent is a source of democratic change. The negotiation of concessions and commitments by government actors to citizens contributes to the transformation. Equally important is the periodic reevaluation of what constitutes a fair policy. The norms of fairness citizens and governments apply are a product of experience with previous practices, but they also may emerge from new ideologies that increase citizen pressure for reform. As standards of fairness change, so, too, do the institutions that demand consent.

The model of contingent consent should be able to explain (and predict) the general pattern of compliance within a society. It cannot, however, offer an account of individual motivation. It is an explanation of the aggregate, not the particular. Yet it is an explanation fundamentally grounded in a conception of citizens as ethically constituted rational actors. Democracies depend on citizens who have an ethical commitment to comply with the demands of their governments. Democracies equally depend on citizens who are rational in the pursuit of their self-interest "rightly understood" (Tocqueville 1990 [1840]: 121–4). When ethics and rationality contradict each other, the result is the loss of self that makes possible either extreme nationalism and fascism or opportunistic disrespect of others. The model of contingent consent offers a perspective on how these two requirements of democratic citizens reinforce each other. Trustworthy and responsive government and citizens concerned with promotion of their individual ends within a context of ethical reciprocity are the foundational elements of democracy – rightly understood.

---

[8] Petersen (1989) offers the best available explanation of this phenomenon, but also see Enloe (1980) and Young (1982).

Bibliography

PRIMARY SOURCES

Australia Commonwealth Bureau of Census and Statistics Australian Bureau of Statistics. 1965. *Census of the Commonwealth of Australia* Vol. VIII.
1974. *Official Yearbook of Australia.*
1983. *Census of Population and Housing.*
1990. *Official Yearbook of Australia.*
Australia House of Representatives. 1968. *Commonweatlh Parliamentary Debates* Vol. 59. Comments by Lance Barnard, Australian Labor Party spokesman on defense (15 May): 1442.
1970a. *Commonwealth Parliamentary Debates.* Vol. 70. Response to Questions by Philip Lynch, Minister for Labour and National Service (20 April): 1730.
1970b. *Commonwealth Parliamentary Papers.* Vol. 70. Debate by B. M. Snedden, Minister for Labour and National Service (13 October): 2009.
1971a. *Commonwealth Parliamentary Debates.* Response to questions by B. M. Snedden, Minister for Labour and National Service (9 May): 622.
1971b. *Commonwealth Parliamentary Debates.* Vol. 73. Response to questions by Philip Lynch, Minister for Labour and National Service (18 August): 279.
1972a. *Commonwealth Parliamentary Debates.* Vol. 81 (26 October): 3443–4.
1972b. *Commonwealth Parliamentary Debates.* Vol. 81 (24 February): 623–4.
Australia Ministry for Labour and National Service. 1970. "Press Release by B. M. Snedden, Minister" (25 August).
1972. "Press statement by Philip Lynch, Minister" (3 September).
Canada. 1919. "Sessional Paper 246: Report of the Director on the Operation of the Military Service Act, 1919." NAC RG 24, Vol 1842, File GAQ 10–44, GAQ 10–47, vol 1.
Canada Bureau of Statistics. 1977. *Statistics of Canada.*
Canada Department of Militia and Defence. 1867–1922. *Annual Report.*
1919. "European War Memorandum No. 6." In file with Canada Sessional Paper 246.

Bibliography

Great Britain. 1912–1913. *Parliamentary Papers (Accounts and Papers), (16) Education (England and Wales)* Session: 14 February 1912 to 7 March 1913, Vol. 64.

1913. *Parliamentary Papers* Vol. [Cmd. 6663] CXVIII. 1. "General Report 1912–13 (Irish Language Census)."

1921. *Parliamentary Papers* Vol. [Cmd.1193]. "General Annual Report of the British Army 1913–1919."

Great Britain Army. 1916. *Report on Recruiting in Ireland.*

Great Britain Army and Militia. 1901. *Annual Report of the Inspector-General of Recruiting for the Year 1900.*

Great Britain House of Commons. 1833. *Parliamentary Papers* Vol. XXXIX.

1843. *Parliamentary Papers* Vol. LI: 321, 459.

1856. *Parliamentary Papers* Vol. XXIX: 4, 22.

1863. *Parliamentary Papers* Vol. LIX: 14.

1872. *Parliamentary Papers* Vol. LXVII: 1.

1881a. *Parliamentary Papers* Vol. XCVI: 159.

1881b. *Parliamentary Papers* Vol. LVIII. "General Annual Return of the British Army."

1892. *Parliamentary Papers* Vol. XC: 1.

1893–1894. *Parliamentary Papers* Vol. CVI: 629.

1899. *Parliamentary Papers* Vol. LIII. "General Annual Return of the British Army": 429.

1902. *Parliamentary Papers* Vol. CXXXIX: 111, 374.

1908. *Parliamentary Papers* Vol. XI. "General Annual Return of the British Army": 101.

1912–1913. *Parliamentary Papers* Vol. CXVIII: 213.

1914. *Parliamentary Papers* Vol. LII. "General Annual Return of the British Army": 360.

République Française Chambre correctionnelle XVII. 1962. *Le Procès du Déserteur.* Paris: Les Éditions de Minuit.

République Française Ministère de la Défense. 1945–1985. *Bilans Officiels.*

République Française Ministère des Affaires Sociales et de la Solidarité Nationale. 1984. *Instruction relative à l'emploi des objecteurs de conscience.* Compiled by Bernard Mansseyre, Le Directeur de l'Administration Générale, du Personnel et du Budget au Ministère des Affaires Sociales et de la Solidarité Nationale.

République Française SIRPA (Service d'Information et de Relations Publiques des Armées). 1989. *Le Service National en Chiffres 1988.* Paris: Ministère de la Défense.

1990. *Le Service National en Chiffres 1989.* Paris: Ministère de la Défense.

United States Congress House Armed Services Committee. 1966. *Review of the Administration and Operation of the Selective Service System.*

United States Congress House Armed Services Committee Special Subcommittee on the Draft. 1970. *Review of the Administration and Operation of the Draft Law.*

United States Congress House Armed Sevices Committee Subcommittee on the Draft. 1969. *Hearings to Amend Military Selective Service Act of 1967.*

221

Bibliography

United States Congress House Judiciary Committee Subcommittee on Courts. 1980. *Hearings on the Judiciary Implications of Draft Registration.*

United States Department of Commerce. 1973. *Statistical Abstract of the United States.*

United States Department of Justice Administrative Office of the United States Courts. 1941–1945. *Report of the Judicial Conference of Senior Circuit Judges.*

    1945–1977. *Federal Offenders in United States District Courts: Annual Selective Service Violation Statistics.*

    1950–1953. *Report of the Judicial Conference of the United States.* Washington, DC: U.S. Government Printing Office.

United States Federal Bureau of Prisons. 1921–1950. *Federal Prisons.* El Reno, Oklahoma, and Leavenworth, Kansas: Federal Prisons Industries Inc. Press.

United States National Advisory Commission on Selective Service. 1967. *In Support of Equity.*

United States Provost Marshal General. 1918–1921. *Annual Report on Selective Service (1917–1920).*

United States Secretary of War. 1919. *Statement Concerning the Treatment of Conscientious Objectors in the Army.*

United States Selective Service System. 1940–. "Record Group 147 (Conscientious Objectors)." National Archives, Suitland, Maryland.

    1942. *Selective Service in Peacetime: First Report of the Director of Selective Service 1940–41.*

    1943. *Selective Service in Wartime: Second Report of the Director of Selective Service, 1941–42.*

    1948. *Selective Service and Victory.*

    1950a. *Conscientious Objection.* Special Monograph No. 11.

    1950b. *Enforcement of the Selective Service Law.* Special Monograph No. 14.

    1952–1956. *Annual Report of the Director of Selective Service.*

    1953. *Selective Service under the 1948 Act Extended.*

    1965–1975. *Semi-Annual Reports of the Director of Selective Service.*

United States Senate Judiciary Committee Subcommittee on Administrative Practice and Procedure. 1970. *A Study of the Selective Service System: Its Operation, Practices and Procedures Together with Recommendations for Administrative Improvement.*

United States Supreme Court. 1965. *Seeger v. United States.* 380 U.S. 163.

    1970. *Welsh v. United States.* 398 U.S. 340.

    1971. *Gillette v. United States.* 401 U.S. 437.

United States War Department. 1866. *Report of the Provost Marshall General.* 39 Congress 1 Session, House Executive Document No. 1, vol. 4, part 2, serial 1251.

Bibliography

INTERVIEWS

Pietri, Geneviève. 2 July 1990. "Interview." Chef du bureau, Protocole, Armée Jeunesse, Ministère de la défense, Paris.

Simkins, Peter. 26 January 1995. "Interview." Museum Historian, Imperial War Museum, London.

SECONDARY SOURCES

Abbott, Andrew. 1990. "Conceptions of Time and Events in Social Science Methods: Causal and Narrative Approaches." *Historical Methods* 23 (4): 140–50.

———. 1993. "Measure for Measure: Abell's Narrative Method." *Journal of Mathematical Sociology* 18 (2–3): 203–14.

Abell, Peter. 1987. *The Syntax of Social Life: The Theory and Method of Comparative Narrative.* Oxford: Oxford University Press.

———. 1993. "Some Aspects of Narrative Method." *Journal of Mathematical Sociology* 18 (2–3): 93–114.

Adams, R. J. Q., and Philip P. Poirier. 1987. *The Conscription Controversy in Great Britain, 1900–18.* London: The Macmillan Press.

Aminzade, Ronald. 1993. *Ballots and Barricades: Class Formation and Republic Politics in France, 1830–1871.* Princeton, NJ: Princeton University Press.

Anon. 1940. "The Fortune Survey XXXII: The War." Supplement to *Fortune* (July).

Armitage, Clyde F., ed. 1919. *Yearbook of the Churches.* New York: Missionary Education Movement.

Armstrong, Elizabeth. 1942. *French Canadian Opinion on the War, January 1940–June 1941.* Toronto: The Ryerson Press.

———. 1974 [1937]. *The Crisis of Quebec, 1914–18.* Toronto: McClelland and Steward, Ltd. [The Carleton Library]. Originally published by Columbia University, New York.

Aron, Jean-Paul, Paul Dumont, and Emmanuel Le Roy Ladurie. 1972. *Anthropologie du conscrit français: D'après les comptes numériques et sommaires du recrutement de l'armée (1819–1826).* Paris: Mouton.

Arthur, Brian. 1989. "Competing Technologies, Increasing Returns, and Lock-in by Historical Events." *The Economic Journal* 99 (March): 116–31.

———. 1993. *The Robber Bride.* New York: Bantam Books.

———. 1995. *Morning in the Burned House.* Boston: Houghton Mifflin.

Auvray, Michel. 1983. *Objecteurs, insoumis, déserteurs: Histoire des réfractaires en France.* Paris: Stock/2.

Axelrod, Robert. 1986. "An Evolutionary Approach to Norms." *American Political Science Review* 80 (4): 1095–1111.

Ayres, Ian, and John Braithwaite. 1992. *Responsive Regulation.* Oxford: Oxford University Press.

Bibliography

Baker, Paul. 1988. *King and Country Call: New Zealanders, Conscription, and the Great War.* Auckland: University of Auckland Press.

Ball, Desmond, ed. 1991. *Aborigines in the Defense of Australia.* Canberra: Australian National University Press.

Barker, Rachel. 1982. *Conscience, Government and War: Conscientious Objection in Great Britain, 1939–1945.* London: Routledge & Kegan Paul (Routledge Direct Editions).

Baron, Jonathan. 1993. *Morality and Rational Choice.* Dordrecht: Kluwer.

Barrett, John. 1979. *Falling In: Australians and "Boy Conscription", 1911–1915.* Sydney: Hale & Iremonger.

Barry, Brian. 1995. *Justice as Impartiality.* Oxford: Oxford University Press.

Baskir, Lawrence M. 1978. *Chance and Circumstances.* New York: Alfred A. Knopf.

Baskir, Lawrence M., and William A. Strauss. 1977. *Reconciliation after Vietnam: A Program of Relief for Vietnam Era Draft and Military Offenders.* Notre Dame and London: University of Notre Dame Press.

Bastian, Peter. 1971. "The 1916 Conscription Referendum in New South Wales." *Teaching History* 5 (1, June): 25–36.

Bates, Robert H. 1991. *Beyond the Miracle of the Market.* Cambridge University Press.

1997. *Open Economy Politics: The Political Economy of the World Coffee Trade.* Princeton, NJ: Princeton University Press.

Bates, Robert H., and Anne O. Krueger. 1993. *Political and Economic Interactions in Economic Policy Reform.* Cambridge, MA: Basil Blackwell.

Bates, Robert H., Avner Greif, Margaret Levi, Jean-Laurent Rosenthal, and Barry R. Weingast. *Analytic Narratives,* in process.

Bearman, Peter S. 1991. "Desertion as Localism: Army Unit Solidarity and Group Norms in the U.S. Civil War." *Social Forces* 70 (2): 321–42.

Beck, J. Murray. 1968. *Pendulum of Power: Canada's Federal Elections.* Scarborough, Ontario: Prentice-Hall of Canada.

Beckett, Ian. 1985. "The Nation in Arms, 1914–18." In *A Nation in Arms: A Social Study of the British Army in the First World War,* ed. Ian Beckett and Keith Simpson, 1–35. Manchester: Manchester University Press.

Beckett, Ian, and Keith Simpson, eds. 1985. *A Nation in Arms: A Social Study of the British Army in the First World War.* Manchester: Manchester University Press.

Belich, James. 1986. *The New Zealand Wars and the Victorian Interpretation of Racial Conflict.* Auckland: Auckland University Press.

Berger, Carl. 1970. "Introduction." In *Conscription 1917,* vii-x. Toronto: University of Toronto Press.

Bianco, William. 1994. *Trust: Representatives and Constituents.* Ann Arbor: University of Michigan Press.

Binmore, Ken. 1994. *Game Theory and the Social Contract: Playing Fair* Vol. I. Cambridge, MA and London: MIT Press.

Birnbaum, Pierre. 1988. "The State and Mobilisation for War." In *States and Collective Action,* 55–66. Cambridge University Press.

224

Bibliography

Bond, Brian. 1962. "Recruiting the Victorian Army 1870–92." *Victorian Studies* V (4, June): 331–8.

Boulton, David. 1967. *Objection Overruled*. London: MacGibbon and Kee.

Brady, Alexander. 1958 [1947]. *Democracy in the Dominions,* 3rd ed. Toronto: University of Toronto Press.

Braithwaite, Valerie. 1995. "Games of Engagement: Postures Within the Regulatory Community." Administration, Compliance, & Governability Program, RSSS, Australian National University: Working Paper No 26.

Brennan, Geoffrey, and Loran Lomasky. 1989. "Large Numbers, Small Costs: The Uneasy Foundations of Democratic Rule." In *Politics and Process: New Essays in Democratic Thought,* ed. Geoffrey Brennan and Loran Lomasky, 42–59. Cambridge University Press.

Brewer, John. 1989. *The Sinews of Power: War, Money and the English State, 1688–1783.* New York: Alfred A. Knopf.

Brown, Robert Craig, and Ramsay Cook. 1974. *Canada: 1896–1921.* Toronto: McClelland and Stewart.

Brown, Robert Craig, and Donald Loveridge. 1982. "Unrequited Faith: Recruiting the CEF 1914–18." *Revue Internationale d'Histoire Militaire* 54: 53–77.

Burawoy, Michael. 1979. *Manufacturing Consent: Changes in the Labor Process Under Monopoly Capitalism.* Chicago: University of Chicago Press.

Callan, Patrick. 1987. "Recruiting for the British Army in Ireland During the First World War." *The Irish Sword* XVII (66): 42–56.

Calvert, Randall. 1992. "Rational Actors, Equilibrium, and Social Institutions." Rochester: University of Rochester, Department of Political Science.

   1995. "Communication in Institutions: Efficiency in a Repeated Prisoner's Dilemma with Hidden Information." In *Political Economy,* ed. W. Barnett, M. Hinich, and N. Schofield, 197–222. Cambridge University Press.

Campbell, David. 1989. "The Social Basis of Australian and New Zealand Security Policy." Canberra: Peace Research Centre, Australian National University.

Castles, Francis G. 1985. *The Working Class and Welfare: Reflections on the Political Development of the Welfare State in Australia and New Zealand, 1890–1980.* Sydney: Allen & Unwin.

Cattelain, Jean-Pierre. 1975. *L'Objection de Conscience.* Paris: PUF. Que Sais-Je #1517.

Challener, Richard. 1955. *The French Theory of the Nation in Arms, 1866–1939.* New York: Columbia University Press.

Chamberlain, W. M. 1982. "Australia's Boer War Volunteers." *Historical Studies* 20: 48–52.

Chambers, John Whiteclay, II. 1987. *To Raise an Army: The Draft Comes to Modern America.* New York: The Free Press.

Chapman, Robert. 1981. "From Labour to National." In *The Oxford History of New Zealand,* ed. W. H. Oliver, and B. R. Williams, 333–68. Oxford: Clarendon Press.

Bibliography

Chong, Dennis. 1991. *Collective Action and the Civil Rights Movement.* Chicago: University of Chicago Press.

Clarkson, L. A. 1981. "Irish Population Revisited, 1687–1821." In *Irish Population, Economy and Society,* ed. J. M. Goldstrom and L. A. Clarkson, 13–35. Oxford: Clarendon Press.

Coates, R. H. 1929. *Origin, Birthplace, Nationality and Language of the Canadian People.* Ottawa: Dominion of Canada, Dominion Bureau of Statistics.

Cohen, Elliot A. 1985. *Citizens and Soldiers: The Dilemmas of Military Service.* Ithaca: Cornell University Press.

Coleman, James S. 1964. *Introduction to Mathematical Sociology.* New York: Free Press of Glencoe.

_____ 1990. *Foundations of Social Theory.* Cambridge, MA: The Belknap Press of Harvard University Press.

Coles, Harry L. 1986. "From Peaceable Coercion to Balanced Forces, 1807–15." In *Against All Enemies,* ed. Kenneth J. Hagan and William R. Roberts, 71–89. New York: Greenwood Press.

Colley, Linda. 1992. *Britons: Forging the Nation 1707–1837.* New Haven: Yale University Press.

Collier, David. 1991. "The Comparative Method: Two Decades of Change." In *Comparative Political Dynamics: Global Research Perspectives,* ed. Dankar Rustow and Erickson. New York: Harper Colllins.

Cook, Karen Schweers, and Margaret Levi, eds. 1990. *The Limits of Rationality.* Chicago: University of Chicago Press.

Coulthard-Clark, C. D. 1988. "Formation of the Australian Armed Services, 1901–14." In *Australia: Two Centuries of Peace and War,* ed. M. McKernan and M. Browne, 121–43. Canberra: Australian War Memorial.

Crawford, Sue, and Elinor Ostrom. 1995. "Studying Rules and Norms: Linking Individuals and Context." *American Political Science Review* 89 (3): 582–600.

Cress, Lawrence Delbert. 1986. "Reassessing American Military Requirements, 1783–1807." In *Against All Enemies,* ed. Kenneth J. Hagan and William R. Roberts, 49–69. New York: Greenwood Press.

Crowley, Frank, ed. 1974. *A New History of Australia.* Melbourne: William Heineman.

Curthoys, Ann. 1990. "Mobilising Dissent." In *Vietnam Remembered,* ed. Greg Pemberton, 138–63. Sydney: Weldon Publishing.

Dalton, B. J. 1967. *War and Politics in New Zealand, 1855–1870.* Sydney: Sydney University Press.

Dangerfield, George. 1979. *The Damnable Question: A Study in Anglo-Irish Relations.* London: Billings and Sons.

Dasgupta, Partha. 1988. "Trust as a Commodity." In *Trust: Making and Breaking Cooperative Relations,* ed. Diego Gambetta, 49–72. Cambridge, MA: Basil Blackwell.

Daunton, Martin. 1996. "Delegation and Constraint: Reflections on British Fiscal Administration Since 1842." Paper presented to the final Workshop of the Administration, Compliance, and Governability Program, Australian National University, Canberra.

Bibliography

David, Paul. 1985. "Clio and the Economics of QWERTY." *American Economic Review* 75 (2): 332–37.

——— 1994. "Why are Institutions the 'Carriers of History'?: Path Dependence and the Evolution of Conventions, Organizations, and Institutions." *Structural Change and Dynamics* 5: 205–20.

Davis, James W., Jr., and Kenneth M. Dolbeare. 1968. *Little Groups of Neighbors: The Selective Service System.* Chicago: University of Chicago Press.

Dawes, Robyn, Alphons J. C. van de Kragt, and John Orbell. 1990. "Cooperation for the Benefit of Us – Not Me, or My Conscience." In *Beyond Self-Interest,* ed. Jane Mansbridge, 97–110. Chicago: University of Chicago Press.

Denman, Terence. 1992. *Ireland's Unknown Soldiers.* Dublin: Irish Academic Press.

Denzau, Arthur T., and Douglass C. North. 1994. "Shared Mental Models: Ideologies and Institutions." *Kyklos* 47 (1): 3–31.

Doyle, William. 1995. *Officers, Nobles and Revolutionaries.* London: Hambledon Press.

Easterbrook, W. T., and G. G. Aitken. 1988. *Canadian Economic History.* Toronto: Toronto University Press.

Elster, Jon. 1978. *Logic and Society.* New York: John Wiley & Sons.

——— 1989. *The Cement of Society.* Cambridge University Press.

Enloe, Cynthia. 1980. *Police, Military and Ethnicity: Foundations of State Power.* New Brunswick: Transaction Books.

Ensminger, Jean, and Jack Knight. 1997. "Changing Social Norms: Common Property, Bridewealth, and Clan Exogamy." *Current Anthropology* 38 (February): 1–24.

Etzioni, Amitai. 1961. *Compliance: A Comparative Analysis of Complex Organizations.* New York: The Free Press of Glencoe.

——— 1988. *The Moral Dimension.* New York: The Free Press.

Faivre, Maurice. 1988. *Les Nations Armées: De la guerre des peuples à la guerre des étoiles.* Paris: Economica (for Fondation pour les Études de Défense Nationale).

Fararo, Thomas J. 1993. "Generating Narrative Forms." *Journal of Mathematical Sociology* 18 (2–3): 153–81.

Faucier, Nicolas. 1983. *Pacifisme et Antimilitarisme dans l'entre-deux-guerres (1919–39).* Série B, n. 124. Paris: Spartacus.

Fearon, James, and David Laitin. 1995. "Explaining Interethnic Conflict." Paper prepared for the American Political Science Association Meetings, Chicago.

Feigert, Frank. 1989. *Canada Votes, 1935–1988.* Durham, NC: Duke University Press.

Filteau, Gerard. 1977. *Le Québec, le Canada, et la Guerre 1914–1918.* Montreal: Éditions de l'Aurore.

Finer, Samuel. 1975. "State and Nation-Building in Europe: The Role of the Military." In *The Formation of National States in Western Europe,* ed. Charles Tilly. Princeton, NJ: Princeton University Press.

Bibliography

Firmin-Sellers, Kathryn. 1996. *The Transformation of Property Rights in the Gold Coast.* Cambridge University Press.

Fitzpatrick, David. 1980. "The Disappearance of the Irish Agricultural Labourer, 1841–1912." *Irish Economic and Social History* VII: 66–83.

———. 1984. *Irish Emigration, 1801–1921.* Dublin: The Economic and Social History Society of Ireland and the Dundalgen Press.

———. 1989a. "A Curious Middle Place: The Irish in Britain, 1871–1921." In *The Irish in Britain, 1815–1939,* ed. Roger Swift, and Sheridan Gilley, 10–59. London: Printer Publishers.

———. 1989b. " 'A peculiar tramping people': The Irish in Britain, 1801–1870." In *A New History of Ireland: Ireland Under the Union I, 1801–1870,* ed. W. E. Vaughan, Vol. V, Ch. XXVIII. Oxford: Clarendon Press.

———. 1992a. "Ireland Since 1870." In *The Oxford History Of Ireland,* ed. R. M. Foster, 174–229. Oxford: Oxford Paperbacks.

———. 1992b. "The Logic of Collective Sacrifice: Irish Enlistment in the Great War." Unpublished paper.

Flathman, Richard. 1972. *Political Obligation.* New York: Atheneum.

Flora, Peter, Franz Kraus, and Winifred Pfenning. 1987. *State, Economy, and Society in Western Europe, 1815–1975,* Vol. II (The Growth of Industrial Societies and Capitalist Economies). London: Macmillan Press.

Floud, Roderick, Annabel Gregory, and Kenneth Wachter. 1990. *Height, Health, and History: Nutritional Status in the United Kingdom, 1750–1980.* Cambridge University Press.

Forrest, Alan. 1989. *Conscripts and Deserters: The Army and French Society During the Revolution and Empire.* New York: Oxford University Press.

Forward, Roy. 1968. "Conscription, 1964–1968." In *Conscription in Australia,* ed. Roy Forward and Bob Reece, 79–142. St. Lucia: University of Queensland Press.

Frieden, Jeffry A. 1991. *Debt, Development and Democracy.* Princeton, NJ: Princeton University Press.

Friends' Peace Committee. c. 1913. "A Blot on the Empire: Conscription in New Zealand." A pamphlet printed in London.

Frohlich, Norman, and Joe A. Oppenheimer. 1992. *Choosing Justice.* Berkeley: University of California Press.

Fukuyama, Frank. 1995. *Trust.* New York: Basic Books.

Gagnon, Jean-Pierre. 1986. *Le 22me bataillon (canadien français): 1914–19.* Quebec: Les Presses de l'Université Laval en collaboration avec le ministère de la Défense Nationale et le Centre d'Édition du Gouvernement du Canada.

Gardner, Roy. 1991. "Resisting the Draft: A Perfect Equilibrium Approach." In *Games and Equilibrium Models: Social and Political Interaction,* ed. Reinhard Selten, Vol. IV, 88–102. New York: Springer-Verlag.

Gardner, W. J. 1981. "A Colonial Economy." In *The Oxford History of New Zealand,* ed. W. H. Oliver, and B. R. Williams, 57–86. Oxford: Clarendon Press.

Geddes, Barbara. 1994. *The Politicians' Dilemma.* Berkeley: University of California Press.

Bibliography

Geyer, Michael. 1989. "The Militarization of Europe, 1945–1986." In *The Militarization of the Western World,* ed. John R. Gillis, 65–102. New Brunswick: Rutgers University Press.

Gibbons, James S. 1971 [1862]. "We Are Coming, Father Abraham." Reprinted in American War Songs, ed. *National Committee for the Preservation of Existing Records of the National Society of the Colonial Dames of America.* Ann Arbor: Gryphon Books (originally privately printed in 1925). Pp. 112–14.

Gibson, P. 1963. "The Conscription Issue in South Australia, 1916." *University Studies in History* IV (2): 47–80.

Giddens, Anthony. 1985. *The Nation-State and Violence.* Cambridge: Polity Press.

Gilbert, Alan D. 1969. "The Conscription Referenda, 1916–17: The Impact of the Irish Crisis." *Historical Studies* 14 (October): 54–72.

1971. "Religion, Loyalty and Conscription." *Politics* 4 (1): 15–25.

Gilbert, Alan D., and Ann-Mari Jordens. 1988. "Traditions of Dissent." In *Australia: Two Centuries of War and Peace,* ed. M. McKernan, and M. Browne, 338–65. Canberra: Australian War Memorial.

Gillis, John R., ed. 1989. *The Militarization of the Western World.* New Brunswick: Rutgers University Press.

Girardet, Raoul. 1953. *La Société Militaire dans la France contemporaine: 1815–1939.* Paris: Plon.

1974. *Problèmes contemporains de défense nationale.* Paris: Dalloz.

Golden, Miriam. 1990. *A Rational Choice Analysis of Union Militancy with Application to the Cases of British Coal and Fiat.* Cornell: Cornell University Press.

1996. *Heroic Defeats.* Cambridge University Press.

Goldsmith, Oliver. 1921. *The Good-Natur'd Man.* Cambridge University Press.

Goldthorpe, John H. 1996. "Rational Action Theory for Sociology." Paper in progress, Nuffield College.

Gooch, John. 1980. *Armies in Europe.* London: Routledge & Kegan Paul.

Goodin, Robert. 1992. *Motivating Political Morality.* Oxford: Basil Blackwell.

Goot, Murray, and Rodney Tiffen. 1983. "Public Opinion and the Politics of the Polls." In *Australia's Vietnam,* ed. Peter King. Sydney: Allen & Unwin.

Granatstein, J. L. 1969. *Conscription in the Second World War, 1939–45.* Toronto: McGraw–Hill Ryerson.

1973. "Le Québec et le plébiscite de 1942 sur la conscription." *Revue d'histoire de l'Amérique française* 27 (1, June): 43–62.

Granatstein, J. L., and J. M. Hitsman. 1977. *Broken Promises: A History of Conscription in Canada.* Toronto: Oxford University Press.

Granatstein, J. L., and Paul Stevens, eds. 1982. *A Reader's Guide to Canadian History 2: Confederation to the Present.* Toronto, Buffalo, London: University of Toronto Press.

Granovetter, Mark. 1985. "Economic Action and Social Structure: The Problem of Embeddedness." *American Journal of Sociology* 91 (3): 481–510.

Grant, David. 1986. *Out in the Cold: Pacifists and Conscientious Objectors in New Zealand During World War II.* Auckland: Reed Methuen.

Bibliography

Gravel, Jean-Yves. 1974. *L'Armée au Québec (1868–1900): Un Portrait Social.* Montréal: Boréal Express.

Gravel, Jean-Yves. ed. 1974. *Le Québec et la Guerre.* Montreal: Boréal Express.

Green, T. H. 1967 [1907]. *Principles of Political Obligation.* Ann Arbor: University of Michigan Press.

Greif, Avner. 1989. "Reputation and Coalitions in Medieval Trade: Evidence on the Maghribi Traders." *Journal of Economic History* XLIX (4): 857–82.

    1993. "Contract Enforceability and Economic Institutions in Early Trade: The Maghribi Traders' Coalition." *American Economic Review* 83 (3): 525–48.

    1994a. "Cultural Beliefs and the Organization of Society: A Historical and Theoretical Reflection on Collectivist and Individualist Societies." *Journal of Political Economy* 102 (5): 912–50.

    1994b. "On the Political Foundations of the Late Medieval Commercial Revolution: Genoa During the Twelfth and Thirteenth Centuries." *Journal of Economic History* 54 (4): 271–87.

    In press. "Micro Theory and Recent Developments in the Study of Economic Institutions Through Economic History." In *Advances in Economic Theory,* ed. David M. Kreps, and Kenneth F. Wallis. Cambridge University Press.

Greif, Avner, Paul Milgrom, and Barry R. Weingast. 1994. "Coordination, Commitment and Enforcement: The Case of the Merchant Gild." *Journal of Political Economy* 102 (4): 745–76.

Grey, Jeffrey. 1990. *A Military History of Australia.* Cambridge University Press.

    1991. "Diggers and Databases: The AIF Project." Paper in process.

Grieves, Keith. 1988. *The Politics of Manpower, 1914–1918.* Manchester: Manchester University Press.

Hall, Robert A. 1989. *The Black Diggers.* Sydney: Allen & Unwin.

Hancock, W. K., ed. 1951. *Statistical Digest of the War.* London: His Majesty's Stationery Office and Longmans Green and Co.

Handler, Joel F. 1987. "Dependent People, the State, and the Modern/Postmodern Search for the Dialogic Community." Madison: University of Wisconsin, Institute for Legal Studies, SPR 19.

Hanham, H. J. 1973. "Religion and Nationality in Mid-Victorian England." In *War and Society,* ed. M. D. R. Foot, 159–82. London: Paul Elek.

Hardin, Russell. 1988. *Morality Within the Limits of Reason.* Chicago: University of Chicago Press.

    1995. *One for All.* Princeton, NJ: Princeton University Press.

    In press. *Constitutionalism, Liberalism, and Democracy.* Oxford: Oxford University Press.

Harrop, A. J. 1937. *England and the Maori Wars.* London: The New Zealand News.

Hart, H. L. A. 1955. "Are There Any Natural Rights?" *Philosophical Review* 64 (April): 175–91.

    1961. *The Concept of Law.* New York: Oxford University Press.

Bibliography

Hasluck, Paul. 1965 [1952]. *The Government and the People, 1939–1941.* Canberra: Australian War Memorial.

———. 1970. *The Government and the People, 1942–1945.* Canberra: Australian War Memorial.

Haswell, Jock. 1973. *Citizen Armies.* London: Peter Davies.

Hayes, Dennis. 1949. *Conscription Conflict: The Conflict of Ideas in the Struggle for and Battle Against Military Conscription in Britain Between 1901 and 1959.* London: Sheppard Press.

Hazlehurst, Cameron. 1971. *Politicians at War, July 1914 to May 1915.* London: J. Cape.

Hechter, Michael. 1975. *Internal Colonialism.* London: Routledge & Kegan Paul.

———. 1987. *Principles of Group Solidarity.* Berkeley: University of California.

Herrnstein, Richard J. 1993. "Behavior, Reenforcement, and Utility." In *The Origin of Values,* ed. Michael Hechter, Lynn Nadel, and Richard E. Michod, 137–52. New York: Aldine de Gruyter.

Herzog, Don. 1989. *Happy Slaves: A Critique of Consent Theory.* Chicago: University of Chicago Press.

Hill, Richard S. 1986a. *Policing the Colonial Frontier: The Theory and Practice of Coercive Social and Racial Control in New Zealand, 1757–1787,* Vol. II. Wellington: New Zealand Department of Internal Affairs, Historical Publications Branch.

———. 1986b. *Policing the Colonial Frontier: The Theory and Practice of Coercive Social and Racial Control in New Zealand, 1767–1867,* Vol. I. Wellington: New Zealand Department of Internal Affairs, Historical Publications Branch.

Hintze, Otto. 1994. "Military Organization and the Organization of the State." In *The State: Critical Concepts,* ed. John A. Hall, Vol. 1, 181–202. London and New York: Routledge.

Hobbes, Thomas. 1985 [1651]. *Leviathan,* ed. C. B. MacPherson. London: Penguin Classics.

Hoffman, Elizabeth, and Matthew L. Spitzer. 1985. "Entitlements, Rights, and Fairness: An Experimental Examination of Subjects' Concepts of Distributive Justice." *Journal of Legal Studies* XIV (June): 259–97.

Holloway, E. J. 1966. "The Australian Victory Over Conscription in 1916–17." Pamphlet published by the Anti-Conscription Jubilee Committee.

Holmes, Richard. 1985. *Acts of War: The Behavior of Men in Battle.* New York: The Free Press.

Honey, Michael K. 1994. "The War Within the Confederacy: White Unionists of North Carolina." *Prologue* 26 (2): 55–72.

Hooks, Gregory, and Gregory Mclauchlan. 1992. "The Institutional Foundation of Warmaking: Three Eras of U.S. Warmaking, 1939–1989." *Theory & Society* 21: 757–88.

Horne, Alistair. 1984. *The French Army and Politics, 1870–1970.* London: Macmillan Press.

Horne, John W. 1991. *Labour and War.* Oxford: Clarendon Press.

Hoy, Claire. 1989. *Margin of Error.* Toronto: Key Porter Books.

231

Huang, Peter H., and David A. Malueg. 1994. "Psychological Remorse in the Prisoner's Dilemma and Folk Theorems for Psychological Games." Unpublished paper.

Hughes, Everett Cherrington. 1943. *French Canada in Transition.* Chicago: University of Chicago Press.

Hume, David. 1947. "Of the Original Contract." In *Social Contract,* ed. Sir Ernest Barker, 145–66. London: Oxford University Press.

Huntington, Samuel P. 1957. *The Soldier and the State.* Cambridge MA: Harvard University Press.

Hyatt, A. M. J. 1942. "Military Studies in Canada: An Overview." *Revue Internationale d'Histoire Militaire* 54: 328–49.

Inglis, K. S. 1968. "Conscription in Peace and War, 1911–1945." In *Conscription in Australia,* ed. Roy Forward, and Bob Reece, 22–65. St. Lucia: University of Queensland Press.

Ingram, Norman. 1991a. "The Circulaire Chautemps, 1933: The Third Republic Discovers Conscientious Objection." *French Historical Studies* 17 (2,Fall): 387–409.

1991b. *The Politics of Dissent.* New York: Oxford University Press.

Jacquet, Jr., Constance H., ed. 1979. *Yearbook of American Churches.* Nashville: Abington Press.

1989. *Yearbook of American Churches.* Nashville: Abington Press.

Jacquin, Daniel. 1990. "L'Objection de conscience en France: Figures d'acteurs." *Archives européennes de sociologie* 31 (2): 239–60.

James, Francis. 1968. "The Anglican View on Conscription and Conscientious Objection." In *Conscription in Australia,* ed. Roy Forward and Bob Reece, 260–8. St. Lucia, Queensland: University of Queensland Press.

Janowitz, Morris. 1980. "Observations on the Sociology of Citizenship: Obligations and Rights." *Social Forces* 59 (1,September): 1–24.

Jauffret, Jean-Charles. 1984. "Typologie de l'Engagement Sous la III République." In *L'Engagement et les Engages,* ed. Renée Remond, 42–89. Paris: Centre d'Histoire Militaire et d'Études de Défense Nationale and Centre de Sociologie de la Défense Nationale.

Jauncey, Leslie C. 1935. *The Story of Conscription in Australia.* London: George Allen & Unwin.

Jones, Richard. 1973. "L'Idéologie de l'action catholique, 1917– 1939." *Revue d'histoire de l'Amérique française* 27 (1,June): 63–76.

1981. "Politics and Culture: The French Canadians and the Second World War." In *The Second World War as a National Experience,* ed. S. Aster. Ottawa: The Canadian Committee for the History of the Second World War, Ministère de la Défense nationale.

Jones, Stephen R. G. 1984. *The Economics of Conformism.* Oxford: Basil Blackwell.

Jordens, Ann-Mari. 1987. "Against the Tide: The Growth and Decline of a Liberal Anti-War Movement in Australia, 1905–1918." *Historical Studies* XXII (88, April): 373–94.

1989a. "An Administrative Nightmare: Aboriginal Conscription 1965–1972." *Aboriginal History* XIII (1–2): 124–34.

Bibliography

1989b. "Conscientious Objection and the Vietnam War." Canberra, Peace Research Centre, Working Paper No. 73.

1990. "Conscription and Dissent: The Genesis of Anti-War Protest." In *Vietnam Remembered,* ed. Gregory Pemberton, 60–81. Sydney: Weldon Publishing.

Kahneman, Daniel, Jack L. Knetsch, and Richard H. Thaler. 1991a [1986a]. "Fairness and the Assumptions of Economics." In *Quasi-Rational Economics,* ed. Richard H. Thaler, 220–35. New York: Russell Sage Foundation.

1991b [1986b]. "Fairness as a Constraint on Profit-Seeking: Entitlements in the Market." In *Quasi-Rational Economics,* ed. Richard H. Thaler, 199–219. New York: Russell Sage Foundation.

Kalyvas, Stathis N. 1996. *The Rise of Christian Democracy in Europe.* Ithaca, NY: Cornell University Press.

Karsten, Peter. 1983. "Irish Soldiers and the British Army, 1792–1922: Suborned or Subordinate." *Journal of Social History* 17 (1): 31–64.

1989. "Militarization and Rationalization in the United States, 1870–1914." In *The Militarization of the Western World,* ed. John R. Gillis, 30–44. New Brunswick: Rutgers University Press.

Kateb, George. 1992. *The Inner Ocean: Individualism and Democratic Culture.* Ithaca, NY: Cornell University Press.

Kennedy, Thomas C. 1981. *The Hound of Conscience: A History of the No-Conscription Fellowship, 1914–1919.* Fayetteville: The University of Arkansas Press.

Ketcham, George F., ed. 1949. *Yearbook of American Churches.* Lebanon, PA: Sowers Printing Company.

Kiernan, V. G. 1973. "Conscription and Society in Europe Before the War of 1914–18." In *War and Society,* ed. M. D. R. Foot, 141–58. London: Paul Elek.

Kiewiet, D. Roderick. 1983. *Macroeconomics and Micropolitics.* Chicago: University of Chicago Press.

Kiewiet, D. Roderick, and Donald Kinder. 1981. "Sociotropic Politics." *British Journal of Political Science* 11 (2): 129–61.

King, Michael. 1981. "Between Two Worlds." In *The Oxford History of New Zealand,* ed. W. H. Oliver and B. R. Williams, 279–301. Oxford: Clarendon Press.

Kiser, Edgar. 1994. "Markets and Hierarchies in Early Modern Tax Systems: A Principal-Agent Analysis." *Politics & Society* 22 (3): 285–316.

1996. "The Revival of Narrative in Historical Sociology: What Rational Choice Theory Can Contribute." *Politics & Society* 24 (3): 249–71.

Kiser, Edgar, and Michael Hechter. 1991. "The Role of General Theory in Comparative-Historical Sociology." *American Journal of Sociology* 97: 1–30.

Kiser, Edgar, and Margaret Levi. 1996. "Using Counterfactuals in Historical Analysis: Theories of Revolution." In *Counterfactual Thought Experiments in World Politics,* ed. Philip E. Tetlock and Aaron Belkin, 187–207. Princeton, NJ: Princeton University Press.

Bibliography

Klosko, George. 1987. "The Principle of Fairness and Political Obligation." *Ethics* 97: 353–62.

    1992. *The Principle of Fairness and Political Obligation.* Lanham, MD: Rowman & Littlefield.

Knight, Jack. 1992. *Institutions and Social Conflict.* Cambridge University Press.

Kohn, Stephen M. 1986. *Jailed For Peace: The History of American Draft Law Violators, 1658–1985.* Westport, CT and London: Greenwood Press.

Kornberg, Allan, and Harold D. Clarke. 1992. *Citizens and Community: Political Support in a Representative Democracy.* Cambridge University Press.

Kreps, David M. 1990. "Corporate Culture and Economic Theory." In *Perspectives in Positive Political Economy,* ed. James Alt and Kenneth Shepsle, 90–143. Cambridge University Press.

Kuczynski, Robert R. 1930. *Birth Registration and Birth Statistics in Canada.* Washington, DC: The Brookings Institution.

Ladurie, Emmanuel Le Roy. 1979 [1973]. *The Territory of the Historian.* Hassocks, Sussex: The Harvester Press.

Ladurie, Emmanuel Le Roy, and Nicole Bernageau. 1971. "Étude sur un Contingent Militaire (1868): Mobilité Géographique Délinquance et Stature, Mises en Rapport avec d'Autres Aspects de la Situation des Conscrits." *Annales de démographie historique* 1971: 311–37. Revised and translated in *The Territory of the Historian.*

    1979 [1971]. "The Conscripts of 1868: A Study of the Correlation Between Geographical Mobility, Delinquency and Physical Stature, and other Aspects of the Situation of the Young Frenchmen called to do Military Service in that Year." In *The Territory of the Historian,* ed. Emmanuel Le Roy Ladurie, 33–75. Hassocks, Sussex: The Harvester Press.

Ladurie, Emmanuel Le Roy, Nicole Bernageau, and Yves Pasquet. 1969. "Le conscrit et l'ordinateur: Perspectives du recherches sur les archives militaires du XIXe siècle français." *Studi storici* X (2,Avril-Juin).

Ladurie, Emmanuel Le Roy, and Paul Dumont. 1972. "Exploitation quantitative et cartographique des comptes numériques et sommaires (1819–1826)." In *Anthropologie du conscrit français,* 7–190. Paris: Mouton.

Laitin, David. 1992. *Language Repertoires and State Construction in Africa.* Cambridge University Press.

    1995. "National Revivals and Violence." *Archives européennes de sociologie* 36: 3–43.

Lake, Marilyn. 1975. *A Divided Society: Tasmania During World War I.* Melbourne: Melbourne University Press.

Landis, Benson, ed. 1958. *Yearbook of American Churches.* New York: National Council of the Churches of Christ in the U.S.A.

    1959. *Yearbook of American Churches.* New York: National Council of the Churches of Christ in the U.S.A.

Laurendeau, André. 1962. *La crise de la conscription 1942.* Montreal: Les Éditions du Jour.

Leach, Jack Franklin. 1952. *Conscription in the United States: Historical Background.* Rutland, VT: Charles E. Tuttle.

234

Bibliography

Levi, Margaret. 1977. *Bureaucratic Insurgency: The Case of Police Unions.* Lexington, MA: Lexington Books.

———. 1988. *Of Rule and Revenue.* Berkeley: The University of California Press.

———. 1990. "A Logic of Institutional Change." In *The Limits of Rationality,* ed. Karen Schweers Cook and Margaret Levi, 402–18. Chicago: University of Chicago Press.

Levi, Margaret, and Sara Singleton. 1991. "Women in the 'Workingman's Paradise.'" *Social Research* 58 (3,Fall): 627–51.

Levi, Margaret, and Shane Fricks. 1992. "Giving and Refusing Consent: Anglophone and Francophone Responses to Conscription." Presented at the Public Choice Society Meetings, New Orleans, and the American Political Science Association Meetings, Chicago.

Levi, Margaret, and Richard Sherman. In press. "Rationalized Bureaucracies and Rational Compliance." In *Institutions and Economic Development,* ed. Christopher Clague. Baltimore: Johns Hopkins University Press.

Levi, Margaret, and Stephen DeTray. 1993. "A Weapon Against War: Conscientious Objection in the U.S., Australia, and France." *Politics & Society* 21 (4): 425–64.

Lind, E. Allan, and Tom R. Tyler. 1988. *The Social Psychology of Procedural Justice.* New York: Plenum Press.

Linteau, Paul-André, René Durocher, and Jean-Claude Robert, eds. 1989a. *Histoire du Québec contemporain: De la Confédération à la crise (1867–1929),* Vol. I. Montreal: Boréal.

Linteau, Paul-André, René Durocher, Jean-Claude Robert, and François Ricard, eds. 1989b. *Histoire du Québec contemporain: Le Québec depuis 1930,* Vol. II. Montreal: Boréal.

Lipsky, Michael. 1980. *Street-Level Bureaucracy.* New York: Basic Books.

Lipton, Charles. 1968. *The Trade Union Movement of Canada, 1827–1959.* Montreal: Canadian Social Publications.

Locke, John. 1965 [1690]. *Two Treatises on Government,* ed. Peter Laslett. New York: New American Library.

Lustick, Ian. 1993. *Unsettled States, Disputed Lands: Britain and Ireland, France and Algeria, Israel and the West-Bank Gaza.* Ithaca, NY: Cornell University Press.

MacKinnon, Mary. 1994. "Canadian Railway Workers and World War I Military Service." Paper prepared in Department of Economics, McGill University.

Maclean, Norman. 1992. *Young Men and Fire.* Chicago: University of Chicago Press.

MacLennan, Hugh. 1990 [1945]. *Two Solitudes.* Toronto: General Paperbacks.

Mahon, John K. 1983. *History of the Militia and the National Guard.* New York: Macmillan.

Main, J. M. 1970. *Conscription: The Australian Debate, 1901–1970.* Melbourne: Cassell Australia.

Mann, Michael. 1986. *The Sources of Social Power: A History of Power from the Beginning to A.D. 1760,* Vol. I. Cambridge University Press.

Bibliography

1993. *The Sources of Social Power: The Rise of Classes and Nation-States, 1760–1914,* Vol. II. Cambridge University Press.

Mansbridge, Jane J. 1990. "On the Relation of Altruism and Self-Interest." In *Beyond Self-Interest,* ed. Jane Mansbridge, 133–43. Chicago: University of Chicago Press.

March, James G., and Johan P. Olsen. 1989. *Rediscovering Institutions: The Organizational Basis of Politics.* New York: The Free Press.

1995. *Democratic Governance.* New York: The Free Press.

Margolis, Howard. 1982. *Selfishness, Altruism, and Rationality: A Theory of Social Choice.* Cambridge University Press.

1990a. "Dual Utilities and Rational Choice." In *Beyond Self-Interest,* ed. Jane Mansbridge, 239–53. Chicago: University of Chicago Press.

1990b. "Equilibrium Norms." *Ethics* 100 (July): 821–37.

Marr, William L., and Donald G. Paterson. 1980. *Canada: An Economic History.* Toronto: Macmillan of Canada.

Martel, André. 1984. "L'Engagement et les Engagés. Tome 1: Approches Historiques, 1872–1962." Montpellier: Centre d'Histoire Militaire d'Études de Défense Nationale, Université Paul Valéry.

Martial, Pierre. 1984. *Objection: Mode d'Emploi.* Paris: Éditions Avis de Recherche.

Martin, Michel. 1993. "France: A Statute But No Objectors." In *The New Conscientious Objection,* ed. Charles C. Moskos and John Whiteclay Chambers, 80–97. Oxford: Oxford University Press.

Marx, Karl. 1974 [1867]. *Capital,* Vol. I. New York: International Publishers.

Maschino, Maurice. 1961. *L'engagement: Le dossier des réfractaires.* Paris: François Maspero.

McCloskey, Donald N. 1991. "History, Differential Equations, and the Problem of Narration." *History and Theory* 30 (1): 21–36.

McKernan, Michael. 1977. "Catholics, Concription, and Archbishop Mannix." *Historical Studies* 17 (68,April): 299–314.

1980a. *Australian Churches at War.* Canberra: Australian War Memorial.

1980b. *The Australian People and the Great War.* Melbourne: Nelson.

1984. *Australians in Wartime.* Melbourne: Nelson.

McNaught, Kenneth. 1988 [1969]. *The Penguin History of Canada,* rev. ed. London: Penguin Books.

McQuilton, John. 1987. "A Shire at War: Yackandandah, 1914–1918." *Journal of the Australian War Memorial* 11 (October): 3–16.

Meyer-Spiegler, Madeleine. 1969. Antimilitarisme et refus de service militaire dans la France contemporaine (1945–1962). Ph.D. Dissertation, l'Institut d'Études Politiques.

Michelat, Guy, and Jean-Pierre Thomas. 1966. *Dimensions du Nationalisme: Enquête par questionnaire, 1962.* Paris: Librairie Armand Colin.

Milgrom, Paul R., Douglas C. North, and Barry R. Weingast. 1990. "The Role of Institutions in the Revival of Trade: The Medieval Law Merchant, Private Judges, and the Champagne Fairs." *Economics and Politics* 2 (1): 1–23.

Miller, Carmen. 1975. "A Preliminary Analysis of the Socio-Economic Composition of Canada's South African War Contingents." *Social History* VIII (16): 219–37.

Miller, Gary. 1992. *Managerial Dilemmas.* Cambridge University Press.

Mitchell, B. R. 1975. *European Historical Statistics, 1750–1970.* New York: Columbia University Press.

Mokyr, Joel. 1983. *Why Ireland Starved.* London: George, Allen & Unwin.

Mokyr, Joel, and Cormac Ó Gráda. 1984. "New Developments in Irish Population History, 1700–1850." *The Economic History Review* XXXVIII (4,November): 473–88.

1996. "Height and Health in the United Kingdom 1815–1860: Evidence from the East India Company Army." *Explorations in Economic History* 33 (2): 141–68.

Monroe, Kristin Renwick. 1996. *The Heart of Altruism.* Princeton, NJ: Princeton University Press.

Moore, Barrington. 1978. *Injustice: The Social Bases of Obedience and Revolt.* New York: The Macmillan Press Ltd.

Morton, Desmond. 1970. *Politics and the Canadian Militia 1868–1904.* Toronto: University of Toronto Press.

1971. "French Canada and War, 1868–1917: The Military Background to the Conscription Crisis of 1917." In *War and Society in North America,* ed. J. L. Granatstein and R. D. Cuff. Toronto: Nelson.

1980. "The Limits of Loyalty: French Canadian Officers and the First World War." In *Limits of Loyalty,* ed. Edgar Denton III, 79–97. Waterloo, Ontario: Wilfrid Laurier University Press.

1990. *A Military History of Canada.* Edmonton: Hurtig.

Moskos, Charles C., and John Whiteclay Chambers II, eds. 1993. *The New Conscientious Objection.* New York: Oxford University Press.

Moskos, Charles C., Jr. 1970. *The American Enlisted Man: The Rank and File in Today's Military.* New York: Russell Sage Foundation.

Murdock, Eugene. 1971. *One Million Men: The Civil War Draft in the North.* Madison: The State Historical Society of Wisconsin.

Murphy, D. J. 1974. "Religion, Race and Conscription in World War I." *Australian Journal of Politics and History* 20 (2): 155–63.

Nelson, D., and E. Silberberg. 1987. "Ideology and Legislator Shirking." *Economic Inquiry* 25: 15–25.

Nicholson, Colonel Gerald W. L. 1964. *Official History of the Canadian Army in the First World War: Canadian Expeditionary Force, 1914–1919.* Ottawa: Roger Duhamel, Queen's Printer and Controller of Stationery.

Niemi, Richard G., John Mueller, and Tom W. Smith. 1989. *Trends in Public Opinion: A Compendium of Survey Data.* Westport, CT: Greenwood Press.

Noël, Alain. 1992. "Politics in a High Unemployment Society." In *Quebec State and Society,* 2nd ed., ed. Alain Gagnon. Toronto: Nelson.

North, Douglass C. 1981. *Structure and Change in Economic History.* New York: Norton.

Bibliography

North, Douglass C. 1990. *Institutions, Institutional Change, and Economic Performance.* Cambridge University Press.

North, Douglass C., and Barry R. Weingast. 1989. "Constitutions and Commitment: The Evolution of Institutions Governing Public Choice in Seventeenth Century England." *Journal of Economic History* 49 (4): 803–32.

O'Connor, P. S. 1967. "The Recruitment of Maori Soldiers, 1914–1918." *Political Science* 19 (2): 48–83.

Offer, Avner. 1995. "Going to War in 1914: A Matter of Honor." *Politics & Society* 23: 213–41.

Olson, Mancur. 1965. *The Logic of Collective Action.* Cambridge, MA: Harvard University Press.

Omissi, David. 1994. *The Sepoy and the Raj: The Indian Army, 1860–1940.* London: Macmillan.

Opp, Karl-Dieter. 1990. "The Attenuation of Customs." In *Social Institutions: Their Emergence, Maintenance and Effects,* ed. Michael Hechter, Karl-Dieter Opp, and Reinhard Wippler, 119–39. New York: Aldine de Gruyter.

O'Rourke, Kevin. 1991. "Did the Irish Famine Matter?" *Journal of Economic History* 51 (1): 1–21.

Ostrom, Elinor. 1990. *Governing the Commons: The Evolution of Institutions for Collective Action.* Cambridge University Press.

Paoli, François-André. 1974. *L'Armée Française de 1919 à 1939: Les Temps des Compromis.* Paris: Ministère des armées, état-major de l'armée du Terre, Service Historique.

Pariseau, Jean, and Serge Bernier. 1987. *French-Canadians and Bilingualism in the Canadian Armed Forces: The Fear of a Parallel Army,* Vol. 1. Ottawa: Canadian Government.

Parker, H. M. D. 1957. *Manpower: A Study of War-time Policy and Administration.* London: Her Majesty's Stationery Office.

Partridge, P. H. 1971. *Consent and Consensus.* London: Pall Mall.

Pateman, Carol. 1979. *The Problem of Political Obligation: A Critique of Liberal Theory.* Berkeley: University of California Press.

Patterson, Douglas A., and James A. Hoskins. 1987. *The Air Force, Conscription, and the All-Volunteer Force.* Maxwell Air Force Base, AL: Air University Press.

Pearson, A. R. 1974. "Western Australia and the Conscription Plebiscites of 1916 and 1917." *RMC Historical Journal* 3: 21–27.

Pedroncini, Guy. 1968. 1917: Les Mutineries de l'Armée française. Thesis, Paris. Collection Archives No. 35 (Julliard).

Peel, Mark. 1995. *Good Times, Hard Times.* Melbourne: Melbourne University Press.

Perry, F. W. 1988. *The Commonwealth Armies: Manpower and Organization in Two World Wars.* Manchester: Manchester University Press.

Petersen, Roger. 1989. "Rationality, Ethnicity and Military Enlistment." *Social Science Information* 28 (3): 563–98.

Bibliography

Pinney, Neil, and John T. Scholz. 1995. "Duty, Fear, and Tax Compliance: The Heuristic Basis of Citizenship Behavior." *American Journal of Political Science* 39: 490–512.

Pitkin, Hanna. 1965. "Obligation and Consent I." *American Political Science Review* 59 (1): 990–9.

    1966. "Obligation and Consent–II." *American Political Science Review* X (1): 39–52. Reprinted in *Obligation and Dissent,* ed. Donald W. Hanson and Robert Booth Fowler, 489–508. Boston: Little, Brown.

Piven, Frances Fox. 1981. "Deviant Behavior and the Remaking of the World." *Social Problems* 28 (June): 489–508.

Plamenatz, J. P. 1968. *Consent, Freedom and Political Obligation.* New York: Oxford University Press.

Przeworski, Adam. 1985. *Capitalism and Social Democracy.* Cambridge University Press.

Putnam, Robert. 1993. *Making Democracy Work: Civic Traditions in Modern Italy.* Princeton, NJ: Princeton University Press.

    1995. "Bowling Alone: America's Declining Social Capital." *Journal of Democracy* 6 (1,January): 65–78.

Rabin, Matthew. 1993. "Incorporating Fairness into Game Theory and Economics." *American Economic Review* 83 (5–6): 1281–1302.

Rae, John. 1970. *Conscience and Politics: The British Government and the Conscientious Objector to Military Service, 1916–1919.* London: Oxford University Press.

Ralston, David B. 1967. *The Army of the Republic: The Place of the Military in the Political Evolution of France, 1871–1914.* Cambridge, MA: The MIT Press.

Rawls, John. 1971. *A Theory of Justice.* Cambridge, MA: Harvard University Press.

Raynauld, André. 1962. *Les Croissance et Structures Économiques de la Province de Québec.* Quebec: Ministère de l'Industrie et Commerce.

Regamey, P. R., and Y.-Y. Jolif. 1962. *Face à la violence: Pour un statut des objecteurs de conscience.* Paris: Les Éditions du Cerf.

Robertson, J. R. 1959. "The Conscription Issue and the National Movement, Western Australia: June, 1916 to December, 1917." *University Studies in Western Australian History* III (3): 5–38.

Robson, L. L. 1970. *The First A.I.F: A Study of Its Recruitment, 1914–1918.* Melbourne: Melbourne University Press.

    1988. "The Australian Soldier: Formation of a Stereotype." In *Australia: Two Centuries of War and Peace,* ed. M. McKernan and M. Browne, 313–37. Canberra: Australian War Memorial.

Rogowski, Ronald. 1974. *Rational Legitimacy: A Theory of Political Support.* Princeton, NJ: Princeton University Press.

Root, Hilton L. 1994. *The Fountain of Privilege: Political Foundations of Markets in Old Regime France and England.* Berkeley: University of California Press.

239

Bibliography

Rosenthal, Jean-Laurent. 1992. *The Fruits of Revolution*. Cambridge University Press.

Ross, Thomas W. 1994. "Raising an Army: A Positive Theory of Military Recruitment." *Journal of Law and Economics* 38 (April): 109–31.

Roy, Gabrielle. 1980 (1945). *The Tin Flute*. Toronto: McClelland and Stewart.

Sablière, Pierre. 1963. "L'Objection de Conscience en France. Depuis la Seconde Guerre Mondiale." Mémoire préparé pour Raoul Girardet, l'Institut d'Études Politiques.

Sales de Bohigas, Nuria. 1968. "Some Opinions on Exemption from Military Service in Nineteenth-Century Europe." *Comparative Studies in Society and History* X (3): 261–89.

Sandburg, Carl. 1948. *Abraham Lincoln*. New York: Charles Scribner's Sons.

Scanlon, Thomas M. 1982. "Contractualism and Utilitarianism." In *Utilitarianism and Beyond,* ed. Amartya Sen and Bernard Williams, 103–28. Cambridge University Press.

   1988. "Levels of Moral Thinking." In *Hare and Critics,* ed. Douglas Seanor and N. Fotion, 129–46. Oxford: Clarendon Press.

Scarrow, Howard A. 1962. *Canada Votes: A Handbook of Federal and Provincial Election Data*. New Orleans: The Hauser Press.

Scharpf, Fritz. 1990. "Games Real Actors Could Play." *Rationality & Society* 2 (October): 471–94.

   1991. "Games Real Actors Could Play: The Challenge of Complexity." *Journal of Theoretical Politics* 3 (3, July): 277–304.

   1994. "Games Real Actors Could Play: Positive and Negative Coordination in Embedded Negotiations." *Journal of Theoretical Politics* 6 (1, January): 27–53.

Schelling, Thomas C. 1978. *Micromotives and Macrobehavior*. New York: W.W. Norton.

Schnapper, Bernard. 1968. *Le Remplacement Militaire en France: Quelques aspects politiques, économiques et sociaux du recrutement au XIX siècle*. Paris: S.E.V.P.E.

Scholz, John T. 1984. "Cooperation, Deterrence, and the Ecology of Regulatory Enforcement." *Law and Society Review* 18 (2): 179–224.

   1994. "The Adaptive Compliance of Citizens: Tax Compliance as Contingent Consent." Canberra: Australian National University, Administration, Compliance and Governability Working Paper No. 21.

Scott, Ernest. 1938. *Australia During the War. The Official History of Australia in the War of 1914–1918,* Vol. XI. Sydney: Angus and Robertson.

Scott, F. R. 1942. "What Did 'No' Mean?" *Canadian Forum* (June): 71–3.

Scott, James C. 1985. *Weapons of the Weak*. New Haven: Yale University Press.

Sen, Amartya K. 1977. "Rational Fools." *Philosophy and Public Affairs* 6 (4, Summer): 317–44.

Serle, W. H. 1976. "A Soldier Explains the Conscription Votes." *LaTrobe Library Journal* 5 (18, October): 43–4.

Serman, William. 1976. Le Corps des officiers français sous le Deuxième République et le Second Empire, aristocratie et démocratie dans l'armée au milieu du XIXe siècle. Thèse d'état, Université de Paris IV, Paris.

1982. *Les officiers français dans la nation: 1848–1914.* Paris: Aubier.

Shields, Neville T. 1968. "National Service Training, 1950–1959." In *Conscription in Australia,* ed. Roy Forward and Bob Reece, 66–78. St. Lucia: University of Queensland Press.

Shy, John. 1976. *A People Numerous and Armed.* New York: Oxford University Press.

1986. "Armed Forces in Colonial North America: New Spain, New France, and Anglo America." In *Against All Enemies,* ed. Kenneth J. Hagan and William R. Roberts, 3–20. New York: Greenwood Press.

Sibley, Mulford Q., and Philip E. Jacob. 1962. *Conscription of Conscience: The American Conscientious Objector, 1940–1947.* Ithaca, NY: Cornell University Press.

Silver, Allan. 1994. "Democratic Citizenship and High Military Strategy: The Inheritance, Decay and Reshaping of Political Culture." In *Research on Democracy and Society,* ed. Frederick D. Weil, 317–49. Greenwich, CT: JAI Press.

Simkins, Peter. 1988. *Kitchener's Army: The Raising of the New Armies, 1914–1916.* Manchester: Manchester. University Press

Simmons, John. 1979. *Moral Principles and Political Obligations.* Princeton, NJ: Princeton University Press.

Singer, Peter. 1974. *Democracy and Disobedience.* New York: Oxford University Press.

Skelley, Alan Ramsay. 1977. *The Victorian Army at Home.* London: Croom Helm.

Skelton, William B. 1986. "The Army in the Age of the Common Man, 1815–1845." In *Against All Enemies,* ed. Kenneth J. Hagan and William R. Roberts, 91–112. New York: Greenwood Press.

Smith, Adam. 1982 [1759]. *The Theory of Moral Sentiments.* Indianapolis: Liberty Fund.

Smith, F. B. 1981 [1966]. *The Conscription Plebiscites in Australia, 1916–17.* North Melbourne: History Teachers Association of Victoria, Ltd.

Smith, Hugh. 1989. "Conscience, Law and the State: Australia's Approach to Conscientious Objection since 1901." *Australian Journal of Politics and History* 35 (1): 13–28.

1990. "Conscientious Objection to Particular Wars: Australia's Experience During the Vietnam War, 1965–1972." *War and Society* 8 (1,May): 118–34.

Smith, Leonard V. 1994. *Between Mutiny and Obedience: The Case of the French Fifth Infantry Division During World War I.* Princeton, NJ: Princeton University Press.

Smith, W. H. C. 1985. *Second Empire and Commune: France 1848–1871.* London: Longman.

Somers, Margaret R. 1992. "Narrativity, Narrative Identity, and Social Action: Rethinking English Working-Class Formation." *Social Science History* 16 (4): 591–630.

1993. "Citizenship and the Place of the Public Sphere: Law, Community, and Political Culture in the Transition to Democracy." *American Sociological Review* 58 (October): 587–620.

Sorrenson, M. P. K. 1981. "Maori and Pakeha." In *The Oxford History of New Zealand*, ed. W. H. Oliver, and B. R. Williams, 168–93. Oxford: Clarendon Press.

Spiers, Edward M. 1980. *The Army and Society, 1815–1914*. London: Longman.

1985. "The Regular Army in 1914." In *A Nation in Arms: A Social Study of the British Army in the First World War*, ed. Ian F. W. Beckett and Keith Simpson, 40–60. Manchester: Manchester University Press.

Stacey, C. P. 1948. *The Canadian Army 1939–1945: An Official Historical Summary*. Ottawa: King's Printer.

1955. *Six Years of War: the Army in Canada, Britain, and the Pacific. Official History of the Canadian Army in the Second World War*, Vol. I. Ottawa: Edmond Cloutier, Queen's Printer and Controller of Stationery.

1963 [1936]. *Canada and the British Army, 1846–1871: A Study in the Practice of Responsible Government*. Toronto: University of Toronto Press.

Stanley, George F. 1974 [1954]. *Canada's Soldiers: The Military History of an Unmilitary People,* 3rd ed. Toronto: Macmillan of Canada.

Stelzle, Charles, ed. 1929. *Yearbook of the Churches*. New York: J. E. Stohlmann.

1931. *Yearbook of the Churches*. New York: J. E. Stohlmann.

Stephens, John. 1979. *The Transition from Capitalism to Socialism*. London: Macmillan.

Stern, Chaim, ed. 1973. *Gates of Repentence: The New Union Prayerbook for the Days of Awe*. New York: Central Conference of American Rabbis.

Stigler, George J., and Gary Becker. 1977. "De Gustibus Non Est Disputandum." *American Economic Review* 67 (2): 76–90.

Stock, Jenny Tilby. 1985. "Farmers and the Rural Vote in South Australia in World War I: The 1916 Conscription Referendum." *Historical Studies* 21 (84,April): 391–411.

Stoezel, Jean. 1983. *Les Valeurs du Temps Present*. Paris: PUF.

Stoker, Laura. 1992. "Interests and Ethics in Politics." *American Political Science Review* 86 (2): 369–80.

Stokes, Susan. In press. "Pathologies of Deliberation." Paper prepared for inclusion in *Deliberative Democracy,* ed. Jon Elster.

Sugden, Robert. 1986. *The Economics of Rights, Co-operation, and Welfare*. Oxford: Basil Blackwell.

Summers, Anne. 1976. "Militarism in Britain Before the Great War." *History Workshop Journal* 2: 104–23.

Symonds, Craig L. 1986. "An Improvised Army at War, 1861–1865." In *Against All Enemies,* ed. Kenneth J. Hagan and William R. Roberts, 155–71. New York: Greenwood Press.

242

Bibliography

Taylor, Michael. 1982. *Community, Anarchy and Liberty*. Cambridge University Press.

1987 [1976]. *The Possibility of Cooperation*. Cambridge University Press.

Teichman, Jenny. 1986. *Pacifism and the Just War*. Oxford: Basil Blackwell.

Tetlock, Philip E., and Aron Belkin, eds. 1996. *Counterfactual Thought Experiments in World Politics*. Princeton, NJ: Princeton University Press.

Tetlock, Philip E., Randall Peterson, and Jennifer Lerner. In press. "Revising the Pluralism Model: Incorporating Social Content and Context Postulates." In *Values*, ed. C. Seligman, J. Olson, and M. Zanna. Hillsdale, NJ: Erlbaum.

Thaler, Richard H., ed. 1991. *Quasi-Rational Economics*. New York: Russell Sage Foundation.

Therborn, Goran. 1977. "Mass Democracy." *New Left Review* 103: 3–41.

Thomas, Jean-Pierre. 1981. "Fonction Militaire et Système d'Hommes." In *Hommes de la Défense* (Tezenas du Moncel et al.) Supplément 12 of *Stratégique*, 17–42.

Thomas, Jean-Pierre, Pierre Saint Macary, and François Veillescazes. 1978. "Les Engagés Volontaires dans l'armée de la terre en 1977: Petit Atlas de Données Socio-Démographique." Invalides: CSDN.

Thompson, John. 1978. *The Harvests of War*. Toronto: McClelland and Stewart.

Thomson, Janice E. 1995. *Mercenaries, Pirates, and State Sovereignty*. Princeton, NJ: Princeton University Press.

Thoreau, Henry David. 1950 (1859). "Civil Disobedience." In *Walden and Civil Disobedience*, ed. Brooks Atkinson. New York: Modern Library.

Tickten, David. 1969. "The War Issue and the Collapse of the South African Labour Party, 1914–15." *South Africa Historical Journal* 1: 59–73.

Tilly, Charles. 1990. *Capital, Coercion, and European States*. Cambridge, MA: Basil Blackwell.

Titmuss, Richard M. 1971. *The Gift Relationship*. New York: Pantheon Books.

Tocqueville, Alexis de. 1990 [1835]. *Democracy in America*, Vol. I. New York: Vintage.

1990 [1840]. *Democracy in America*, Vol. II. New York: Vintage.

Toulat, Jean. 1971. *Les grévistes de la guerre*. Paris: Fayard.

Townshend, Charles. 1983. *Political Violence in Ireland: Government and Resistance Since 1848*. Oxford: Clarendon Press.

Tsebelis, G. 1990. *Nested Games: Rational Choice in Comparative Politics*. Berkeley: University of California Press.

Turner, Ian. 1965. *Industrial Labour and Politics: The Dynamics of the Labour Movement in Eastern Australia 1900–1921*. Canberra: Australian National University Press.

Tussman, Joseph. 1960. *Obligation and the Body Politic*. New York: Oxford University Press.

Tyler, Tom R. 1990. *Why People Obey The Law*. New Haven: Yale University Press.

Ullmann-Margalit, Edna. 1977. *The Emergence of Norms*. Oxford: Oxford University Press.

Urquhart, M. C., ed. 1965. *Historical Statistics of Canada*. Toronto: Macmillan of Canada.

Bibliography

Useem, Michael. 1973. *Conscription, Protest, and Social Conflict: The Life and Death of a Draft Resistance Movement.* New York: John C. Wiley and Sons.

Vamplew, Wray, ed. 1987. *Australians: Historical Statistics.* Sydney: Fairfax, Syme and Weldom Associates.

Van Holde, Stephen. 1993. State Building and the Limits of State Power: The Politics of Conscription in Napoleonic France. Ph.D. Dissertation, Cornell University, Ithaca, NY.

Veillescazes, François. 1978. "L'engagement volontaire dans l'armée de terre: Une analyse exploratoire." *Révue française de sociologie* XIX: 341–72.

Verdier, Daniel. 1994. *Democracy and International Trade: Britain, France, and the United States, 1860–1990.* Princeton, NJ: Princeton University Press.

Verlet, Martin. 1967. "A Protest of the Young." *Liberation* (January): 29–33.

Wade, Mason. 1968. *The French Canadians,* Vol. I and II. Toronto: Macmillan.

Walzer, Michael. 1970. *Obligations: Essays on Disobedience, War and Citizenship.* Cambridge, MA: Harvard University Press.

1977. *Just and Unjust War: A Moral Argument with Historical Illustrations.* New York: Basic Books, Inc.

1983. *Spheres of Justice: A Defence of Pluralism and Inequality.* Oxford: Basil Blackwell.

Wanless, Newton. 1929. *The History of the Fourteenth Battalion, AIF.* Melbourne: Arrow Printing.

Weatherley, Richard. 1991. "Doing the Right Thing: How Social Security Clients View Compliance." Administration, Compliance and Governability Program, Research School of Social Sciences, Australian National University, Canberra, Working Paper No. 3.

Weber, H. C., ed. 1939. *Yearbook of American Churches.* Elmhurst, NY: YAC Press.

Weber, Max. 1949 [1905]. "Objective Possibility and Adequate Causation in Historical Explanation." In *The Methodology of the Social Sciences,* ed. Max Weber. New York: Free Press.

1968. *Economy and Society.* Berkeley: University of California Press.

Weigley, Russell F. 1973. *The American Way of War.* New York: Macmillan.

Whitman, Lauris B., ed. 1969. *Yearbook of American Churches.* New York: National Council Press.

Wilcox, Craig. 1994. The Citizen Soldier Tradition. Ph.D. Dissertation, Australian National University, Research School of Social Sciences, Department of History, Canberra.

Willms, A. M. 1970 [1956]. "Conscription 1917: A Brief for the Defence." In *Conscription 1917,* ed. A. M. Willms, 1–14. Toronto: University of Toronto Press.

Wilson, Barbara M., ed. 1977. *Ontario and the First World War, 1914–1918: A Collection of Documents.* Toronto: University of Toronto Press.

Winter, J. M. 1985. *The Great War and the British People.* London: Macmillan.

Withers, Glenn. 1972. *Conscription: Necessity and Justice.* Sydney: Angus and Robertson.

Bibliography

1982. "The 1916–1917 Conscription Referenda: A Cliometric Re-Appraisal." *Historical Studies* 20 (78): 36–47.

Woloch, Isser. 1994. *The New Regime: Transformations of the French Civic Order, 1789–1820s*. New York: Norton.

Wright, Gordon. 1942. "Public Opinion and Conscription in France, 1866–70." *The Journal of Modern History* XIV (1,March): 26–45.

Yamagishi, Toshio, and Midori Yamagishi. 1994. "Trust and Commitment in the United States and Japan." *Motivation and Emotion* 18 (2): 129–66.

Young, Oran R. 1979. *Compliance and Public Authority: A Theory With International Implications*. Baltimore: The Johns Hopkins University Press.

Young, Warren L. 1982. *Minorities and the Military: A Cross-National Study in World Perspective*. Westport, CT: Greenwood Press.

Index

Abbott, Andrew, 6
Abell, Peter, 6
accountability, community, 26
Adams, R. J. Q., 57, 58, 112, 113, 115
Aitken, G. G., 146
Allen, James, 70, 116, 117
Aminzade, Ronald, 6, 94
analytic narrative, techniques and use, 6–9, 14, 44, 78, 81
Armstrong, Elizabeth, 67, 119, 146, 148, 149, 151, 152
Arthur, Brian, 8
Asquith, Herbert Henry, 112–13
Atwood, Margaret, 1, 200
Atzioni, Amitai, 30n11
Australia: compulsory military training, 73–5, 177; conscription, 73–5, 178, 180; formation of Commonwealth (1901), 71–2; issue of conscientious objection, 177–85, 191–3; military policy in colony of, 70–5; opposition to conscription during World War I, 128–9; participation in Boer War, 71; post-1840 volunteer militias, 71; referenda on conscription (1916, 1917), 121–2, 129; Sydney and Parramatta Loyal Associations, 70; War Precautions Act, 121
Australian Freedom League, 74–5
Australian National Defence League, 73, 75
Auvray, Michel, 45, 186, 187
Ayres, Ian, 10, 209, 213, 216

Baker, Paul, 70, 116–17
bargaining model of normative change, 206–7
Baron, Jonathan, 213
Barrett, John, 73, 74, 75
Barry, Brian, 203–4, 206

Baskir, Lawrence M., 174, 199
Bates, Robert H., 7
Bearman, Peter S., 63, 214
Beck, J. Murray, 120–1, 139
Becker, Gary S., 199
Belich, James, 69–70
Belkin, Aron, 8
Berger, Carl, 141
Bernageua, Nicole, 91, 94
Bernier, Serge, 68, 140, 154, 156, 159
Bianco, William, 211
Birnbaum, Pierre, 4, 46, 48
Black Panthers, 29
Block, Fred, 198n19
Bloc populaire canadien, le, 159–60
Boer War (1899–1902), 56, 57, 68, 70–1
Bonaparte, Louis, 94
Borden, Robert, 119–20, 128, 129, 139–40, 149, 159, 163
bounty system for volunteers for Union Army in U.S. Civil War, 98–100
Bourassa, Henri, 119, 139, 148, 152
Braithwaite, John, 10, 209, 213, 216
Brennan, Geoffrey, 199, 209
Brewer, John, 51, 53
Brown, Robert Craig, 139, 142, 143, 146, 147
Burawoy, Michael, 17, 215
buying out (see also commutation; exonération; replacement; substitution): abolition of, 103; during Civil War in United States, 96–102; in France, 85–96; of military service, 80–2, 206; Pareto optimality of, 206

Callan, Patrick, 113–14
Calvert, Randall L., 217
Canada: conscription crisis (1917), 134; history of military service, 66–8;

246

Index

Index

Index

Labor Party, Australia, 12, 75, 121, 128–30

Labour Party: New Zealand, 116; United Kingdom, 12, 112

Ladurie, Emmanuel Le Roy, 49–50, 88–9, 91, 94

Laitin, David, 6

Lake, Marilyn, 122

Lapointe, Ernest, 153

Laurendeau, André, 150, 159, 160

Laurier, Wilfred, 120, 139

Lecoin, Louis, 188, 189

legislation (see also policymakers, government): approving conscription policy bargain, 109; British militia law after reform (1757), 51; French authorization of conscientious objection, 188–9; French law (loi Jourdan), 46–8, 85, 212; French law (Saint-Cyr) of military service principles, 49–50, 88; militias, 67, 69, 169; for national draft in U.S. Civil War, 63–4; related to French military service (1872–1914), 50–1, 85; in United States related to militia on national and state levels, 60

legislative median: game of military service policies, 34–5; in government demand and citizen compliance in World War I, 123–4; during nation-building era in countries studied, 76–7

legislator, median: change in preferences related to replacement and substitution, 104–6; in conscription games with policymakers, 82–4; decisions based on demand during nation-building era, 77–8; hypotheses explaining shift in position, 81–2; in large-demand conscription-volunteer games, 110–11; shift in position on French replacement system, 93

Lerner, Jennifer, 211

Levi, Margaret, 4n4, 7, 9, 20, 22, 26, 33, 40, 51, 204, 209, 213

Liberal Government: United Kingdom, 57

Liberal Government/Party: New Zealand, 70, 116

Liberal Party: Canada, 120, 128, 139–40, 153–4; United Kingdom, 112

Liberal Party of Quebec, 159

Lincoln, Abraham, 100

Lind, E. Allan, 23

Linteau, Paul-André, 68, 154, 156, 159

Lipsky, Michael, 23

Lloyd George, David, 112, 113–15

Locke, John, 201

Lomansky, Loran, 199, 209

Long, Walter, 112

Loveridge, Donald, 139, 142, 145, 146, 147

McCloskey, Donald, 6

Mackenzie King, William Lyon. See King, William Lyon Mackenzie.

McKernan, Michael, 122–3

MacKinnon, Mary, 147, 161

McLauclan, Gregory, 4

Maclean, Norman, viii, 200

MacLennan, Hugh, 160

McNaught, Kenneth, 153, 156

McQuilton, John, 123

Mahon, John K., 60–1, 62, 65, 96

Main, J. M., 73

Malueg, David A., 217

Mann, Michael, 4, 43

Mansbridge, Jane J., 26, 209, 213

Margolis, Howard, 26, 209, 213

Marr, William L., 145, 146, 147, 157, 158

Martial, Pierre, 186, 187, 188

Martin, Michel, 189, 193, 199

Marx, Karl, 14

Massey, William, 70, 116, 117

Meighten, Arthur, 156

Meyer-Spiegler, Madeleine, 186, 187, 188

Milgrom, Paul R., 22, 216

military service: abolition of buying out, 103; bargain in policy for, 33; buying out of, 80–1, 206; factors in transformation of military sector, 43–4; hypotheses related to government demands and citizen response, 44; hypotheses related to shift in position on buying out, 81–2; Prussian example of universal, 103–4, 106; stylized policy game, 31–3

military service, Canada: voluntary system at beginning of World War I, 139–40

military service, France: (1872–1914), 50–1, 85; avoidance under, 47–8; experience of, 12; principle of wartime conscription (1789–1815), 45–9, 85; principles based on voluntarism, 49–50

military service, United Kingdom: British Army in nineteenth century, 53–4; British forces in New Zealand in eighteenth and nineteenth centuries, 68–9; British nineteenth-century apparatuses, 52–3

military service, United States: buying out in political debate, 96; changes in military sector, 61; during Civil War, 62–6; obligation under Constitution, 60; selective service system, 119

military service policy: choices of policymakers given preferences of legislators and citizens, 82–4; differences in countries studied during nation build-

251

Index

Plamenatz, J. P., 202
Poirier, Philip P., 57, 58, 112, 113, 115
policymakers, government (*see also* conscription policy bargain): change in position related to replacement and substitution, 104–6; in conscription games with median legislator, 82–4; dependence in democracies on citizen approval, 109; negotiations with citizens over conscription, 107–9
Polk, James K., 61
preferences: large- and small-demand conscription games, 111; permitted by democratic institutions, 218–19; of pivotal legislator and voter in World War I conscription, 130; shaping of, 211
Provisional Army Act (1789), United States, 61
Przeworski, Adam, 215
public opinion: in Australia on conscription, 121–3; in British colony of Australia, 74–5; Canadian francophone opposition to conscription, 119–20; conscription in France during Napoleonic era and Revolution, 46–9; toward conscription in U.S. Civil War, 96–102; toward French military service policy, 92–6; issue of conscientious objection in Australia, 181–2; Korean War, 176–7; on military service in United States during World War I, 117–19; on military service in United States from colonial era to Civil War, 58–62; in New Zealand related to conscription, 116–17; opposition to replacement and substitution, 104–6; in United Kingdom during World War I, 111–15; Vietnam War, 177, 182–4; on war and conscription in Australia (1962–8), 183–4
Putnam, Robert, 8

Quakers: American, 29, 58, 169, 194; Australian, 74
quasi-voluntary compliance. *See* compliance.
Quebec Act (1774), Canada, 66–7

Rabin, Matthew, 217
Rae, Saul, 155
Ralston, David B., 51
rational choice model, 2–3, 14–15
Rawls, John, 204
reciprocity for mutual advantage, distinct from ethical reciprocity, 25
recruitment: avoidance in France (1819–26), 88–9; British voluntary recruitment at beginning of World War I,

111–13; Canada at beginning of World War I, 139–40; *milice royale* of French *Ancien Régime*, 45; mobilization in France (1792), 46; for nineteenth-century British Army, 53–4; in pre–World War I British army, 56–7; with reforms of French army, 46; standing army of French *Ancien Régime*, 45; under U.S. Enrollment Act (1863), 63–5
Redmond, John, 113–14
Reform Government/Party, New Zealand, 70, 116
refusal to consent: conditions for, 31, 132; in conscientious objection, 198; contingent, 23; Ireland, 55
replacement system (*see also* commutation; substitution system): arguments for and against, 104–5; of European countries during nineteenth century, 102; France, 46–7, 85–95, 106; Pareto optimality, 103
Republican Party (Jeffersonian), United States, 60
Revenue Act (1764), Canada, 67
Robertson, J. R., 122
Robson, L. L., 73, 123
Roy, Gabrielle, 160

Sablière, Pierre, 186, 187–8
Saint-Cyr, Gouvion, 49, 88
Sales de Bohigas, Nuria, 94, 102, 103, 109
Sandburg, Carl, 80
Scanlon, Thomas, 203
Scarrow, Howard A., 120
Scharpf, Fritz, 9, 11, 213
Schelling, Thomas, 8
Schnapper, Bernard, 50, 85, 87f, 88, 89, 90f, 91, 92, 94
Scholz, John T., 10, 209, 214, 215, 217
Schools Controversy (1914–16), Ontario Province, 148–50, 152
Scott, Ernest, 122
Scott, F. R., 159
Scott, James C., 17, 18, 33, 206, 215
Seeger v. United States (1965), 173
selective service system, United States, 118–19, 170–1
Sen, Amartya, 213, 217
Sherman, Richard, 22
Shy, John, 58–9
Sibley, Mulford Q., 171–2, 195
Silberberg, Eugene, 209
Silver, Allan, 5, 187
Simkins, Peter, 111, 112, 113
Simmons, John, 202
Singer, Peter, 5n5
Singleton, Sara, 33